NAKED IN THE WOODS

ALSO BY JIM MOTAVALLI:

*Forward Drive: The Race to Build
    "Clean" Cars for the Future* (2000)
*Breaking Gridlock: Moving Toward
    Transportation That Works* (2001)

AS AUTHOR/EDITOR:

*Feeling the Heat: Dispatches from the
    Frontlines of Climate Change* (2004)
Green Living: The E Magazine *Handbook
    for Living Lightly on the Earth* (2005)

NAKED
☆ IN THE ☆
WOODS

Joseph Knowles
and the Legacy of
Frontier Fakery

JIM MOTAVALLI

DA CAPO PRESS
A Member of the Perseus Books Group

Designed by Pauline Brown
Set in 11.5 point Bodini by The Perseus Books Group

Cataloging-in-Publication data for this book is available from the Library of Congress.

ISBN-13: 978-0-7867-2008-8
ISBN-10: 0-7867-2008-5

Published by Da Capo Press
A Member of the Perseus Books Group
www.dacapopress.com

Da Capo Press books are available at special discounts for bulk purchases in the U.S. by corporations, institutions, and other organizations. For more information, please contact the Special Markets Department at the Perseus Books Group, 2300 Chestnut Street, Suite 200, Philadelphia, PA, 19103, or call (800) 255-1514, or e-mail special.markets@perseusbooks.com.

10 9 8 7 6 5 4 3 2 1

For Andrew Kimball Weegar
and my Nature Girls

CONTENTS

————•◆•————

"The world is glorious—the sea, the sky, the sunlight, the solemn woods—and the voices of all its wild inhabitants. But man, oh man, how you are tearing things to pieces! With my paint and brushes I am making a record of the works of nature while the making is good."

—JOE KNOWLES

PREFACE

———— ·◆· ————

In the summer of 1999, I had the good fortune to be chosen as a fellow of the Institutes for Journalism and Natural Resources (IJNR), which meant a total-immersion study of the environmental issues of Maine. With a group of journalists from all over the country—many of whom subsequently became friends and colleagues—I went out on lobster boats; visited logging camps, sardine canneries, and salmon hatcheries; discussed the benefits of dam removal and the evils of urban sprawl; and much more.

Our IJNR guide was Andrew Kimball Weegar, a Maine-born environmental journalist and naturalist whose list of accomplishments and interests was seemingly endless. According to his friend Wayne Curtis, even in cities he trailed the smell of freshly cut pine. His love for the Maine woods was total, and he had "the zeal of a missionary intent on converting heathens who lived amid asphalt and concrete."

Weegar could tell a great story, discuss arcane points of religious doctrine (he had a master's degree from Harvard Divinity School), build fine furniture and both wooden and canvas canoes, restore historical homes, raise obscure animal breeds (including Black English pigs and Scottish Highland cattle), and guide whitewater rafting trips.

Actually, he could guide a whitewater rafting trip and tell a great story simultaneously, as he proved by telling me everything there was to know about Joseph Knowles, son of Maine and Nature Man, as we proceeded helter-skelter down the Kennebec. Weegar said that Knowles had gone into the woods naked in 1913 to prove that modern man could live off the land; but after he came back out, some people said he was a fraud. Soon after Weegar finished the story, an errant current turned me out of the boat, but the brief immersion in the swirling river did not dislodge the particulars of his tale.

It took me seven years to get to the Nature Man's story, and by that time Andrew Weegar was dead, having been killed in a tragic tractor accident at his home in Fayette, Maine in 2005. He was only forty-one. At the time of his death, according to the obituary in the *Bangor Daily News,* he was restoring a timber-framed Yankee barn dating to 1840 and working on a study of the American eel, "which he considered to be one of the most fascinating and under-appreciated animals on earth." Weegar had so many ongoing projects that he was forced to leave many of them unfinished. Given enough time, I'm sure he would have gotten around to telling the Nature Man's story himself. With that no longer possible, I'm sure he'd appreciate that this quintessential Down East story did at last get set down, even if it had to be told by someone less well equipped than himself.

Fairfield, Connecticut
March 2007

———•◆•———

ONE

A Modern
Adam in Maine

PERHAPS HE DIDN'T EXPECT IT TO RAIN ON THE MORNING OF AUGUST 4, 1913, but Joseph Knowles appeared resolute as he stood on the Spencer Trail before a crowd of onlookers that included hunting guides and reporters. He slowly removed the drenched brown suit he was wearing. Soon he was wearing nothing but an athletic supporter.

Knowles, a stocky figure in early middle age whose most prominent feature was a big beak of a nose, was not lacking in confidence for the experiment he was about to conduct. This moment marked the beginning of a two-month sojourn in the Maine Dead River wilderness with only his wits and the materials he found on the forest floor. It would be a period of total solitude and silence, with no human contact, and he was ready.

Knowles had been raised in rural Maine and had worked as a trapper and hunting guide in these very woods ten years earlier. He considered himself an expert on both animal behavior and wilderness survival. He could skin a bear, build a shelter, and make a fire.

"When I emerge in October, I shall be sufficiently clothed to walk the city streets," he proclaimed in the *Boston Post*, the newspaper that was sponsoring his escapade in the woods. "From cap to heels, I shall be fitted out with at least one [outfit], and may possibly have a variety to suit weather conditions. I shall go before medical experts for examination immediately after I come out of the woods."

Knowles, then forty-three, most recently employed as a part-time newspaper artist, predicted that he would live off berries and wild vegetables, from native cherries to artichokes, until something more substantial came along. "My first meat luxury will be frogs' legs," he told the paper's readers. "The frogs are easy to catch, as all schoolboys know. My only requirement will be a club to secure them." To keep the newspaper apprised of how things were going, he would send out regular birchbark dispatches to the newspaper, written in charcoal taken from his cooking fires.

A group portrait shows a naked Knowles, his body below the waist discreetly shrouded by shrubbery, surrounded by no fewer than sixteen grown men and a scattering of youths. Many were hunting and fishing guides who were enjoying a semi-holiday, having "laid aside reel and rod for the day." Two were New York doctors, Forbes Munson and T. A. Buckley, drawn by the widespread publicity and said to be keenly interested in the scientific value of Knowles's experiment. Together, they signed a statement reading:

> On August 4, 1913, the undersigned observed Joseph Knowles disrobe and deliver his effects to [camp operator] Harry M. Pierce on the shore

of Spencer Lake, after submitting to our examination to see that he concealed no material of any kind that would aid him in any way. He entered the forest at 10:40 A.M. alone, empty handed and without clothing.

A joking Knowles was seemingly in his element as the time for leave-taking approached. He had made many friends in the isolated hunting camps where he'd prepared for his ordeal. "Knowles was the most jovial man in the party that gathered to bid him goodbye," wrote the *Post*. "He dropped none of the rollicking good humor that had made him popular in the camps." He laughed off the idea of postponing his experiment until better weather prevailed and dismissed the threat of bears and wildcats. Still, several onlookers told the intrepid explorer that they expected to see him back that same night. "Here's your last cigarette!" someone cried. Knowles, a dedicated smoker, took it, enjoyed a few thoughtful puffs, then threw the butt on the ground and shook hands all around.

His naked body glistening with rain, he stepped onto the trail. "At the top of the incline, where, in another moment, I would be out of sight among the trees, I paused and waved once more to the waiting crowd below," Knowles wrote in the bestselling book—*Alone in the Wilderness*—that he would release later that year. "Then I struck out straight along the trail. I had left civilization!"

Knowles's final words were a cocky but understated "See you later, boys!" He may have been naked, but he did carry some baggage with him: the historical record. Knowles was hardly the first man to wave goodbye to home and hearth and vanish into the unknown vastness; in fact, the stoic backwoodsman, living by his wits, was already part of the American tradition.

KNOWLES SAYS GOODBYE TO WELL-WISHERS AT THE FOOT OF SPENCER TRAIL, AUGUST 4, 1913. *BOSTON POST* PHOTO, FROM *ALONE IN THE WILDERNESS*

There was an historical oddity at work here, since Knowles was not the kind of person the public expected to see clad in buckskin, wresting a living from the primordial forest. He was born and bred a Yankee, a rural man of the woods but a long way from any frontier. But in manner and temperament, Knowles was decidedly not a Yankee "type." He more closely resembled the storied Southeastern backwoodsman of tall tale and legend. Those sons of the South Daniel Boone (or Boon) and David ("Davy") Crockett were broadly known in 1913, well before the coonskin-cap mania of 1955.

As described in Constance Rourke's 1931 *American Humor: A Study of the National Character*, the penny-pinching, sharp-dealing Yankee was a preeminent figure in eighteenth- and early nineteenth-century folklore. Yankee peddlers would leave you in nothing but your underwear, wondering what had hit you.

The Yankee was never a romantic figure, and, while extravagant, his character was somewhat earthbound. After the War of 1812, a new and more inspirational figure began to supplant the Yankee in the national consciousness: the backwoodsman. His character can be glimpsed as far back as 1822, when an actor with a rifle over his shoulder stepped onto a New Orleans stage in buckskin shirt, moccasins, and a fur cap. He sang a song about the hunters of Kentucky, and it spread quickly through the South and West.

The character of the backwoodsman was one part historical fact mixed with five parts absurdity, said to be, like Davy Crockett, half horse and half alligator, "a ring-tailed roarer," and the "gamecock of the wilderness." Joe Knowles's larger-than-life public persona fit the bill perfectly. The backwoodsman set out to conquer nature, to demonstrate his prowess against tooth and claw; and that's exactly what Knowles said he was going to do.

Though Knowles was indeed walking into a wilderness teeming with bears and other wildlife, the *Post*'s description of the land as "virgin forest" was a bit of hyperbole. As Knowles himself acknowledged, his new base near Big Spencer Lake, 275 miles north of Boston, was surrounded in all directions by hunting and fishing camps. Knowles's jumping-off point was Harry Pierce's 34,000-acre King & Bartlett hunting camp (set up by the first governor of Maine, William King, in the nineteenth century and still extant today). To reach it, Knowles took the train from Boston

KNOWLES WAS ENTERING ROUGH COUNTRY, FULL OF DENSE UNDERGROWTH AND FALLEN TREES. *BOSTON POST* PHOTO, FROM *ALONE IN THE WILDERNESS*

to Bigelow, Maine, the stagecoach for eight miles to Eustis (population fifty), and then the final sixteen miles on a rutted buckboard trail, which Knowles described as "something worse than living two months alone in the forest."

It was rough country, full of dense undergrowth and fallen trees, but it was not totally isolated. All around were familiar landmarks for outdoorsmen. To the north was Bear Mountain (the state has eleven peaks with that name) and Big Spencer Lake. To the south, Horseshoe Pond and Spencer Stream. To the east, Little Spencer and, beyond, Heald Mountain. On the west, King and Bartlett Lake, named for his camp's founders.

Spencer Trail climbs steeply up Bear Mountain, then winds its way down the other side and through thick woods to Big Spencer Lake. Knowles was out of sight, but not yet quite alone. The newspaper reported that Pierce and guide Fred Allen followed him for four miles along the trail and were the last to catch a glimpse of this modern Adam. Allen was reportedly concerned that the task was daunting, but respected Knowles's wilderness skills. Finally, even these two shadows were left behind. From then on, any message to the outside world would come in the form of his scrawled birchbark notes.

Knowles continued in a jaunty mood, though he found the wet trail slippery. As soon as he was out of sight of humanity, he threw away the athletic supporter that had protected his modesty. "With no clothing or burden to hamper me," he wrote in one of his first nearly illegible missives to the *Post,* "I felt the full freedom of the life I was to lead." He crossed open timber land on the south shore of Spencer Lake, then ran into trouble in the cedar swamps at the edge of Lost Pond, becoming tangled in thick underbrush and thistles. With legs looking like they'd been torn up by a wildcat, he paused at the edge of the lake and watched a doe drinking water on the opposite shore.

"She looked good to me, and for the first time in my life I envied a deer her hide," Knowles told the *Post.* "I could not help thinking what a fine pair of chaps her hide would make and how good a strip of smoked venison would taste a little later. There before me was food and protection, food the millionaires would envy and clothing that would outwear the most costly suit the tailor could supply."

But Knowles decided to let the deer keep her skin because he lacked a hunting license and was at that point trying to live within the game laws of the state of Maine. He would later abandon that pledge, a decision that was to play a dramatic role in the end game in October.

With his legs smarting, Knowles finally struggled out of the swamp and into open timber once more. Evening was drawing near, and he made camp under a clump of spruce trees, which gave him some protection from the rain. Though he had not eaten since morning, he was clearly still excited by the day's events, and on a stout spruce limb he did a set of chin-ups to build up his arms. "I did not feel the need of sleep, and still retained that feeling of freedom and exhilaration that I experienced when I stepped into my domain," he told the *Post* in his daily journal. The appearance of this curling parchment, covered with tightly spaced revelations, is preserved in a photograph in Knowles's book.

Alone in the Wilderness offers a markedly different—and much more somber—account of Knowles's first night in the woods. He doesn't mention the iconic deer (though she appears in his account of the following day). Instead, he poetically describes three ducks flying around in a circle over the water. Knowles tries to start a fire using pine root as a base, a stick for a spindle, and inner cedar bark as kindling, but everything is wet and he gives up the task in frustration. He begins to consider the precariousness of his situation, alone in a spruce thicket "without food or fire, naked, and miles from a camp." Absent the exhilaration he described to the newspaper, he is much occupied with keeping warm, alternately resting against a tree and pacing back and forth. He admits to "jumbled thoughts." The rain keeps falling until what he guesses to be three A.M. "Thus running and resting, I spent the first night alone in the wilderness. Daylight came very slowly," he wrote.

It's not surprising that the feelings he described ran in that tentative direction. The jaunty figure that strode into the woods without a care was a character in a play that now had no audience. Knowles was a gregarious person, one of the boys in the back room, happiest when recounting his wilderness adventures in a Boston bar with a full glass in front of him and a crowd gathered around. Now, in solitude, he could admit to more complex feelings than those that occupied the famous backwoodsmen who, at least as portrayed in legend, were relatively one-dimensional. With the woods growing dark around him, Knowles was challenged in his view of nature as a benign force; his thoughts were colored by the convictions of an earlier day, when wilderness was seen as a forbidding, godless place full of dangerous wild beasts, best cleared as soon as possible to make way for sunshine, salvation, and civilization.

The early settlers of North America saw the untouched forests of Maine not as a majestic paradise, but as a dreary wasteland. The Jesuit Father Pierre Biard wrote in his book *Relation de la Nouvelle France* (1616) that the untamed Nova Scotia, "though capable of the same prosperity as ours, nevertheless through Satan's malevolence . . . is a horrible wilderness, scarcely less miserable on account of the scarcity of bodily comforts than for that which renders man absolutely miserable, the complete lack of the ornaments and riches of the soul." Similarly, William Bradford, a passenger on the *Mayflower* and the future governor of the Plymouth Colony, saw in Massachusetts "a hideous and desolate wilderness, full of wild beasts and wild men."

As Knowles shivered through his first rainy night, his thoughts may have turned as dark as those of the title character in Daniel Defoe's *Robinson Crusoe* (1719), who in the early days on his desert island saw no prospect before him "but that of perishing with Hunger, or being devour'd by wild beasts. . . ." Crusoe had only a pipe, some tobacco, and a knife, and this threw him into "terrible Agonies of Mind, that for a while I [ran] about like a

Mad-man; Night coming upon me, I began with a heavy heart to consider what would be my Lot if there were any ravenous Beasts in that Country, seeing at Night they always come abroad for their Prey."

But Knowles had an advantage in that he was not a reluctant castaway, but a volunteer. In fact, he had been born in the woods, and at an early age frequently disappeared into them. The howling wilderness probably held fewer terrors for him than for the European used to cultivated fields and city streets. Like Crusoe, he was not formally religious, but became closer to god through his experiences with nature. "My god is the wilderness," Knowles said. "My church is the church of the forest." But, on that first night, he was still mightily unsure of the prospect before him, and absent the companions who listened enraptured to his tall tales set in the forests of Maine. Crusoe had his Friday, but Knowles was alone.

On his second day in the woods, Knowles's mood was improved, and he started to feel hungry. He trapped a couple of trout in a shallow pool of Little Spencer Stream, dispatching them with a sharp stick. With the sun out, he began to feel sunburn and missed his clothes. He again tried to set a fire, but, finding his materials too wet, he parked the trout in a spring and built a crude shelter that left him fairly comfortable. "Outside the shrinkage around my waistline and a few scratches on my legs and body, I was in just as good condition as when I left the shore of Spencer Lake on Monday," he wrote on his birchbark paper.

Again, the story as told in Knowles's book is somewhat different. Instead of the relatively restful night he described to his newspaper readers, he recounts a second night that was "a rep-

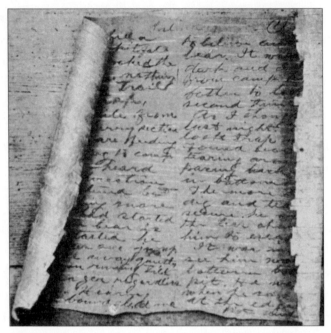

ONE OF KNOWLES'S BIRCHBARK PARCHMENTS, WITH TEXT WRITTEN IN CHARCOAL FROM THE NATURE MAN'S FIRES. *BOSTON POST* PHOTO, FROM *ALONE IN THE WILDERNESS*

etition of the first, spent in alternately walking back and forth and resting. I didn't suffer terribly, but it was not altogether comfortable out there without any clothes."

Boston Post readers, who could not learn of these events as they unfolded, were kept in suspense for more than a week at a time as the paper ran stories like "Can Knowles Live Two Months as Cave Man?" While stirring their breakfast coffee, the men and women of Boston were informed that it was a giant who had strode forth into the wilderness: "And what manner of man is this, who, realizing full well his task, has set forth to throw down the gauntlet to all the ages and prove the 20th century Bostonian is the equal in physical hardihood to any bullet-headed anthropoid who ever swung down from the trees to brain the sabre-toothed tiger with a mace of flint?"

There was something of the carnival barker at play as the paper added breathlessly: "In fact, so far as is known, no civilized man, since the world began, ever deliberately threw off all the conventionalities and associations of a civilized community and plunged into the fastness for an attempt at life as lived by his primeval ancestors."

The publicity worked wonders, because by the time the first word came from the man of the woods on Friday, August 15, the paper's circulation was growing and it was front-page news. That first birchbark dispatch, left in the appointed hiding place and discovered by a hunting guide, was brief and had been made almost illegible by rain. Knowles, the readers were informed, was somewhat scratched up and still naked, but physically intact. "He's all right, boys!" announced the unnamed guide, to the general relief of his fellows. "The boy has got it in him," added another Knowles confederate, guide Fred Allen. "And he knows the woods with the best of us."

The brief report was an appetizer for the main course, held for the larger-circulation Sunday paper, an enticing montage of color comics, sob-sister columns, theatrical and movie coverage, illustrated fiction, and even long essays about everything from dinosaurs to medical cures. "Even at a distance of one hundred years, there is something extraordinarily exhilarating about reading through a turn-of-the-century Sunday newspaper," writes David Nasaw in *The Chief,* his biography of William Randolph Hearst. "Like continuous vaudeville in the 1890s . . . and the amusement parks in the 1920s, the Sundays were intentionally oversized, overstocked, and overwhelming."

For the Sunday readers, Knowles wasn't writing short notes, but detailed accounts of each day's activities that probably required whole forests of birch trees to record, illustrated with his own vivid charcoal sketches of the animals around him. On the third day, fire! He found some dry punk and was able to coax a flame with it, which somewhat compensated for the disappointment resulting from the loss of his stream-stored trout to a passing mink.

Knowles was living on berries and wild onions, but he was able to give his legs some relief by weaving witchgrass into crude leggings. He was no longer naked, but he must have been quite a sight—strange enough to scare a swimming otter into dropping the trout it held in its mouth, thus "getting square with the mink." Knowles had his first hot food, roasted trout, which he complained was not all that enjoyable without salt. Still, he felt like "a new man," and reported a new confidence driving away the despair he'd felt during his first restless nights. "The idea of going out of the forest had left me," he wrote in *Alone*. "I began to go about things as if I were a man of the forest itself."

Knowles told his *Post* readers that even as he pursued his survival tasks, the scientific value of his experiment was uppermost in his mind. "My object is not to show how many wild creatures I can destroy, but rather how few I will need to supply me with the absolute necessities of life and comfort." The birds and animals, he said, "are my friends and neighbors." The kind-hearted Maine hunter who preferred a camera to a gun was still very much alive. Knowles's essential sweetness and good nature come through clearly in both his own writing and the many interviews he granted after the adventure.

Even in the first week, the newspaper was delighted with the success of the back-to-nature story. It watching circulation climb

KNOWLES'S CHARCOAL SKETCH OF A WILDCAT HE HAD SEEN. *BOSTON POST* PHOTO, FROM *ALONE IN THE WILDERNESS*

rapidly against the hated *Boston American,* and its reporters were having a good deal of fun with the Knowles story. During the week, with no treasure troves of birchbark notes to write about, they teased the readers with reports of bare footprints found on distant shores. There was also a tantalizing sighting that at first glance was taken to be a muskrat in the water, but a guide's keen eyesight declared to be "a man's head that bobbed above the surface of the water." Could it be the Bostonian "whose novel experiment all are informed [about] and deeply interested in"? There was even high drama when Knowles was "feared injured"— because there'd been no message from him for eleven days. It wasn't until August 20 that the public finally learned that Knowles was indeed still out there, and still naked too. He sent out a striking charcoal portrait of a wildcat he'd seen, and the *Post* displayed it in its office window.

Even so, Knowles was not the only big story of the day. His adventures in the wild had to compete with the sensational news about wealthy murderer Harry Thaw, who had just escaped from the New York asylum he'd been sentenced to after shooting the well-known architect Stanford White. Since they'd quarreled over the attentions of chorus girl Evelyn Nesbitt, the beautiful "girl on the red velvet swing" (Thaw's wife), this was pretty hot stuff. While the *American* was known as Boston's scandal sheet, the *Post* also had a pretty garish idea of what was fit to print. Murder and mayhem filled its front section. Next to Knowles was a story about a six-year-old drowning in Boston Harbor; the "death pier" had claimed another victim.

Readers responded with hundreds of letters, offering Knowles free advice. A woman from Concord, New Hampshire, said the woodsman should have followed Adam's example and taken along a wife, who would have "made him a costume to protect him from sun, wind, rain and insect pests." A man offered to go into the woods with his bloodhounds to find Knowles if necessary. A joker from Boston was worried he'd be mistaken "for a bare" and shot. *The Boston Traveler*, also in a joking mood, suggested that Knowles create Neolithic hieroglyphics for future generations to ponder. A Dorchester man put paintings by Knowles in his shop window. And young drugstore clerk Benjamin F. Pickering piped up to say that he'd been going into the woods naked for years, spending two days to a week at a time living the primitive life "clad in nature's garb." Said Pickering, "Joe Knowles has nothing on me!"

The author and traveler Haliday Witherspoon of Dorchester opined that if Knowles had sharp flints for skinning animals and striking sparks, he'd get through his ordeal well enough, despite the cold nights. His biggest problem would be mosquitoes,

Haliday said; and he had a point, since humorists refer to the mosquito as Maine's unofficial "state bird." The insect problem would indeed seem to have loomed large. Maine has, for instance, at least forty species of black flies, many of them fierce biters, though their season generally ends in July.

Knowles doesn't mention any significant harassment by insects in his newspaper journals or in his book, though he did note that the subject frequently came up in his public appearances. The flies are over by the end of July, he said, and the few mosquitoes he encountered were in the swamps. In 1935, he told an interviewer from the state of Washington that he had "sought a 4,000-foot level to get away from the mosquitoes."

On August 24 (a Sunday, of course) came the sensational news that Joe Knowles had caught a bear in a homemade pit and now had not only food, but clothing too. Knowles told his readers of having built a snug lean-to with a roof covered in birch bark and walls chinked with moss. His bed was of fir boughs. Knowles had made a rough calendar, so he was aware of passing his forty-fourth birthday in the woods on August 13. He told his readers in typical homespun prose:

> What a strange place to pass a birthday—alone in the wilder-
> ness. It is a holiday for me. Perhaps it is because I am more
> comfortably situated that my thoughts are drifting to my out-
> side friends. I hear the voices of my woodland neighbors and
> feel the presence of my mother. It was she who guided my
> footsteps along the trail that has led me to nature. She knows
> where I am and that today I think of her. She will wonder what
> I have to eat and if I am comfortable at night. But she will have
> no fear. . . . I have worked for nine days with my hands and

brain to secure the comfort which I enjoy today. I am satisfied
on this birthday, and it will long be remembered as the most
notable of my life.

The bear he trapped was pretty notable too. It was a yearling,
and Knowles caught it in a deadfall trap he made in berry country a mile from his camp. If the bear had been a cub, he might
have tried to make a pet of it, but as it was beyond taming he
sought its immediate demise with a stout club. After nearly falling
into the pit himself, Knowles wrote that he "finally landed a blow
on the bear's head that put an end to him." The seasoned hunter
described the skinning of the bear in great and graphic detail, but
he also admitted to feelings of guilt that came over him for de-
priving the animal of its life and liberty. Knowles worked the hide
for three days until the skin was pliable and soft. With a bearskin
coat, Knowles was naked no more.

But he was still lonesome. Far more than in his generally up-
beat newspaper reports, *Alone in the Wilderness* emphasizes the
"alone" part. The reader, he wrote, might think his biggest problem was living on berries and roots, or being cold and exposed
in the dark woods. They would be wrong, he explained, because
the biggest problem was something he hadn't expected at all. "I
did not experience any physical suffering to speak of," he wrote,
"though I did suffer greatly in another way. My suffering was
purely mental and a hundredfold worse than any physical suffering I experienced."

In admitting to human weakness, Knowles's accounts are considerably more nuanced than previous rip-snorting wilderness adventures by other writers. His frequently expressed sympathy for
animals, and regret at their necessary killing, was also something

new. In one engaging passage, he befriends an albino fawn and her mother, describing them as "great company." He saves the fawn from a stalking wildcat, and depicts her in an affecting charcoal portrait. Clearly, there was more to this man than bravado and woodcraft skills.

But he needed more than deer for company. Sitting around his campfire, missing the sound of human voices, Knowles began to entertain dark thoughts about quitting his experiment. "I remember one night when I was in despair," he wrote. "I sat looking dejectedly into the fire, vowing fervently to myself—and I meant it just then—'This is my last night in this wilderness. I don't care if my time isn't up. Life is too short to be spent voluntarily suffering the way I am suffering.'"

THE DEER DRAWINGS PROVED POPULAR WITH NEWSPAPER READERS. *BOSTON POST* PHOTO, FROM *ALONE IN THE WILDERNESS*

He vowed to go the next day (August 29) to King & Bartlett Camp, and almost gave up right there when he ran into a Maine guide on the trail. "Hello, Joe!" the man said to him. "An almost overpowering desire came upon me to talk to him—just a word or two with another human being!" But with those words the experiment would be over, so Knowles turned away and walked back into the woods.

Finding a deer killed by a wildcat helped supply his needs and made Knowles feel a bit better. He resolved to stick it out. Among the primitive messages he sent out, which were full of plans to create a color picture using pigments taken from nature, was a letter to President Woodrow Wilson. The object of his experiment, he told Wilson, was to "demonstrate that modern man is not only the equal of primitive man in ability to maintain himself, but that civilization has so improved the human mind that he may add to primitive life accomplishments which our early ancestors never knew."

The *Post* continued to fill the dead spots between Sunday spectaculars with think pieces about Knowles's chances for success, interviews with the guides hanging around King & Bartlett Camp, and even some observations by a minister who predicted that Knowles would "share the fame of [Henry] David Thoreau." This kind of material would eventually flag the interest of even the most dedicated Knowles watcher, so it was with some relief that on September 14 the paper reported drama in the form of a high fever and another close call. Aching all over, Knowles had determined to give up his adventure in the woods. He was "all in" and on his way back to civilization when he came upon two moose engaged in a terrific struggle, smashing tree branches and tearing up the underbrush. They fought for an hour and did tremendous damage to each other, but eventually separated. Knowles was transfixed, and he forgot all about being sick as he watched their primordial battle.

Knowles did approach King & Bartlett Camp later that day; but after the encounter with the moose he was revived a bit and, despite being visited by guide Harry Pierce's Airedale terrier on the outskirts of the camp, did not give himself away. Instead, he napped and awoke feeling better in every way. "I guess I won't give up today," he proclaimed. It was a turning point.

The leaves were beginning to turn as Knowles had another of his great adventures: catching a deer with his bare hands. Waiting on the trail, with the wind carrying away his scent, Knowles pounced on a young buck, caught him by his front feet, grabbed on to his horns, and broke his neck with a quick twist.

Again, he was apologetic: "I want to apologize for killing the deer in that manner," he wrote in *Alone*. "But under the circumstances, it was the only way I had. I needed the skin badly." He was soon wearing it in combination with his bearskin, and looked the very picture of the backwoodsman of legend. In a photograph taken for the book shortly after he came out of the woods, Knowles lacks only the coonskin cap to resemble a Hollywood version of Davy Crockett. Ironically, this photograph of an "authentic" woodsman is heavily retouched—aside from the head and shoulders, it looks like one of Knowles's own paintings.

Knowles had several times enjoyed windfalls from fresh animal kills, but now he had downed a deer and a bear on his own, and the news was splashed all over the Boston newspapers. The seasoned hunter and trapper nevertheless lacked hunting and trapping licenses from the Maine Fish and Game Commission, and in any case deer season wasn't set to begun until October 1.

IN HIS BEARSKIN AND DEER LEGGINGS, HE LOOKED THE
IMAGE OF THE FRONTIERSMAN. NOTE THAT THE PHOTO, POSED
SHORTLY AFTER THE EXPERIMENT ENDED, IS HEAVILY
RETOUCHED. *BOSTON POST* PHOTO, FROM *ALONE IN THE
WILDERNESS*

According to his account in *Alone*, before his trip he had applied
through friends for the necessary permits, but was turned down.
He applied again, citing Section 17 of the game laws, which permitted out-of-season hunting and trapping when some scientific
purpose was involved. "Noted men" were endorsing the experiment, he said. But again Knowles was turned down, with the
board declining to be put "in the position of endorsing violations
of our Inland Fish and Game Laws."

In fact, Massachusetts resident Knowles was in violation not only of the licensing law, but also of another statute, which required any non-resident of Maine to engage a guide when building fires or camping on hunting and fishing trips. The *Post* editorialized on September 21 to purple effect that the Maine game laws "are a deep and devious system," and urged the wardens to consider the scientific, artistic, and practical value of Knowles's experiment. But they were up against hard men who allowed no sentiment to interfere "with their great and sworn duty toward protecting the network of game regulations."

Rumors flew that the wardens were planning to go into the woods to "interview" Knowles and perhaps drag him out. Whether this was true or not, it certainly added drama to the story. By September 28, Knowles was ready to modify his plan to simply walk out of the woods at the end of his two months, because being carted off in handcuffs by game wardens would have hardly been a fitting end to the noble experiment.

The chase was on. Knowles decided that if he made it across the (fairly) nearby Canadian border, he'd be out of the Maine wardens' jurisdiction. "I would have undergone anything rather than be taken by game wardens in the woods," he wrote in *Alone*. Time was short because, as the newspaper put it, "The wardens are mustering up courage to tackle the Forest Man in his lair and drag him out." Though it was a journey of some thirty miles (exaggerated to sixty in the breathless newspaper accounts) through rough terrain to the nearest substantial town, Lake Megantic in Quebec, this didn't seem to faze Knowles. He was now only a week away from the planned end of the experiment on Saturday, October 4, 1913.

The story of Knowles's race to the Canadian border had all the high drama of a televised police chase, and it's hard to resist the conclusion that the paper manipulated events to make it even more so. The fugitive from justice might as well have shouted "You'll never take me alive, coppers!" It's not surprising that the *Post* coverage was now enjoying a huge readership; indeed, the paper claimed that its daily circulation had doubled, from 200,000 to a perhaps-inflated 436,585, in the two months Knowles was in the woods.

In another pouring rain, Knowles portaged through the brush, staying away from logging roads and well-known pathways, "fearing such places would be watched." Moving along natural game trails, he moved relentlessly toward Canada, using the north-pointing moss on trees as guides. An exultant *Post* knew just how to play up this modern odyssey, adding the *frisson* of fear. Knowles, it said, had "taken his very life in his hands" by wearing his bearskin as deer-hunting season opened in the state of Maine. "[T]he intrepid Boston artist has traveled through a forest country where hunters might appear at any moment," the paper wrote, "and there would have been the best of excuses for any hunter firing at Knowles for a deer, clad as he is in his forest garb."

Now carrying a bow and arrow he had fashioned and used to kill a deer, he shot spruce partridges (known as "fool hens" because they're easy to catch) on the wing and ate them raw. By the evening of October 3, he had reached Boundary Mountain, marking the Canadian border. "It was not until I had crossed the line that I drew my first free breath," he wrote in *Alone.* "They couldn't touch me now!"

Meanwhile, back in Maine, not everyone had gotten the word that Knowles was to emerge not at King & Bartlett Camp but miles north in Canada. A contemporary Canadian account by Alphonse Gauchon that appeared in *Les Annales de St. Gerard* says

THE AUTHOR'S FIRST SHOES, MADE OF THE INNER LINING
BARK OF THE CEDAR

KNOWLES'S HANDMADE SANDALS. *BOSTON POST* PHOTO,
FROM *ALONE IN THE WILDERNESS*

that at the appointed time, canoes dotted King and Bartlett Lake scanning the shoreline for signs of Joe Knowles. "The hour was getting near the rendezvous time and there was concern whether Knowles had died from starvation, or been devoured by wild beasts more starving than himself. None of this had happened. Knowles was very much alive, but six miles from Lac Megantic."

On the morning of October 4, he covered the few miles remaining and was rewarded by a distant train whistle. And at four P.M. that day, he came out on a clearing and found himself face to face with the tracks of the Canadian Pacific Railroad. He was seven miles from Megantic, and the great experiment was over. But as *Yankee* magazine put it, a welcome fit for a Roman general was about to begin.

TWO

The Makings of a Nature Man

KNOWLES, SOMETIME ARTIST, FORMER HUNTING GUIDE AND NAVY MAN, claimed that "the book of nature has been sadly neglected," and he aimed to be the sage who reconnected America to its roots. It may seem bizarre to suggest that a nation so recently forged, and only recently expanded to its natural limits, would be out of touch with frontier life and the woodcraft skills necessary for survival. But such anxiety did indeed characterize the period, and Knowles's timing was propitious.

Instead of blazing the trail west with horses and covered wagons, Americans in 1913 were starting to drive cars, dancing to early jazz, and working in factories. The sons and daughters of farmers now saw the fields only in the far distance from the shop floor or their office windows. When they found time to read, they often turned to fanciful Western novels like Zane Grey's bestselling *Riders of the Purple Sage* (1912). Edgar Rice Burroughs's *Tarzan of the Apes* was first serialized in 1912, and it similarly gave city dwellers a chance to escape their confines and dream of wild places. *Tarzan* was another story of a natural man who lived among animals in the wilderness, and it captured the public imagination as did few other stories of its time. The adventures of Joseph Knowles captivated these same audiences, because here was the natural man leaping off the fictional page and into the news headlines.

This man of the woods was native to Maine, specifically the little town of Wilton, in Franklin County. Wilton, directly south from the wilderness Knowles would haunt as the Nature Man, was settled in 1785 and owes its existence to an act of historical violence. According to an 1886 history by George J. Varney, the land that became Wilton was granted to a Captain Tyng of Concord, Massachusetts, in gratitude for his role in the capture and slaying of "a dangerous savage called Harry." Indeed, the town was initially known as Harrytown ("in memory of the ill-fated Indian"). There's some irony in the fact that Knowles, who admired the teachings of Native Americans and was later to live among them, would be a native son.

Wilton, around the time of Knowles's birth in 1869, was a thriving mill town, home to Moosehead Mills and Holt scythes. From its factories came woolen goods, leather boots, shingles, notable Wilton cheese, canned corn, first-grade flour, and the lightning hay cutter. Because the town is blessed with the 190-acre Wilson's Pond, which reaches a depth of 175 feet, it was able to take part in the lucrative international ice trade. As Geoffrey Wolff notes in his book *The Edge of Maine,* ice from the state's lakes and ponds was cut by horse-drawn teams in the days before re-

THE GIANTESS SYLVIA HARDY. BARNUM'S GALLERY OF WONDERS, NO. 10, "THE MAINE GIANTESS," UNDATED. PUBLISHED BY N. CURRIER. MUSEUM OF THE CITY OF NEW YORK, THE HARRY T. PETERS COLLECTION

frigeration and large blocks of it sent by ship (packed in sawdust so that the inevitable melting was slowed) as far away as India and the Caribbean.

Wilton was a long way from the vaudeville stages whose boards Knowles would eventually tread, but the town did produce one theatrical notable of sorts, "The Maine Giantess" Sylvia Hardy.

Born in Wilton in 1823, she was briefly on exhibition at P. T. Barnum's American Museum in New York. An 1855 *New York Times* story describes her appearance (alongside the bearded lady) at Barnum's celebrated "baby show" of that year. The reporter describes her as having weighed only three pounds at birth, but, now that she was at least seven feet tall (estimates went all the way up to seven feet, eleven inches), she topped the scales at 330. "Thunder, ain't she a whopper!" exclaimed a newsboy in attendance.

The population of Wilton in 1880 was 1,739. The town was still making leather boots as late as 1997, but the following year the G. H. Bass factory closed, taking hundreds of jobs to Puerto Rico, the Dominican Republic, and other locations. The 2000 census found 4,123 people living in Wilton, which by then no longer had much of an industrial life. "This is a dying town in some ways," says Pam Brown, president of the Wilton Historical Society. "Bass took our jobs overseas."

The Wilton that Knowles knew was a lovely village at the bottom of a picturesque valley, at a remove from the mills along Wilson's Stream. Bordering the settlements of East Wilton and Wilton Village were dense forests, which served as Knowles's classroom when he was a boy.

Knowles's father, Joseph Greenleaf Knowles, was a Civil War veteran (a private in the Eighth Maine Infantry) of English and Native American heritage who came home from the conflict "crippled and unable to help support the family," according to *Alone.* The 1890 census lists J. G. Knowles as suffering from malarial poisoning, chills, and fever as a result of his wartime experience. Knowles's Scotch-Irish mother, Mary Hitchcock Knowles, the more formative influence on him, "was born in the wilds of Canada, near the Indians." Knowles calls her "the most courageous per-

Mary Hitchcock Knowles, family matriarch. photo courtesy of ilwaco heritage museum

son I ever met"; later, after his months in the woods, he would have
his picture taken greeting this short, black-clad, and grandmoth-
erly figure on the front porch of the family homestead. It was his
mother who taught him the ways of the woods and animals, he says.

Knowles wrote that he grew up in poverty in "an old-fashioned
house in a forest clearing," with his mother the family's sole source
of support for ten years. "His first recollection of food was cornbread, and for many years thereafter it was his constant companion," he wrote in the third person. He added that at age four he

built a crude homemade sled and dragged it to school, where he experienced ridicule from wealthier children with steel-shod store sleds. A fight broke out, and Knowles was pummeled by many mittened fists, his face (and the sled) pushed under the snow. "This was his initiation into the society of schoolmates," he wrote.

Knowles showed artistic talent early on, but he was eleven before he got his first crayons. With four children, including young Joseph's two brothers and a sister, to feed and clothe, the matriarch would haul wood from the forest in the winter and pick berries in the summer, walking six miles into the village to sell them. She also made moccasins, wove baskets, and took in piecework. It wasn't always enough. During one snowbound winter, the family of six was left with only a single turkey egg, which Knowles's mother mixed with the remaining flour to make a batter that the family lived off for three days (she herself ate nothing, claiming that she wasn't hungry).

Despite these difficulties, Knowles seems to have had much to give him solace. And rural Maine in the nineteenth century was not the cultural wasteland many would imagine. There were spelling bees, Grange programs, and competitive debating societies called lyceums, with speakers vying to outdo each other with comic essays, dialogues, and mock trials. Women read homemade literary "newspapers" aloud at community gatherings. It may be that Knowles honed the first of his tall tales at events like these.

The woods lay just outside the door, and Knowles decided early on to supplement the family's meager diet with the bounty in the forest. At age ten, he took his father's gun into the winter woods and went after big game. Shooting at what he thought was a bear cub in a tree, he dropped his weapon (and his shoes) in terror and ran home after seeing the animal come down the trunk in his direction.

KNOWLES'S PORTRAIT OF HIS NEPHEW MAY HAVE AUTOBIOGRAPHICAL OVERTONES. NOTE THE RIFLE'S ODD RESTING PLACE. COURTESY OF THE WILTON FARM AND HOME MUSEUM / PAUL TAITT

"There's a bear after me!" he shrieked, but Knowles's ever-wise mother convinced him that since bears happened to be in hibernation at the time, the murderous beast was actually a hedgehog.

There are no known pictures of Knowles as a boy or young man. A camera—or professionally shot photographs—would have been a considerable luxury for a nineteenth-century family in those circumstances. But clues to Knowles's appearance are offered by a pair of paintings in the collection of the Wilton Farm and Home Museum. In an oil self-portrait done in 1913 (the year he went into the woods), he depicts himself as he appeared perhaps in his early twenties. Looking extremely fit, he is seen traipsing through a wintry scene, his Indian-like features somewhat shrouded by a Western hat. This version of Knowles is carrying a rifle in one hand and using the other to hold up an immense moose head.

In the second work, an undated painting of one of his nephews, the ten-year-old boy is clearly a stand-in for Knowles himself. Again, it is a winter scene and the boy, wearing a jaunty cap, has removed his mittens as he bends to the task of tying his snow-shoes (the correct making of which was one of Knowles's many obsessions). A rifle is rather improbably leaning against his body as he works.

Many years later, Knowles told of an incident that had occurred when he was a boy around the age of the one in the painting. In a surviving fragment, he wrote that his grandfather had a flintlock rifle that he'd brought home from the Mexican-American War (1846–1848). Since it was simply a display piece, young Knowles worked for a local farmer for a week in exchange for powder and six bullets to load into it. He then, in a rare display of caution, rigged the gun with a string and fired it remotely. "There was a terrific explosion," Knowles wrote. "I'd used too much powder and not enough lead. The barrel had split wide open full length, and the stock was busted. It was a lucky thing for me that I had thought to lash the thing to a tree." He got a licking for this prank.

Knowles told many stories like this, and it's revealing that he was often the butt of his own jokes. His self-effacing humor aided considerably in his later popularity. Another explosive incident from this period, told and very likely embellished by Knowles's boyhood friend Howard Noble, occurred during the family's brief move to the bright lights of Lewiston, Maine, south of Wilton. Knowles, then probably eleven or twelve, and his younger brother, Leander, came across two twenty-five-pound kegs of powder left over from a blasting operation. The brothers hauled their find into the family kitchen and attempted to manufacture homemade fireworks. A scrap of burning paper landed in one of the barrels and ignited the powder, causing the roof of the house to lift off "into the empyrean blue," as Noble describes it. "Each of the four walls took a different course through space. Even the floor went upward. Horses and pedestrians were knocked down and windows in neighboring buildings were blown out. It was some explosion!"

Knowles himself was immediately reduced to a pathetic form lying prostrate in the dust of Main Street. "The poor fellow," cried an onlooker in the crowd that gathered. "He's all blown to pieces." There was a collective sigh, and men and boys removed their hats in respect. But then the limp form raised itself from the ground and, instead of intoning a few last words, asked merely, "Which way did Leander go?" Leander had, in fact, landed some distance away, and despite powder burns that kept doctors occupied for some time neither was the worse for wear. The family moved back to Wilton, taking with it "the boy who had given Lewiston its biggest sensation in years."

The young Knowles carried a meager lunch of cornbread and sowbelly to school in a lard pail. He would eat in the woods so the other kids, who lunched on "dainty sandwiches," would not see his pathetic meal. But Knowles's main memory of his school days involved a dramatic fight with a classmate. He was to write of this encounter several times and mentioned it as a key moment of his youth in several interviews. In the most detailed account, he describes his opponent as "the Harrington boy, handsome, red-headed and a favorite with the girls." He bedeviled the young Knowles terribly, at one time holding his head under water "until I nearly drowned."

Knowles took this vexing problem to his often-disappointing father, who told him, "You are afraid of the Harrington boy. There are no cowards in my family. All you will get if you stand up for

your rights can't be as bad as what you've already taken for laying [*sic*] down like a coward."

To his credit, Knowles's account of his own actions is far from
heroic; in fact, it somewhat embraces the "coward" diagnosis.
That night, he got so worked up about having to confront Harrington that he had a nightmare and fell out of bed, breaking his nose.
Still, he went to school the next day with a plaster on his face,
and Harrington had a field day, chanting "He has a patch on his
nose, and a patch on his pants." Finally, Harrington said it one
too many times and Knowles punched him in the middle of a
recitation, sparking a wild melee. To his great surprise, Knowles
emerged the victor as a bleeding Harrington was led away. "The
girls were off me for life for mussing up their pretty boy's face,"
Knowles wrote. But the boys granted him a new respect.

Knowles's trips into the woods grew longer and longer as he approached his teen years, according to his parents. The *Post,* in one
of the filler pieces that appeared between birchbark dispatches,
reported that he would cause his mother and father considerable
worry by disappearing for two or three days at a time, "defying
anyone to find him in his forest lairs." One time, they said, he was
gone for a record eleven days, forcing his parents to organize a
posse and go in after the wayward youth. But Knowles had not been
eaten by a bear, as they feared; he was found "enjoying himself
to the utmost in his favorite haunts."

Given the family's poverty, it's perhaps not surprising that
Knowles ran away to sea when he was only thirteen. His father
had filled his head with fascinating stories about his early life on
board full-rigged ships that sailed across the ocean. And while
Knowles's primary allegiance was always to his mother (to whom

A KNOWLES SELF-PORTRAIT, DONE IN 1913 BUT HEARKENING BACK TO AN EARLIER TIME, IS A CLUE TO HIS YOUTHFUL APPEARANCE. COURTESY OF THE WILTON FARM AND HOME MUSEUM / PAUL TAITT

Alone in the Wilderness is dedicated), his father helped instill his lifelong love of adventure.

In leaving rural New England, Knowles was also following a general stampede toward the bright lights of a larger world. Americans were becoming less sentimental about New England villages in the period following the Civil War, as opportunity and excitement shifted to the rapidly growing cities and to the unexplored frontier.

Knowles's life on the high seas began impulsively, after a parental scolding. Throughout his life, he would similarly act on whims; long-range planning was not part of his makeup. With vague thoughts of shipping out, Knowles walked for two days to Portland. According to Noble, he managed to elude his pursuing parents and, after haunting the Portland docks for some days, succeeded in being taken aboard a three-masted coasting schooner en route to Pensacola, Florida.

His ship was wrecked in the Florida Keys, and Knowles was picked up by a passing steamer and taken to Havana, Cuba, where he got lucky again and boarded a "New Brunswick booker bound light to St. John." What romance! Robert Louis Stevenson's *Treasure Island*, starring an adventurous seafaring boy not unlike Joseph Knowles, had been published to great acclaim in 1881, just the year before, so its vivid tales were still very fresh. The tanned and confident Knowles who arrived back in Wilton with two $10 bills (the equivalent of roughly $400 today) in his pocket was greeted as a conquering hero by the town boys. But Knowles was soon off again, and this time he stayed away several years.

"When next Joe appeared in Lewiston he was wearing the uniform of the U.S. Navy," wrote Noble in the *Post*. "He paid a visit to the old folks in Wilton and then came back to Lewiston, where he was idolized by his former chums. He had numerous tattoo marks on his body. I recall that upon his breast was a fascinating young woman twirling a long snake around her waist. Each of his wrists was encircled with elaborate bracelets done in red and blue India ink. Between his shoulders was a map of the western hemisphere."

One can imagine the scene as Knowles agreed to tattoo the gathered boys of Lewiston. It was probably the first flowering of his artistic aspirations, and it left Noble with a blue India-ink design on his left arm. "To us youngsters, Joe Knowles became a fetish," Noble wrote. "We worshipped him. To us, he represented all the romance of youth—the embodiment of half-baked, callow dreams inspired by the literature of the day."

In 1924, Knowles gave a lengthy account of his younger days to the *Four L Bulletin,* the magazine of the Loyal Legion of Loggers and Lumbermen. Editor J. B. Fitzgerald commissioned a cover illustration by Knowles and praised the Nature Man's life story as "one of the most thrilling human interest yarns I have ever read." Predictably, given his interlocutor's gregarious nature, Fitzgerald also visited Knowles at what was then his home in Seaview, Washington, and described the visit as "going to a gurgling spring of cool water in the summer's heat."

In the *Four L* story, Knowles said he joined the U.S. Navy at nineteen, serving an enlistment and a half. Unjustly denied shore leave during his second enlistment and put in the brig for insubordination, he says he picked the locks, jumped overboard, and was taken in by a passing oyster boat. Later, he says, the officer who had disciplined him was censured and Knowles's discharge changed from dishonorable to honorable.

We may have to take Knowles's word for that Navy enlistment. Genealogist Hazel Standeven, who produced a detailed dossier on Knowles and his family, attempted to obtain his service record between 1888 and 1892 from the National Archives, but was told that no information was available.

Knowles says he also served in the merchant marine, where a Japanese sailor taught him karate. He became "a deep water man," and served as second mate on many voyages. A 1933 account in the *Portland Sunday Oregonian* says that Knowles's travels took him to Europe, Africa, Asia, the West Indies, and South and Central America. He presumably came out of these adventures a far more cosmopolitan person than the boy who had loitered on the Portland docks or the peers he left behind. His backwoods charm remained, however.

"After that, I decided I would like to try sailing on the fresh-water lakes," Knowles wrote. "So I left the coast and sailed on the Great Lakes for another 12 months." It was there, on the west coast of Michigan, that he encountered tribes of Sioux and Chippewah Indians, hunted and trapped with them, and from them "picked up valuable knowledge about the woods under these conditions."

After his adventures in the wide world, Knowles came back to Maine, where for five years he worked as a hunting guide and trapper. He also worked in lumber camps—driving horse and ox teams, riding logs down the river, and living on sourdough bread, blackstrap molasses, and pork and beans. Laboring with a hard-bitten crew of French-Canadians, Yankees, and what he called "half-breed Indians," he found that his fighting skills came in handy. "Rum, whiskey, gambling and jealousy resulted in a good many scraps in which fists, knives and hatchets were used," he told the *Four L Bulletin.*

Knowles and his brother Dick would frequently volunteer to break up logjams. On one memorable occasion, he fastened nine sticks of dynamite to a pole, lit it off, and tried to find the key log to blast the jam free. At that moment, he was knocked into the water by an errant log, and the smoldering dynamite fell from his hands. "The stick with the dynamite [was] chasing me around the eddy, while I desperately tried to get out of the water," he told *Four L.* Fortunately, the dynamite was carried by currents over the nearby dam, where it exploded and threw a log high enough to land near a passing team of horses, thus "giving them the surprise of their lives." Knowles was unhurt.

Around this time, in 1893, Knowles married for the first time. His new wife was the former Sadie Andrews, two years older than Joe. In the census of 1900, they are listed as living together in Eustis, Maine, near the King & Bartlett Camp. The marriage was childless and not enduring. Knowles left no remembrance of this union, good or bad. By 1910, Sadie was divorced, living with her sister, and working as a hotel chambermaid. Perhaps she had grown tired of the Nature Man's perpetual wandering. She was soon married again, to a much younger man, and resettled in Wilton. Knowles, meanwhile, had gone on to other adventures.

In 1895, as if in training for his test in the woods two decades later, he was asked to take a young woman on a sixty-mile sleigh ride in a sparsely settled section of northern Maine. The small party encountered calamity when the sleigh and its passengers fell into a snow-covered river, and Knowles spent a harrowing seven hours in an almost-Herculean effort to get both the nearly frozen woman and the horse to the safety of a distant farm. The ordeal is vividly described in *Alone*, complete with Knowles "beating and pulling and rubbing" the unfortunate woman to keep her alive. He did the same to the horse, and all three survived.

Harry B. Center, who worked alongside Joe in the woods, remembered him as a practical joker, a daredevil, and a soft heart who would rather photograph the plentiful moose than shoot them. After catching a single trout, he would put his rod away, take out his watercolors, and create a portrait of the fish. Fly-casting on Spencer Stream one day, Center was taken by Knowles to hear beavers "talk." Writing in the *Post*, Center says he and Knowles crept up on a beaver dam. "It was so still that the voices of the beaver, a low squeal something like the whine of a dog, could plainly be heard. 'They're eating the bark,' said Joe. 'Pretty soon you'll hear 'em arguing about who'll go out and get the next feed stick.' We heard them, too."

Later, Knowles gave Center the scare of his life when he tried to push him out of a canoe on Big Spencer Lake just shy of a sixteen-foot waterfall. "I came out of that canoe like a yeast cake and bawled Joe out for trying to drown me," Center wrote. But he later learned that Knowles had actually taken a canoe over that same waterfall and through the rapids below on a bet.

Knowles was one of the boys, but the men who worked along-side him were often amused when he took out his paints or sketch-pad. If no paper was available, he'd draw on a piece of mushroom. "I used to tell him he was a cussed fool and was wastin' good time that ought to be used for makin' snowshoes," one of Knowles's old acquaintances told the *Post* in the spring just before he went into the woods. The old campaigner added, with some apparent cha-grin, "There he is up in Boston paintin' pictures for books and mag-azines and I'm—I'm going to Lewiston and get good and drunk."

The middle-aged Knowles, weighing more than two hundred pounds and by his own admission considerably softened by civilized life, was no longer quite as inspirational as he once had been. His life in the woods eventually came into conflict with his desire, nurtured since childhood, to succeed as an artist. Knowles was no longer content to make occasional sketches of wildlife and hand them out to his uncritical friends; he was uncertain about the quality of his work, and he wanted the approval of a wider world.

His break came when a magazine bought one of his nature paintings for cover art. "It meant a great deal to me," he said. Fi-nally, the woodsman's quest to become a painter took him out of

the woods around 1903 and to an attic room in Boston, where he
spent ten years perfecting his craft. He and a partner, Bernice
Lambert, created a small business burning and painting leather
novelties "for dens, camps, canoes, etc." Paintings of sport fish
and local game animals were also offered.

Although he continued to design covers for magazines, including *Field and Stream* in 1908 and *National Sportsman* and *Baseball,* both in 1910, Knowles was not professionally trained. His
one encounter with formal study was a brief stint in a Boston art
class. The instructor became convinced that this apt pupil would
be hired in his place, and so after three classes reportedly asked
Knowles to leave. "I never went to an art school, but I studied the
works of successful artists and won what success has been mine
through my own efforts," he writes in *Alone.*

Some work from his period as a newspaper artist survives,
although the very stylish fashion illustrations in Knowles's archives
depicting chic clothes from the first two decades of the new century were actually drawn by his equally talented wife. Knowles's
first known writing in the *Boston Post* was a series on New
England game fish he both wrote and illustrated (with vivid
pen-and-ink sketches) in 1908. The story on the "Muscalonge,"
or "muskie," concludes that it is "not properly a New England fish,
for it is seldom found in New England waters proper. . . . You can
spell muscalonge any way you want to and nobody can seriously
dispute you. There are about 40 accepted spellings, and one is
about as correct as any other." ("Muskellunge" is favored today.)

At the time he went into the woods, Knowles had left his job
(which he'd held from 1907 to 1910) as a part-time artist on the
evening staff of the *Post,* and was a woodsman no longer. "My skin
is not toughened; my muscles have grown flabby because I have

wielded the brush and palette instead of the axe and paddle," he told the paper before setting out. "My stomach is used to seasoned and well-cooked foods; my feet are as soft and sensitive as any city man's; the luxuries of clothing to suit all weathers has almost eradicated my ability to withstand heat and cold in severe degree."

How did this out-of-shape artist morph into the Nature Man? In *Alone in the Wilderness,* he wrote that he had gotten the idea while painting in the woods of Bradford, Vermont, near the Connecticut River, where he then had a studio. Much later, in an unpublished fragment, he sketched in some details. "At the time I was painting wild animals and outdoor life for illustrations and covers of magazines. I was painting the picture of a moose, and, as I added touches of color, I wondered how many would notice [these subtle but accurate details]."

Knowles considered enhancing his picture with a background image of a modern hunter, or a man with a camera, but neither seemed quite right. Then he thought of adding "a primitive man armed with club and spear, a man as wild as the moose himself." The man he saw in his imagination was "well fed, healthy and free," a "real hunter who killed only when necessity demanded." The image stuck in his mind, and it led to an illuminating dream that same night.

In a bylined 1914 story for the *San Francisco Examiner,* written just before he plunged into the mountains for his second trip, on the Oregon–California border, Knowles wrote: "Dreams are wonderful things," he said. "It was a dream that first suggested to me to live alone, independent of civilization. I had a dream that I was lost in the woods. No one was within sight or sound of me. My first thoughts were what I would do to get in touch with civilization."

But in his dream state, without food, gun, or knife, Knowles says he was able to reason through what he would need to survive, from eating wild berries to setting snares made from the fibers of trees and catching fish without benefit of a hook. And so "the fear of being lost and alone in the woods entirely left me and I had perfect confidence in my ability to live. When I awoke, the dream seemed real. . . . I told many of my friends. They argued that a man in that position would be helpless. I doubted and at last decided to make an experiment."

In a 1936 interview with Stewart H. Holbrook of the *American Mercury,* he adds a few curious details about his dream, which he says was "a damned real one." He dreamed he was "lost in the woods, alone and *naked* [emphasis in the original], with no hope ever of getting out. When I woke up I got to thinking if and how a civilized man could get along in such a situation. A day or so later I related my dream at a small hotel dinner. How a New York newspaperman happened to be present I have forgotten, but there was one; and next day the [New York] *Tribune* carried an interview with me, telling of my claims. In a day or two, mail started flooding me."

In his unpublished account, Knowles says the hotel was in Bradford, where he painted the moose, and he quotes the unnamed New York reporter: "Such an experiment as you have outlined would be very interesting and valuable. . . . Your primitive man idea is original and should make a great news feature, but who would attempt such a test?"

"I would," Knowles replied, "if I thought the experiment would be appreciated and not taken as a joke." After the article was published, Knowles wrote that he received proposals from "various newspapers and magazines" containing "bids for the news rights of my proposed woods venture." He doesn't say if the *Tribune* itself was interested in being the sponsor.

The paper in which the story allegedly appeared, the *New York Tribune,* was then a bitter rival of the *New York Herald.* But they were later to merge and form the *Herald Tribune.* There's no evidence that the story about Knowles was actually written. If it was, one might expect the Nature Man to have had New York—not Boston—sponsorship for his first trip. But Holbrook relates that after the flood of letters in New York, both the *Boston Post* and Hearst's *Boston American* wrote to say they'd like to meet this Nature Man. By this account, the *Post* made the only offer. "You're losing the chance of a lifetime," Knowles reportedly told the *American*'s editor.

The New York reporter and his story have proven elusive. Knowles told other versions of this story in which he had morphed into a Bostonian. The most likely scenario is that the Nature Man scheme was hatched in Boston; and that after it was cooked up in a smoke-filled room somewhere, it was shopped to several papers there.

The *Post* was an older paper in a very competitive market with as many as nine other dailies. The *Post, Globe,* and *American* were all based on Washington Street's "Newspaper Row" in downtown Boston. "It was the densest geographical concentration of newspapers in an American city, and helped fuel competition," wrote historian Mark Neuzil in a lengthy essay on Knowles.

The *Post* was suffering heavy circulation loss at the hands of what Holbrook calls the "young and rowdy" *American.* The *Post*'s new Sunday editor, Charles E. L. Wingate, who had just come over from another rival, the *Journal,* was more receptive. He said he would undertake the experiment "to learn whether the human race has become so sissified that it could no longer combat the rigors and dangers which beset Primitive Man."

Knowles's timing was good, because the *Post* was willing to try anything. The idea of a naked man in the woods fit right into a series of increasingly brazen promotional schemes it had undertaken in order to stay afloat. This one wasn't likely to cost much; and if Knowles died out there, well, that made good copy too.

The paper was nothing if not creative. One of its best ideas was the "Boston *Post* Cane." Introduced in 1909 by *Post* owner and publisher Edwin Grozier, the ebony canes (with engraved gold caps) were distributed to 700 small New England towns to be awarded to the oldest resident, then passed on to the next. (Originally the cane was for men only; women were not allowed to receive it until long after they got the vote in 1920.) All in all, it was a promotion that continued to deliver circulation bounty long after its modest expenses had been amortized. The tradition is still followed in many host communities.

The "Boston *Post* Cane" was Grozier's brainchild, one of many. Grozier, a Cape Cod native whose father piloted clipper ships, had graduated from Boston University and worked for newspapers there, but moved to New York in the 1880s. He became not only an editor of the *New York World* (William Randolph Hearst's nemesis there) but a close confidant and secretary to its publisher, Joseph Pulitzer.

When Grozier bought the *Post* in 1891, it was in poor financial health and had a circulation of only 20,000; but through his efforts it was at least pulled back from the brink of bankruptcy. *Post* reporter Kenneth Roberts, hired by Grozier despite his lack of experience (and eventually to become a bestselling author), described his boss as a "newspaper genius" with a special gift for promotion.

According to Mitchell Zuckoff's book *Ponzi's Scheme,* one of his ideas involved circus elephants. Encountering an Englishman and his wife with three surplus pachyderms, Mollie, Waddy, and Tony, Grozier decided they'd make ideal denizens of the city's Franklin Park Zoo. But rather than buy them himself, he enlisted the city's children to make contributions toward the $15,000 purchase price. Many thousands of kids sent in money at a rate of pennies apiece, and all got their names in the paper as "part owners." Some 70,000 youngsters turned up at the zoo when the animals were delivered.

"Every child who had given even one cent wanted to see his name in the paper and was thrilled by the thought that he owned part of an elephant," Grozier said. "Of course, it added thousands to the circulation of the *Post,* but it was a gain that was based not on appealing to the worst elements in human nature but to the best. . . ."

According to Zuckoff, "Barely a day went by [at the *Post*] without some kind of promotion or gimmick." He sent a reporter incognito into the streets, and the first person who said "Good morning, have you read the *Post* today?" to him got $100. He offered free Model T cars to readers who came up with the best human-interest stories. He hired a "movie scout" to find young women who were right for film careers, and put their pictures in the paper. For "the headless lady," a *Post* photographer snapped shots of women on the street from the neck down. If the unidentified woman appeared at the *Post*'s office wearing the identical outfit, she won $10 in gold. The only way to know if you were the "headless lady" was to buy a newspaper.

In addition to the gimmicks, the *Post* did more than a bit of muckraking: It exposed the truth behind Charles Ponzi's financial pyramid, which had promised investors a 50 percent return on their money within forty-five days. Grozier loved lurid crime stories, and in 1911 poured resources into an investigation of the sensational murder of beautiful Avis Linnell by prominent minister Clarence Richeson. (The *Post* found the druggist who sold Richeson the cyanide.) Knowles probably cost the *Post* less than the gold-handled canes or the circus elephants.

Knowles repaired to his studio in rural Bradford, Vermont, to prepare. According to Holbrook, he donned his G-string for the first time and spent a week catching trout with his bare hands, making fires, and deterring insects with wild spearmint rubbed on his body. This, presumably, is the trip that allowed the *Post*'s photographers to take the shots of Knowles in action that adorn *Alone in the Wilderness*.

It made a captivating tale, but a far different and darker chain of events, suggesting that money, not lofty ideals, was the key motivator, emerged in 1938. And more than sixty years after that, in 1999, a column by a former *Post* insider suggested that the whole thing was cooked up in the *Post*'s newsroom as a circulation-building response to the then-popular Tarzan stories. No one tried to reconcile the conflicting stories, because by 1938 the Nature Man had long since gone into retirement and the question of what Joe Knowles did in the woods (and how he got there) no longer burned as brightly.

KNOWLES AND HIS G-STRING, A PHOTO PRESUMABLY TAKEN IN BRADFORD,
VERMONT, BEFORE THE EXPERIMENT BEGAN. *BOSTON POST* PHOTO, FROM
ALONE IN THE WILDERNESS

On the eve of his trip, Knowles was examined by Dr. Dudley
Sargent of Harvard, who tactfully agreed that the would-be man
of the woods was a bit out of shape. Sargent suggested that the
onetime woodsman's "considerable fat . . . should aid him in re-
sisting the cold." This pudgy habitué of city garrets and barrooms
bore little resemblance to a rugged outdoorsman, but Knowles
believed this urban veneer would soon wear off; he had confidence in the restorative powers of the wilderness.

Knowles's newspaper readers undoubtedly identified with his
slow transformation from city dweller to nature warrior, as it was
a path they too might take some day. Here, at last, was a frontiersman tailor-made for changing times.

THREE

The Toast of Boston

IF AN EDWARDIAN BOY'S ADVENTURE STORY COULD HAVE COME TO life, it would have disgorged a figure resembling Joseph Knowles on those Quebec railroad tracks on October 4, 1913. As *American Heritage* described it, he "looked half-man, half-bear, with his matted hair, skin dark as an Indian's, fur-lined chaps and bearskin cloak." His skins were tied together with thongs of deerhide, and on his feet were buckskin moccasins. A crude cedar bark–lined pack was on his back, filled with forest treasures. This vision from another time—"a replica of what the cave man must have looked like when the world was young," said the *Post*—encountered a fourteen-year-old girl, Frieme Gerard, who said later that the fur-clad creature reminded her of a picture of Stone Age man from a history book. Nonetheless, she stood her ground and accosted him in an avalanche of French. Joe Knowles was back in civilization. "She was the first human being I had spoken to in two months," Knowles later wrote.

With his bearskin stinking and upsetting the other passengers, Knowles hopped a passenger train and rode the few miles into the town of Lake Megantic on the plush cushions of a first-class rail car. *Yankee Magazine* describes a tumultuous welcome in the little French town, "replete with brass bands, bunting, bevies of British and American officials—and four genial Maine Game Wardens, come to escort him home." The *Post* said the game wardens were complemented by Megantic's mayor, a local parish priest, and "prominent Boston and New York sporting men." Knowles, whose weight had dropped from 204 pounds to 174, was taken to the flag-draped Queen's Hotel, where he stretched out on a "real bed" for the first time in sixty days. He told the assembled dignitaries that he'd never felt better in his life, and—echoing the beginning of the adventure on August 4—he asked for a cigarette.

A *Boston Globe* story offers an intriguing addition to the story. It says that the *Post*'s reporter Paul Waitt (a newspaper stylist of some merit and later the likely ghostwriter of Knowles's autobiography) was deputized to stage-manage Knowles's emergence in Megantic. The *Globe* reported that "a local booster" in Megantic had viewed with interest the capture in another Canadian town of New York society murderer Harry K. Thaw. Because the town had reaped international publicity from the incident, the booster reasoned that if Megantic arrested Knowles on some trumped-up charge, it would also win a place on the map. "The poo-bah was all set to arrest him for setting a fire in the woods of Canada," according to the *Globe*.

The irrepressible Waitt took the local official out for a lavish dinner, and the liquor flowed. "When Waitt finally stood up, the local official could not. He was the only man in town who could make the arrest." Knowles, sequestered in the local barbershop, according to this account, escaped custody and "left town at three A.M. on the milk train."

As the train pulled away from Megantic, three A.M. or not, the great Joseph Knowles circus of 1913 was underway. With it went a publicity machine that would last for many weeks. It compared in intensity to the 1850 concert tour of P. T. Barnum's find, "Swedish Nightingale" Jenny Lind. "She has won all hearts," the *New York Herald* wrote in September of that year. "Wherever her carriage goes, there is a crowd collected around it, and the people feast their eyes upon her as if she were an angel, and not a mere woman." If the account is to be believed, they did more than look at Lind—they rushed her carriage and had to be beaten back. Knowles experienced similar public adulation.

Even allowing for the artificial energy infused by the media (mostly print) of the day, the public's reaction to Knowles's homecoming was undoubtedly heartfelt, genuinely enthusiastic and almost over the top. He was mobbed everywhere he went, as crowds surged forward to shake the Nature Man's hand and congratulate him for his epochal feat.

In 1910, according to the U.S. Census, more than half the population still lived in rural areas (compared to less than a quarter today). Basic woodcrafting skills were not as distant to the average American as they are today. And yet Knowles was viewed with awe nearly everywhere he went.

People even crowded around to see Knowles's amazing fire-making apparatus, at a time when the necessary skill would likely have been in the possession of a typical Woodcraft Indian or Son of Daniel Boone. The U.S. branch of the Boy Scouts was still in its infancy, having been organized in 1910, but a section titled "How to Make a Fire by Rubbing Sticks" was in the very first edition of the handbook that year.

One explanation for Knowles's nearly hysterical reception is offered by Richard White, professor of American history at Stanford and co-author of *The Frontier in American Culture.* In an interview, White offered this intriguing thesis: "My guess, and it is only a guess, is that since he was playing to a largely urban audience, they identified with him because he could do what they could not. I think he was in some ways the flip side of the Mark Twain character in *A Connecticut Yankee in King Arthur's Court.* Twain's character could recreate the machinery of industrial civilization from scratch; Knowles could supposedly recreate the necessities of living in the wild when all he had was his own naked body. I think both play to the people of a complex, industrial society whose members, individually, seem largely helpless."

Another specialist in this historical period is Louis S. Warren, professor of Western history at the University of California, Davis, and author of *Buffalo Bill's America: William Cody and the Wild West Show.* He said in an interview about Knowles's experience that "something about the progress of Americans out of the wilderness and into modernity seems to be at stake here." While noting that the frontier had long been closed by 1913 and the automobile was proliferating, Warren adds,

There's something here about mass society and the rugged individual man who can still revert to his 'inner savage' and tame the wilderness. The psychologist G. Stanley Hall, [who lived from 1844 to 1924 and is known as the father of the child-study movement] argued that the stages of human development mimic the stages of civilization, ontogeny recapitulates phylogeny. We can escape neurasthenia and other modern maladies, he said, if we just cultivate the savage instincts. This seems important especially in light of the gathering war clouds in Europe, and the fear that modern American men weren't up to savage combat like their frontier ancestors were.

It seems relatively safe to say that modern society had bred modern anxiety, and that Knowles's feat was a comforting reversion to a less-complicated time. Emerging from the woods intact, clad in the symbols of wilderness, he was saying something positive about the human spirit. He could do it, so maybe they could also do it. A "me too" chorus would soon emerge.

Boston was definitely hungering for Knowles, but a victory lap of northern New England was first on the agenda. In the absence of the real Knowles, the *Harvard Lampoon* published a parody diary with entries like "Spent all day making a birch bark suit, Norfolk style. Very becoming, but cracked in two when I sat down." Harvard's comic version of Knowles confronts a subject that the real one mostly avoided: the cold October nights. "Beginning to get deuced chilly in the evening," the *Lampoon* "quotes" him as saying.

Knowles made his way south slowly, stopping at one banquet after another. One of the first and more colorful ones was held at a northern Maine lodge (still in operation today) on an island in the middle of Attean Lake. The woods banquet sponsored by the "Six Thirty Club" was attended not only by local officials but by a director of the New England Telephone & Telegraph Company and the treasurer of the Maine Central Railroad. Soup, partridge, champagne, and ice cream were served in a log-cabin dining room decorated with autumn leaves.

After a buckboard-borne reunion at King & Bartlett Camp, it was time for Knowles to make a highly sentimental visit to his parents in Wilton. A photograph shows the Nature Man, still clad in his skins, greeting his venerable seventy-five-year-old gray-haired mother on the steps of his ancestral home.

School was closed for the day, and a sizable contingent greeted Knowles at the Wilton train station as a brass band played and cries of "Three cheers for our Joe" rent the air.

A parade moved down the Depot Road while, from a rooftop, a cameraman filmed the whole spectacle. Wilton town lawyer Cyrus Blanchard delivered a speech in the town square, praising Knowles for "the discoveries he has made along scientific lines," a preview of the reception he would later get from the learned scholars at Harvard University.

Knowles's Civil War veteran father, then eighty-one, described as a "splendid old gentleman in a brown coat, buttoned high up under a bearded chin," admitted to having been "kind of worried" about his son, adding that "it must have been terrible to have sat in the cold on those wet nights." Mother Mary Knowles, ever the booster, admitted that she worried, too, but considered her son to be "the biggest thing in the world!"

Many years later, Knowles would write a two-page description of this day, putting it in context as a triumphant homecoming that made up for his youthful humiliations. He describes having been taunted and beaten as a child in Wilton for wearing homemade moccasins and shirts made from empty flour sacks. "I solemnly swore that I would have revenge for the injury they had done me and their insult to my mother," he wrote.

Now Knowles was being cheered in these same streets. "I was the hero of the hour, and I shall never forget how it feels to be a hero," he wrote. But as he watched the crowds surge forward, he also concluded that "some of these same men who were lauding me were the boys who mussed me up and kicked me out of their town 30 years before." But by this time, thoughts of revenge had flown and he had a more benevolent attitude toward his fellow men. The former outcast "was invited to every social function in the village," he said with much satisfaction.

The game wardens who had bedeviled Knowles and threatened to forcibly remove him from the woods were now his traveling companions and allies, offering testimonials to his courage and bravery. Knowles proclaimed them his "best friends."

The triumphal march through Maine took five days, including a major stop in Portland, where he attracted 10,000 people. Cheering crowds also showed up in Saco and Biddeford. In Augusta, Knowles drew 8,000 and rode by automobile to the offices of the State Fish and Game Commission. There, Knowles solemnly admitted to violating state game laws, and fines totaling $205 were assessed for killing deer and partridge out of season, hunting and trapping without a license, and making an illegal fire.

The crowds may have been expecting an orator who would expound on the wider meaning of the Stone Age experiment, but what they got was a man—though he was usually quite loquacious and sociable—of relatively few words, plainspoken and somewhat bemused by it all. In Portland, he pleaded fatigue as he confined his remarks to a few sentences. "My friends, I am overwhelmed

with this magnificent reception," he said. "It is all perfectly wonderful to me, these repeated ovations all along the line."

Knowles's southward progress toward Boston was lavishly covered in the *Post* by reporter Waitt, who'd been given carte blanche
to detail the Nature Man's every move. Among much else, Waitt
records a reunion on the southbound train between Knowles and
one of the leading sopranos of the day, the forty-year-old Lillian
Blauvelt, who, it turned out, had borrowed his violin four years
before at King & Bartlett Camp. She told the reporter that, in his
woodland finery, Knowles resembled the warrior character Hund-
ing from Wagner's opera *Die Walküre.*

Waitt evidently formed a strong bond with the modern Adam.
When *Alone in the Wilderness* appeared two months later, Knowles
thanked his "good friend" Waitt "for his kindness in helping me
in the preparation of this book. . . ." Waitt was almost certainly
Knowles's ghostwriter. They made a complementary pair, since
the newsman (who later in his career profiled poet Robert Frost)
had at his command a veritable thesaurus of ennobling allegory.

Having triumphed in northern New England, Knowles arrived in
Boston on October 9, on the noon train from Portland. As described
in Roderick Nash's book *Wilderness and the American Mind,* "[A]
huge crowd jammed North Station to meet Knowles's train and
shouted itself hoarse when he appeared." According to Paul Waitt
in the *Post,* "The subway stairs inside the station were a mass of
people—the effect resembling a grandstand at a football game.
Men had climbed up on top of the cars on adjoining tracks, while
a fringe of humanity adorned the top of the iron gateways."

American Heritage estimated that as many as 200,000 people
(nearly a third of Boston's population, an amazing proportion)

Just a portion of the Boston crowd that welcomed Knowles on October 9, 1913. *BOSTON POST* PHOTO, FROM *ALONE IN THE WILDERNESS*

welcomed the prodigal Nature Man home at various points in the city that day. The crowd, the magazine wrote, "filled the station and spilled over into Causeway Street and around the corner of Canal." The police struggled to maintain order. When the Nature Man's face appeared in the window of the train's drawing room, several women reportedly tried to climb in after him.

Nash writes that pandemonium reigned in a procession that lacked only ticker tape: "Thousands more lined the streets through which his motorcade passed. Still clad in the bearskin, Knowles went to Boston Common where an estimated 20,000 people waited."

But even the *Post* had to acknowledge Knowles's shortcomings as a spellbinding orator. Under the heading "Finds Speechmaking Hard," it recounts very brief remarks on Boston Common that were

nearly identical to what he had said in Portland, with one memorable addition. "It is a whole lot easier being in the woods than it
is making a speech," he said. By all accounts, Knowles was a man
at ease holding forth to a group of cronies in an alehouse, and he
could be a delightful raconteur under those circumstances, but big
crowds unnerved him. The *Boston Transcript* made the most of his
brief appearance, noting that Knowles mounted the wooden grandstand with "the quick, graceful movements of a tiger."

The momentous day also included a side trip to Harvard University's Hemenway Gymnasium, where he was reunited with that
eminent authority on physical culture, Dr. Dudley A. Sargent. In
the late nineteenth century, working alongside (and sometimes
fighting with) Beacon Hill philanthropist Mary Tileston Hemenway, former acrobat Sargent had built what the *New England
Quarterly* called "a model university physical training program."
He also ran afoul of the university administration after serving on
a faculty committee that banned football for a year, and so was
stripped of his Harvard teaching post after 1889. Sargent's School
of Physical Training in Cambridge became part of Boston University in 1929, five years after he died. He was the first-call physician in Boston to investigate claims of physical prowess. And he
was very impressed with his reexamination of Joseph Knowles.

"If you want to see what the pink of condition means, just look
at Mr. Knowles," the doctor said. At the YMCA in Cambridge
later that day, Dr. Sargent personally stripped Knowles to the
waist and called the rapt audience's attention to the velvety con-
sistency of the Nature Man's "perfect" skin, which he said was
so healthy that "its pores close and shield him from sudden chills."
In a strength test, Knowles topped the university's rowing crew,
and lifted 1,000 pounds with his legs.

DR. DUDLEY A. SARGENT EXAMINES KNOWLES AT HARVARD. HE ALSO INTRODUCED THE NATURE MAN AT SPEAKING ENGAGEMENTS. *BOSTON POST* PHOTO, FROM *ALONE IN THE WILDERNESS*

Dr. Sargent compared Knowles favorably (complete with detailed body measurements) to Eugen Sandow, a vaudeville attraction known as "the physical marvel of the age" and considered the strongest man in the world. "[Knowles] has probably the staying power of three Sandows," said Dr. Sargent.

Knowles's feat proved instructive for a cross section of Boston society. Herbert S. Johnson, the pastor of Warren Avenue Church, could not ignore this most useful current event. "The Almighty has raised up such men as he to go forth into the wilderness," he said from the pulpit that Sunday. "And behold a sermon two months long for the people of the United States!" Editorials praised Knowles as "a naked man against the tooth and claw of nature," and proclaimed him "a noble piece of poetry." He was even compared to John the Baptist.

Harvard students, not content to go after the Nature Man in print, made Harvard Square their stage and enacted a comic version of the fight between Knowles and the bear he had trapped in the woods. An Olympic-level tennis player played the bear, and the president of Harvard's sophomore class was Knowles, declaring to gales of laughter that his month [*sic*] in the woods consisted of "one week in the forest and the other three in a neighboring farmhouse." At the old Howard Theater, meanwhile, burlesque comics were doing routines about "Kno Jowles."

An economics professor at the Massachusetts Institute of Technology instructed his students that, for Knowles, "capital" did not have its usual meaning in the business world, but was "the capital of the cave man, consisting of a knowledge of woodcraft and a manual ability to make tools and clothing." Much the same point was made in the book *Natural Capitalism,* which came out eighty-six years later.

On October 10, Knowles fought his way through crowds for visits to Governor Eugene Foss and Boston's first Irish Catholic mayor, John Francis "Honey Fitz" Fitzgerald (John Fitzgerald Kennedy's grandfather). Like so many other admirers, Governor Foss was most interested in how Knowles had made fire, and he had kind words for the Nature Man's physical prowess. "I wouldn't mind if I had some of that vigor you possess," Foss said, "as I have a campaign ahead and it would be mighty useful." The words proved prophetic, because Foss ran on a Prohibition platform in 1914 and lost badly.

Dr. Sargent was a champion of physical education for women, so Knowles's next stop was the doctor's female training school in Cambridge. With 400 youthful admirers gathered around him (and serenading him with a special song), Knowles was made to stand on a platform in the center of the gymnasium. "Did you attempt to make strawberry shortcake?" was one of the more inane questions directed his way. But then, once again, Dr. Sargent removed the bearskin in dramatic fashion and exposed the rippling, sun-bronzed muscles of the world's most perfect specimen. With Knowles's permission, the young women were allowed to approach and stroke the velvety skin of his back.

The day had other high points ahead, and Knowles was whisked to the famous Filene's where, after a hearty meal of "Brook Trout Knowles" and partridge, he was put through a public makeover. The bearskin fell to the floor and, after barbering, manicuring, and chiropody, he was outfitted in a suit of the latest cut, topped with a soft black hat and a walking stick. He might have looked dapper, but he didn't look like the Nature Man, so the bearskin was soon back in place.

A climax to the round of festivities that night was a dinner at the Copley Plaza Hotel, built just the year before. The white linens were strewn with "leaves of the woods," and an eagle ice sculpture was illuminated from within. Attorney William A. Morse presided, calling Knowles a "Robinson Crusoe without a man Friday" and "a Robin Hood without his archers." The ever-present Dr. Sargent lamented that fire-making skill was sorely lacking among Harvard undergraduates.

Naturalist James H. Thornton brought a few of his own primitive implements and a specially commissioned poem:

> He goes into the woods, naked and bare;
> He goes through the woods with trouble and care;
> He comes out of the woods, God only knows where.

The *Post* ran a bylined story by Knowles the next day, October 12, and a tone of modesty prevailed. What he had accomplished, he said, "wasn't a whole lot. There are many men today who could do the same thing. All that is necessary to live the primitive life . . . is a combination of health, resourcefulness and a little brains." He declared, "I think that any man to be complete must have a touch of nature in his makeup."

The article was accompanied by a solemn declaration, signed by a dozen men who had been in Megantic, attesting that Knowles "has been successful in his attempt to live on his resources in the forest." How merely seeing him emerge in skins proved that point was unclear, but affidavits of this kind would soon come in handy.

The *Post* was running short on Knowles material, so it tried to keep the public's interest up by running some of his illustrations in full-page format with a framed border. They were probably crowd pleasers, especially the two-panel *The Call* and *The Answer*, depicting a hunter luring a moose. The paintings were more than a little reminiscent of a popular Frederic Remington work titled *Coming to the Call*, from 1905. But having been a Maine hunting guide, Knowles certainly had personal experience of the subject.

By November 2, not even a month after he emerged from the north woods, the *Post* was already announcing the impending publication of the "profusely illustrated" *Alone in the Wilderness* by Small, Maynard and Company. Aimed at "sportsmen, scientists, hunters, nature lovers and the entire reading public," the book would show how a naked man without tools of any kind "made Nature his complete ally." An initial printing was set at 25,000 copies.

As a way to sell newspapers, Joseph Knowles had few rivals up to that point. His story doubled circulation. As *Sunday Post* editor Charles E. L. Wingate wrote in a 1919 letter, "We made a tremendous gain in circulation, 37,000 in the summer, and created an immense amount of interest in the *Sunday Post* all through New England." The naked man in the woods had been masterfully handled; he was a true Edwin Grozier enterprise surpassing the legendary "Boston *Post* Cane."

"Of course," wrote Wingate, "a great deal depends on the handling. I arranged, for example, with all the Mayors of the Maine cities through which Knowles passed on returning to give him receptions. We had a parade in Boston when he got here and gave him a banquet to which the leading sportsmen of the town were invited, etc." (Knowles liked Wingate's letter so much that he later retyped it, word for word. The clincher may have been the line praising him as "a very experienced woodsman" who "can do what he says he does.")

The Knowles experiment indeed played well all over New England. The *Hartford Courant* praised the Nature Man's "wonderful feat" in late October, adding, ". . . no one ought to begrudge the hardy woodsman any rewards that may come to him." But it added, in remarks that would prove prescient, that Knowles had made good his boast "unless the biggest fake of the century has been palmed off on a credulous public."

Still, anyone could see that the Nature Man extravaganza was beginning to wind down by the end of November. Knowles certainly did what was asked of him. After his round of promotions for the *Post,* he was booked by B. F. Keith's Theatre, a famous Boston vaudeville house, for a few days of Nature Man appearances.

Dressed in his woods attire, he demonstrated how he made his crude tools and described "his thrilling experience with the black bear."

By this time, Knowles may already have been screening some of the copious film footage that had been shot since he emerged from the woods. A list of scenes from this footage (titled *A Trip Through the Wilderness with Joe Knowles "The Nature Man"*) survives, and it includes "the value of a sharp-edged stone"; "making a fire drill from wood"; "kindling fire from friction with two pieces of wood"; "chipping arrowheads"; "hunting with bow and arrows"; "tanning the skins of animals in primitive ways"; "building a raft from logs"; "making coffee from roasted acorns"; "making clay pottery"; and the very intriguing "luxuries of a primitive life."

The reviews of Knowles's vaudeville work were balanced. In a comment echoed by other observers, the *Boston Herald* of October 14 noted that Knowles "is obviously not a man of the stage, and its technique is for others than himself." But on a brighter note, it added: "Happily, he avoids any attempt at being theatrical, and his act is a simple and direct story of his life in the wilderness." This show at B. F. Keith's was "well received by the audience."

Knowles's act was not unique. One contemporary vaudeville performer was Charles Kellogg, "The Nature Singer," also a regular on the B. F. Keith circuit. Kellogg's claim to fame was that he could duplicate bird songs and, like Dr. Doolittle, "talk" to them in their own languages. Kellogg decorated his stages in imitations of forest scenes, and his ability to start fires by rubbing sticks was also a showstopper. In his 1929 book *The Nature Singer,* Kellogg claimed, rather dubiously, that he found, backstage at vaudeville theaters, "conditions that are congenial to my own habits of the woods."

Kellogg was a respected conservationist in his time, and toured in the "Travel Log," a motor home whose body was made entirely from a hollowed-out redwood log. He counted naturalists John Muir (for whom he created fire by rubbing redwood sticks) and John Burroughs among his friends, and neither seemed bothered that he was also a vaudeville star.

Knowles's local engagement led to weeks of bookings in vaudeville theaters around the country. The *American Mercury* reported that he was on the road for twenty weeks, receiving "24-sheet billing and $1,200 a week." Knowles also found time for a triumphal second return to his hometown of Wilton on November 18. A poster from that momentous occasion survives in the collection of Sean Minear, president of the Historical Society of Weld, Maine. "The Primitive Man Himself," it proclaims, offering "a two-hour lecture describing his experiences in the wilds of Maine, augmented with 1,500 feet of sensational motion picture film, especially posed by Mr. Knowles, including his reception en route to Boston." Admission was fifteen and twenty-five cents for the afternoon show, twenty-five and fifty cents in the evening. The flyer was illustrated with a picture of Knowles reclining in full regalia, holding a handmade bow.

Minear's cousin, recently deceased at age ninety-seven, vividly recalled being taken to the State Theater in Portland to see Knowles around this time, and for the rest of her life spoke of being "terrified" at the sight of him in his bearskin. Meanwhile, back in Boston, the Knowles story was beginning to die down.

On November 30, however, the dying embers were fanned back into life by a sensational lead story in the *Post*'s bitter rival, the Hearst-owned *Boston Sunday American*. "The Truth About

AN UNDATED JOE KNOWLES SELF-
PORTRAIT, ATTIRED AS HE ENTERED
THE WOODS. COURTESY OF KAYE
MULVEY-COWAN

Knowles," the banner read, "Real Story of His 'Primitive Man' Adventures in the Maine Woods." The lengthy exposé, which initially appeared only in some editions, was written by Bert Ford, who claimed to have been the first reporter to interview Knowles when he emerged in Canada. Further, he wrote that his sleuthing had taken him deep into the Nature Man's lair, where he found more than a few discrepancies in the now-burnished, twice-told tale.

Ford was particularly indignant because Knowles at that time was recounting his experiences as a "latter-day aborigine" to colleges, schools, societies, and sporting clubs for an unheard-of income totaling $700 to $1,200 per week. "He has been deluged with offers from theatre managements, motion picture concerns, lecture bureaus and publishers," Ford complained.

Far from a heroic nature man, the *American* charged, Joe Knowles was the "Dr. Cook of the North Woods." This comparison lacks sting today, but in 1913 those were fighting words. Dr. Frederick A. Cook had claimed to reach the North Pole before Commander Robert Peary in 1909, and was widely disbelieved. Interestingly enough, among Dr. Cook's admirers in later years was one Joe Knowles, who believed his claims.

Ford's lengthy piece made much of the ardors of his seven-week investigation and took quite a while to get to the point. But when it did, the charges were dramatic. In place of the naked man arrayed against the forces of nature, Ford sketched a portrait of indolence: Knowles had, according to him, spent his two months luxuriating—fully clothed—with an unnamed "manager" in a log cabin near Spencer Lake. Regular provisions and even a mysterious woman friend (who might have been Bana Douglas, "a girl whose father was a friend of Knowles," said the *Maine Sunday Telegram*) were supposedly delivered to him. The alleged go-between was Flagstaff-based hunting guide Allie "Tripe" Deming, who the *American* said was on Knowles's payroll (charged with retrieving the birchbark messages, among other things).

Ford attempted to dismantle the Knowles legend, piece by piece. Since the bearskin was the Nature Man's pride and joy, Ford took particular aim at it, writing that trapper William Hall had actually sold it to Deming. The sale price was $12 ($7 more than the market value at the time). To add insult to this injury, Ford claimed to have found four holes in the skin, which "experts" had validated as bullet holes. Was Deming, reported to be flush with cash, put on the payroll because he had come across a fully clothed Knowles and had to be kept silent? So Ford alleged.

Ford said that, after days of arduous searching with trapper Henry E. Redmond, he had found Knowles's bear pit near Lost Pond on September 30. The pit, wrote Ford, "was a scant four feet wide and bare three feet deep. . . . A cat could have hopped out of it with ease." The mustachioed Redmond is shown in an accompanying photo standing in the pit, which fails to reach his waist. The investigators also said they couldn't find any signs of bear habitation in the pit: no claw marks or blood. And the club Knowles had supposedly used to dispatch the bruin? Discovered leaning against a tree, it was a "stub of decaying moose wood." In a low blow, Ford proclaimed this rotted twig "just such a club as an artist would be expected to select for the role." (Of course, whatever else he may have been, Knowles was an experienced Maine trapper and guide, thus hardly a neophyte babe in the woods, putting the kibosh on at least some of these claims.)

Moreover, Ford claimed to have evidence of pencil lead on Knowles's birchbark messages, which he said appeared to have been worked from their host trees with a sharp blade.

The quality of the evidence against Knowles varied, however. "College graduate" and "former artist" Frank Brown had only visited the general area where the Nature Man lurked, but picked up plenty of local gossip. "I saw and heard enough to convince me Joe isn't suffering much discomfort," Brown told the *American*. "He's having his three square meals, all right, plenty to smoke and nice, snug blankets. There have been strange things happening since Joseph settled here."

The *American* initially wilted at the first threats of a libel lawsuit from the *Post* and withdrew the story from the day's later editions. Runners were even sent out to retrieve copies of the bulldog edition that had already hit the newsstands outside of the city. But the *American* then reacquired a backbone and confidence in its Knowles exposé, reprinting the story in full on December 2, two days later. The *Post* reportedly filed its $50,000 libel lawsuit, though the matter never reached a courtroom. Knowles's reputation had definitely suffered a blow, but the newspaper continued to support him fully, soon announcing that Knowles, who'd been out of town on "an important professional engagement," was racing back to the city to answer his critics.

James B. Connolly, a friend of Knowles, former Olympic medalist (in 1896) and a highly regarded writer of sea-based adventure stories, stepped into the breach and proclaimed, "These little local fellows produce no evidence against Knowles. . . . The little knockers are always standing by."

A full defense had to wait, of course, until the *Post*'s much-anticipated Sunday edition of December 7. Knowles was still out of town, though he wrote in to complain that the need to answer these "flimsy" charges had caused him to cut short a lucrative trip to the northeast Canadian province of Prince Edward Island and lose "a large sum of money."

The record shows, however, that Knowles did appear on the island. According to the *Island Patriot* of December 6, he drew a large crowd to the People's Theater. Again it was noted that "Mr. Knowles does not pose as an orator," but the account added that he was "a clear, fluent, distinct talker." He told the crowd that he was in the process of writing his book, said to be 80,000 words, and was dictating the material while on the road. While on the island, he visited a black fox ranch and was filmed by the cameras of the International Film Company with the foxes swarming all over him and the resident bear cub saying hello.

As a finale at the end of his Prince Edward Island lecture, Knowles offered to demonstrate his bare-handed bear-killing technique—as long as someone could produce a bear. Amazingly enough, one Reg Fraser did know of an available bear that had appeared recently at a provincial exhibition. "Would it do?" According to the *Charlottetown Guardian,* a plan was hatched that night to dig a pit in a nearby field, put the bear in (anchored for the safety of the spectators, with sharpshooters standing by), and then have Knowles jump in and dispatch it with a club.

Alas, events did not go as planned. Knowles failed to rouse himself at the appointed time, and when he finally did get up the ground was found to be frozen. A great effort with pick and shovel produced only a shallow hole, which was nonetheless deemed sufficient for the purpose. The crowd gathered, and the cameramen made ready.

But now the bear was late. It was a passenger on the island railway, which was behind schedule. By the time it was unloaded and transported to the field, the afternoon was waning and the cameramen were complaining there wasn't enough light to shoot.

Knowles had an unsporting suggestion: Let the bear loose to climb a tree, then have the sharpshooters pick it off for the delight of the crowd. But bystanders pointed out that it might decide to climb them instead of a tree. In the end, the bear won a temporary reprieve, and Knowles agreed to buy it to serve as an attraction on his ongoing lecture tour. Back in Maine, the bear would soon come in handy.

Much of Knowles's own response to the *American* exposé consisted of indignation that Ford (who had apparently used the alias "Adams" during his time in the woods) had turned out to be an ungrateful recipient of the Nature Man's hospitality. Knowles and company had made sure there was a seat for Ford at the banquets from Megantic to Boston, though they knew he worked for a rival newspaper. "I invited him to join my party," Knowles wrote. "I answered every question he put to me."

Knowles said that Ford was, at best, a reluctant investigator. He quoted the *American* reporter as having told him, during a buckboard ride to Spencer Lake, "I want to tell you that I believe you have lived every day in the woods just as you claim to have lived. I may lose my position on my paper when I return to Boston, but since meeting you I have wired my paper to hold all previous stories I have written concerning you." Might this moral dilemma help explain the nearly two-month gap between Ford's meeting Knowles in Megantic and the *American*'s story?

And Knowles had ready explanations for Ford's charges. Allie Deming did indeed buy a bearskin from William Hall—Deming was, after all, "a fur buyer in that country"—but it was a *different* bearskin. "I have no doubt that Hall shot a bear," Knowles wrote. "There are plenty of them there to shoot." Knowles volunteered to let any taxidermist or qualified expert look at *his* bearskin, which he noted had been on near-constant public view since October 4, without a bullet hole in sight.

Knowles admitted that Ford had found his bear pit, but he stoutly defended its construction. "Such a pit as I built, and Ford found and described, will easily catch a bear in the Maine woods," he declared, adding that "squaws among the Western Indians" catch grizzly bears in similar pits. The relatively shallow pit was covered with logs weighed down with stones and embedded in dirt on the sides, which Knowles said made it escape-proof (for a bear, at least). Knowles did concede, however, that a cat might have been able to jump out of it.

The Nature Man laughed off the lack of blood or fur, asserting that any real woodsman would know that such spoor disappears quickly in the woods. And that rotted moose wood club? Not his, since the authentic article was "a piece of stout hornbeam."

Knowles's reply was every bit as lengthy as Ford's attack, because there were a considerable number of charges to refute. Ford had claimed that Knowles was incapable of navigating his way to Canada by studying the moss on the north side of trees, and had instead hired a part-Indian known as Joe St. Ober to guide him to Quebec. When St. Ober left him a dozen miles from Megantic, Ford charged, Knowles got lost and so ended up on the train tracks instead of in the town.

"I know Joe St. Ober!" Knowles roared in reply. "I have hunted and trapped with him in this same country, and the idea that I needed him to pilot me is so ridiculous that if Joe ever hears the statement he'll laugh until he cries." But St. Ober definitely had some involvement, because he was in Megantic when Knowles emerged from the woods. His name appears as one of the signatories on an October 4 affidavit attesting that Knowles had lived "on his own resources in the forest." It's unfortunate that St. Ober's actual thoughts on all this are lost to history.

There were more charges and countercharges. Knowles went on stage at the old Tremont Temple and challenged anyone with firsthand knowledge of his supposed fraud to come forward. There were no takers. But an *American* follow-up piece quoted former *Post* chief of photography Thomas A. Luke as confirming the *American*'s charges. The *Post* countered that Luke had been let go for drunken behavior. The basic outcome was that Knowles was battered and bruised, but still standing. It's telling, however, that the *Post*'s lawsuit rather countered Knowles's public position that the sunshine of truth was the best antiseptic. It did eventually silence the *American*.

Knowles must have felt that further vindication was needed, because, with the *Post*'s active assistance, he staged a somewhat farcical reprise of his adventures in the woods. In mid-December, he had the 250-pound black bear he'd bought in Canada shipped through Portland to Farmington, from which it traveled overland to Knowles's famous bear pit. The *American*'s reporter, Bert Ford, was invited along, and Knowles added, rather gratuitously, that if necessary he would build a special bear-proof shelter for Ford, "so that he may view the entire proceedings without danger of attack from the bear."

The *Post* played up the journey, reporting breathlessly that a hapless express company employee in Portland "had a narrow escape from serious injury" when the enraged bear reached out and tore a big piece out of his trouser leg. Though housed in a stout cage with a grating of iron bars, the wily bruin had somehow managed to make a significant hole. "Anybody who approached the crate was met with a rumbling growl and a swift pass of a clawed paw," the *Post* wrote. Willis Sargent, the employee who'd narrowly escaped those terrible paws, reported that Knowles was likely to have a lively time with the bear, because it was "wide awake, crafty, and not slow in taking advantage of an opportunity."

The bear was hauled off to the woods, and with some effort tied up with clothesline and dragged the last few miles to the famous bear pit. Unfortunately, the bear was no longer the roaring ursine menace encountered by the Portland postman, but, according to the *Post*, chose to "sulk" in the pit, forcing Knowles to "stir him up" by prodding with a stick. But nothing could induce any satisfying behavior. "The bear wasn't doing very well," said one witness, fifteen-year-old Helon Taylor, in an account published in the *Maine Sunday Telegram* in 1973 (when Taylor was seventy-five).

"He'd had a long trip and wanted to hibernate, but we got him into the pit, which wasn't very deep—about up to my waist."

With some observers protesting that he didn't give the bear enough time to try to climb out, Knowles unceremoniously clubbed the poor creature to death (a death blow to the nose) and skinned it in front of a dozen witnesses. "Joe killed it quickly with a club," said Taylor. "Then he dug around until he found a sharp piece of shale and in less than 10 minutes he had the hide off one of the bear's legs. We were all impressed." The local Society for the Prevention of Cruelty to Animals was not, however, and according to the *American* threatened to contact the authorities.

And so the grand adventure of Joseph Knowles in the woods of Maine ended not with a bang but with the whimper of a half-tame and worn-out bear from Canada. But the public still had not had its fill of Joe Knowles. When the hastily written *Alone in the Wilderness* appeared that same month, December, from the Boston publisher of Small, Maynard and Company (for $1.20), it was an immediate hit. Many sources say the book sold an unbelievable-for-its-time 300,000 copies. The *American Mercury* reported that figure in 1936, and it also made it into Roderick Nash's *Wilderness and the American Mind* some thirty years later. But Knowles himself reported a more realistic (and still impressive) 30,000 copies, so it's likely that an extra zero sneaked in at some point.

The reviewers were not all kind. In February 1914, *The Nation* proclaimed that "the dream of a thoroughgoing return to nature had been realized." But it also faulted Knowles's grammar and diction, complained that the book's conclusions had been "set forth in a disorganized, slapdash manner," and noted warily that the author had attracted "a considerable public attention of a cap-flinging kind." It is hoped, the intellectual journal noted, that "Mr. Knowles will use his influence, such as it is, wisely."

The average book buyer did not share *The Nation*'s concerns, since likely author Paul Waitt's prose is serviceable enough and the story he told both uplifting and satisfyingly adventurous. The *Boston Transcript* praised the book as "remarkably interesting reading." Overseas readers seem to have also appreciated it; a review in London's *Chronicle* in March 1914 said "Mr. Knowles has given us a lesson in self-independence." The paper added that it was a "'great stunt' (one must drag in this American language)." A 1997 *Washington Post* account describes the book as "more than a survivalist's diary. It is also an exercise in homespun philosophy and self-examination." For a rush job, it is perhaps surprisingly reflective.

There, you could say, the matter rested for more than twenty years. With the *Post*'s lawsuit keeping the *American* quiet, Joe Knowles quietly faded from New England headlines. His bearskin would go into hibernation, its provenance escaping further questioning.

The Maine trail grew cold until June 18, 1938, when, of all publications, the *New Yorker* magazine reopened the controversy. The "Where Are They Now?" series contained a bemused piece, "The Nature Man," by Richard O. Boyer, about Knowles's first foray in the woods.

Here was the dark underbelly of the Knowles story, as told to Boyer by one Michael McKeogh, presumably the unnamed "manager" described in the *American*'s long-ago exposé. It's unclear what led McKeogh to talk in 1938 after keeping his own counsel for so many years, but perhaps it was the prospect of an appearance in the august *New Yorker*. Or simply the need to have history remember his role in such a fantastic stunt.

According to McKeogh (who got to tell his story without challenge), the idea for the Nature Man was hatched in a Washington Street bar in Boston. Knowles, "a huge, hairy man with a huge beak of a nose," was holding forth, boasting that he could "enter the woods unclothed and weaponless and maintain himself endlessly through his extraordinary woodlore." Knowles's strength and backwoods savvy, McKeogh explained, had been built during a youth spent trapping in the wilds of Maine.

McKeogh was thirty years old in 1913 and a freelance newspaperman. He was a man of letters and had read *Robinson Crusoe*. "He had been much impressed that the book was written in 1719 and was still selling well. He believes he was thinking about this when Joe's booming voice in the smoke-filled saloon suddenly leaped to meaning in his mind. 'We'll make a million,' he told Joe, and they began to talk it over."

With Knowles as willing partner, McKeogh took up pencil and pad and sketched in a schedule for two months in the woods, with such notations as "Tuesday, kills bear." Knowles assured McKeogh he was up for it, and enumerated a half dozen ways of killing a bear without a rifle. It was McKeogh who sold the story to the *Post*, says the *New Yorker* account.

Boyer's account of Knowles's entry into the woods is at odds with both the contemporary newspaper reports and the photographic evidence. They had him cocksure and joking, but Boyer says he was "despondent" as he "slowly bared his soft whiteness to a group of vacationists [actually a mixed group of guides and admirers] at the foot of Bear Mountain."

McKeogh's version alleges that soon after striding into the woods, Knowles made his way to the other side of Bear Mountain and entered a cabin two miles away on Kempshall Point. There, waiting, were Fred Allen, the guide charged with retrieving Knowles's weekly messages, and McKeogh at his typewriter, furiously tapping out messages from the Nature Man. A morose Knowles had to be coerced to go back out into the woods and acquire a tan.

The splendid physique so admired by Dr. Sargent of Harvard was built with exercise no more strenuous than occasional between-meal strolls in the woods, Boyer wrote. On one lazy day, reports the *New Yorker*, Knowles was reportedly caught clothed and relaxing at the cabin by trapper Allie Deming, who was promptly offered $2.50 a day in the *Post*'s hush money to keep quiet about it. But whose side was Deming actually on?

One of the weaker aspects of the *New Yorker*'s story is its reliance on the veracity of Deming, a key player also in the *American*'s exposé. The *Maine Sunday Telegram* reported in 1973 that rumors around Flagstaff and Eustis had Deming being offered $1,000 by the *American* to tell his tale, which included reports of buying the bearskin from a hunter. Deming was not paid the money, however, and it may be for that reason that he later testified on Knowles's behalf. In *Yankee Magazine*, Deming is described as an "odd character."

Knowles still felt aggrieved by Deming's behavior many years later. An undated fragment among his papers is a three-page diatribe against Deming, calling him "a despised, hated, cowardly wretch, cunning as a fox, tow-headed, beatle [*sic*] browed, narrow chested, narrow minded, deceitful and conceited." Deming is described in Knowles's fragment as capable in the woods, but a serial exploiter of them. "What was the song of a bird to him?" Knowles asked. "He would rather stone a bird out of a tree than hear it sing. . . . Anything that was beautiful should be destroyed, especially the things that [were] defenceless and harmless." A half century later, too late to do Joe Knowles any good, the *Sunday Telegram* reported that Deming's "reliability was doubted by many local people."

McKeogh, according to the *New Yorker,* was distressed by the behavior of his moody collaborator, reporting that Knowles alternated between fits of vigor and melancholy lassitude. The Nature Man was stirred to finally dig his bear pit, however, by the newspaperman's assertion that the citizens of Boston were building a statue of Knowles on the Common. "In a bearskin, Joe," McKeogh reportedly said, "in a bearskin."

Though some later deemed it inadequate for the purpose, the bear pit was eventually completed, and in one of his fits of vigor Knowles also hauled in and skinned a dead deer he had found in the woods. McKeogh couldn't take the smell of the stinking hide hanging on the cabin door, and threw it away—further estranging the two men. The rift got even bigger when Knowles furtively stole a pie McKeogh had left out on a windowsill to cool. "Now the breach was too wide to heal," Boyer reported. "Knowles and McKeogh never spoke as friends again."

When the game wardens came knocking on the cabin's door—looking for Knowles, to fine him for allegedly killing the bear—the Nature Man was forced to flee a dozen miles away to a haunt near Eustis. Almost as scary as the wardens was *American* reporter Bert Ford, who was accompanying the authorities on the hunt for Knowles. While he was on the run, McKeogh became concerned that Knowles would emerge on October 4 without the bearskin he had supposedly worked so industriously to acquire. Fortune smiled, when—as Ford reported in the *American*—William Hall shot a bear and Allie Deming was able to buy it from him for $12. Knowles's costume was complete.

It was decided finally that Knowles would emerge from the woods thirty miles to the north at Megantic, but Knowles was not at all confident that he could find the place on his own. With Joe St. Ober indeed guiding, Knowles trudged off, "low in mind but high in odor." He did indeed get lost after St. Ober met him, Boyer reports, and was trying to hire a horse and buggy in a settlement near Megantic when a train came by and he flagged a ride. This account has him reuniting with McKeogh in the Canadian city, after which they entered together into the teeth of a media maelstrom. When they finally reached Boston after five frantic days, McKeogh said to Knowles, "I suppose you don't need me any more." Knowles replied, "No, I don't." According to McKeogh, that was that and they never saw each other again.

Joseph Knowles, who in 1938 was living in semi-retirement on a peninsula in rural Washington State, was not one to take such charges lying down. He responded in a lengthy diatribe on the front page of the local *Chinook Observer* three months later, though he couldn't even bring himself to name the "certain New York magazine" that had slandered him.

"If the charges were less ridiculous, the article might have been more convincing," he averred. "From the back-stage of 1913 appears the ghost of McKeogh with a fantastic tale defaming Knowles. What a break for the writer [Boyer]."

Knowles wrote that he had never met nor entertained Boyer. And he seemed most unsettled by the fact that his "former friend McKeogh" had turned on him. The "suave Michael in his younger

days, now grown old and grey," had waited twenty years "to get a
wallop at the man who befriended him and at the newspaper that
called him in off the streets as a freelance rover and gave him a
chance."

Knowles cited a mountain of "affidavits, signed statements, letters and press notices" that confirmed his version of events, but
he made no specific refutation of the charges. By Knowles's account, McKeogh had been hired by the *Boston Post* to write honest journalism about the experiment in the Maine woods, but was
terminated after his return to the city "for reasons well known to
himself." McKeogh then played a behind-the-scenes role in the
Boston American exposé and an upfront one in the *New Yorker*
piece. "In his sober moments," Knowles says, McKeogh wouldn't
have dared play such a role.

McKeogh's name does not actually appear on any of the *Post*
stories (most are signed by Paul Waitt or not at all). But Knowles
quotes from several of the paper's admiring accounts to show that
McKeogh had once thought favorably of him. Perhaps inadver-
tently, Knowles bolstered the notion of McKeogh as a cabin-bound
ghostwriter. Another curious footnote is that, according to a *Washington Post* account in September 1913, Knowles's letter to President Wilson had been "forwarded from Spencer, Maine, by M.
F. McKeogh," suggesting that they were indeed working together.
It's a pity that Waitt, a prolific writer, never published his own account of these events.

The *New Yorker* exposé, coupled with the rambling but detailed
account in the *American,* amount to a damning indictment against
Knowles. But there was more. Telling his story many years later
in the *Maine Sunday Telegram,* Helon Taylor reported that on the

way back from watching Knowles skin a bear, the party came across a "nice, tight, little log cabin" on the bank at Lost Pond. It was so new, the peeled logs hadn't even begun to change color; and what's more, out behind it was "a pile of beer bottles and tin cans about four feet high."

Though Knowles denied he'd ever seen the cabin, the damage was done. "Lost Pond was small and round, and I don't think there was one spot on shore from which you couldn't see that camp," Taylor said. "Joe was lying to us. I lost all faith in him right there. I never saw Joe's bow and arrow or any of his tools, but I did see his basket. It had two bullet holes in it. That had bothered me before, but the Lost Pond camp clinched it. He was a fake."

Taylor makes a credible witness, one whose hero had failed him. He had strongly admired Knowles, calling him a "big, strong guy" and "an excellent woodsman" who knew how to weave pack baskets and make all manner of things out of cedar bark. "He was the man to go into the woods alone," he said in 1973. After his boyhood adventure, Taylor went into the woods himself, eventually becoming superintendent of Maine's Baxter State Park (site of Mount Katahdin, the terminus of the Appalachian Trail for people headed north). The Helon Taylor Trail is named after him.

Taylor was convinced that Knowles *could* have done it, and he remained regretful many years later that the Nature Man hadn't bothered to exert himself. "I don't know why," Taylor said. "I guess he was just too lazy. Isn't it too bad." Another woodsman and former Knowles acquaintance quoted in the *Telegram* story, Viles Wing of Eustis, came to the same conclusion. "He really knew the woods and its creatures," Wing said, but he was also "awfully lazy" and "didn't work any more than he had to."

A curious addendum to this strange tale is provided by one of Maine's sages, John Gould, who wrote rustic tales for the *Christian Science Monitor* for more than sixty years. In 1999, four years before he died, Gould wrote his own account of Knowles's time in the woods. Gould's version is informed by the fact that he had himself written features for the *Boston Sunday Post* in the early 1940s, when some of the crustier newsroom denizens probably still remembered the Knowles saga.

But Gould's folksy account is filled with known errors, such as the supposition that Knowles's charcoal dispatches were "written in berry juice with a porcupine quill." In his version, Knowles's foil and muse was not McKeogh but *Post* reporter and native Mainer Roy Atkinson, whose name appears in no other account (although he definitely existed at the paper at that time).

Gould does offer a credible and fascinating alternative account of the Nature Man's genesis. As he tells it, the staff of the *Sunday Post* was sitting around one Monday morning discussing upcoming stories, and Edgar Rice Burroughs's then-popular Tarzan saga came up. "Could a modern man brave the wilderness?" Atkinson piped up and said that northern Maine was full of men "who could outdo Tarzan in any context." The editor said if a "State-o'-Maine Tarzan" could be located, he'd reserve space. Atkinson supposedly went straight to Joe Knowles, then an artist living in the Hub. The rest, with Atkinson as guide and ghostwriter, was history. Gould doesn't mention that Knowles would not have been hard to find, since he was a former employee of the *Post*.

In Gould's account, Knowles emerged from the woods "without a single black-fly bite," which squares with the curiously insect-free account in the *Post* and *Alone in the Wilderness*. And even if the black flies had ceased their unique torment by August, the mosquitoes should have been horrible—although Knowles stated at the time that he had avoided them by staying out of swamps.

The columnist puts Atkinson into every scene that, for Boyer, starred McKeogh. The *Monitor* story, however, has a strong "as told to" flavor and lacks the rigor of research. It could well have been the result of a long-ago afternoon's jawboning in the old *Post*'s newsroom, with the veteran reporter Atkinson holding forth to the young recruit. The most likely scenario is that both McKeogh and Atkinson were involved in the Knowles affair, and that both inflated their own roles to willing interviewers. But Gould's piece does provide a fascinating insight into one possible origin of the Nature Man story. Who could deny the appeal of a real-life, modern-day Tarzan? For a month or so, as Gould points out, *Alone in the Wilderness* outsold the King of the Apes.

———— •◆• ————

FOUR

Faking It
in the
Fading Frontier

WHEN JOSEPH KNOWLES WENT INTO THE WOODS IN 1913, HE probably knew that his timing was propitious. The America of that period had lost the confident swagger that characterized its westward expansion, and instead had entered a period of anxiety as the end of the frontier era was reached and industrialization began to move people whose families had worked the land for generations into dirty, noisy, and increasingly crowded cities. Former outdoorsmen were now likely working swing shifts in dark factories and emerging to skylines of belching smokestacks.

Though he was a product of long-settled New England, Knowles came to embody a rekindling of the frontier spirit. Dressed in buckskin and his undoubtedly pungent bear hide, carrying primitive tools and weapons, he lacked only a coonskin cap to embody the heroes

FREDERICK JACKSON TURNER CALLED ATTENTION TO THE PASSING OF
THE FRONTIER.

of dime novels and pulp fiction. For even as the frontier was disappearing, interest in it—and identity with it—were not.

A startling announcement had accompanied the U.S. Census
of 1890. "Up to and including 1880," it said, "the country had a
frontier of settlement; but at present, the unsettled area has been
so broken into by isolated bodies of settlement that there can
hardly be said to be a frontier line. In the discussion of its extent, the western movement, etc., it cannot therefore any longer
have a place in the census reports."

Historian Frederick Jackson Turner cited this passage in his
pioneering paper "The Significance of the Frontier in American

History," delivered at the 1893 World's Columbian Exhibition (better known as the Chicago World's Fair). While its significance was not immediately recognized (Turner's own parents, in Chicago for the fair, didn't bother to attend), the paper has since been lauded as critical to understanding the making of the American character.

As Turner pointed out, the major, dominating fact of U.S. history up to that point had been westward expansion, and this was now coming to an abrupt end. This was hugely significant, he wrote, because the primitive conditions of the frontier fostered independent thinking that was essential to the building of a freedom-loving American character—throwing off the bonds of the stifling Old World, bonds that had been imported from Europe.

"The frontier is the line of most rapid and effective Americanization," Turner wrote. "The wilderness masters the colonist. It finds him a European in dress, industries, tools, modes of travel, and thought. It takes him from the railroad car and puts him in the birch canoe. It strips him of the garments of civilization and arrays him in the hunting shirt and the moccasin. It puts him in the log cabin of the Cherokee and Iroquois and runs an Indian palisade around him." Before long, he even "shouts the war cry and takes the scalp in orthodox Indian fashion."

And with the passing of the frontier and the onset of early industrialization, said Turner, "Western social and political ideas took new form"—the free, unfettered life of the frontiersman was giving way to more centralized control. "It is not strange that the Western pioneers took alarm for their ideals of democracy. . . ." And that alarm helped fuel a growing sense that Americans were losing touch with nature as the wilderness disappeared. For many, then, the appearance of the red-blooded Joseph Knowles was a perfectly timed salve.

Jim Tantillo, a present-day lecturer in environmental ethics at Cornell, includes Knowles in his lectures as an "interesting case history." He said, in an interview, "At the turn of the century there was a general uneasiness, overall cognitive dissonance about how fast society was moving. That feeling helped spur the back-to-the-wilderness movement, and it explains the attraction of primitivism at that time."

As the western boundary was reached, American attitudes toward the frontier began to change. In the place of the manifest destiny to conquer new territory, nostalgia grew over a way of life that was abruptly ending. Western writers on natural themes, including John Muir, began to grow in popularity among the voracious readers of the settled East. Muir founded the Sierra Club in 1892, helping organize a small but growing body of Americans who worried not only about the loss of a natural heritage, but about the effects of such a loss on their well-being.

"Climb the mountains and get their good tidings," Muir instructed his readers in the 1901 *Our National Parks*. "Nature's peace will flow into you as sunshine flows into trees. The winds will blow their own freshness into you, and the storms their energy, while cares will drop off like autumn leaves." His belief that "in God's wildness lies the hope of the world" resonated powerfully.

In striving to reconnect Americans to "God's wildness," Knowles would seem to be on a positive, even noble, mission. But Roderick Nash, in his important book *Wilderness and the American Mind*, also sees a somewhat darker side. Knowles's story, he says, "added to the evidence suggesting that by the early twentieth century, appreciation of wilderness had spread from a relatively small group of Romantic and patriotic literati to become a national cult." And as we shall see, this "cult" was absorbing a fair amount of disinformation about nature from self-appointed experts in the field.

Also getting under way in the early 1900s were the boys' clubs that would soon evolve into the Boy Scouts, with the goal of exposing young men to the character-building rigors of manly outdoor pursuits. The beckoning woods had a unique role to play at this turn in history. In the absence of a war, it was where boys could prove their worth and grow into their masculinity. Just as the American Indians observed certain rites to mark the passage from youth to manhood, so too did the white frontier American have unwritten codes that could only be acted out against a wild backdrop.

There was also a distinct layer of anxiety at work in this period—had boys forgotten how to be boys? Michael Ferguson develops this theme in his book *Idol Worship*. "Western culture was screwing itself up over fears of inadequacy," he writes,

> and Teddy Roosevelt's admonition to 'stave off effeminacy' presaged the 'Boy Reform Movement.' Fearing industrialization's diminishing effects on manliness, society wrestled with fears of breeding a generation of over-domesticated males, the 'mollycoddle,' singularly speaking.
>
> Boys were being pampered, the argument went, not allowed to be the mischievous little savages nature intended. Too many were being sissified at home by their mothers, who tended to rein in their sons' natural urges to be wild beasts. Physical activity, the outdoor life, camping, hunting and same-sex bonding were the remedies.

Roosevelt and others clearly felt that in the absence of the frontier, the "over-civilized" European would reassert himself.

You'd expect Ferguson to bring in Knowles at this juncture, and he doesn't disappoint. Joe Knowles, in his opinion, went into the woods "bare assed" to prove just this point—that the American male could reclaim his identity in the woods. It's not surprising that some modern feminist writers have noted that in this vision, women were often excluded; their "domestic sphere" did not extend far past the kitchen door. But Knowles was soon to give a woman a starring role in one of his productions.

The public was hungry for information about the world beyond the treeline. Ralph H. Lutts writes, in his book *The Nature Fakers,* "By the beginning of the century the public's appetite for nature was enormous. Nature study became a part of the school curriculum. Eager readers made some nature writers wealthy. City dwellers tramped off into the woods." Henry David Thoreau's books enjoyed a renaissance, and many people made pilgrimages to Walden Pond.

In his unpublished paper on Knowles, journalism professor and historian Mark Neuzil writes, "Adults experienced nature through the Audubon Society, the Boone and Crockett Club, the Mazamas and countless others. The books of Liberty Hyde Bailey, a Cornell University educator, gave voice to the nature movement, as did the magazine he edited, *Country Life in America,* founded in 1903." Joyce Kilmer wrote the simple twelve-line poem "Trees" in 1913, and its enduring popularity has eclipsed any of his other verse. In its first thirty years, the Boy Scout handbook sold seven million copies in the United States, second only to the Bible. In its first edition, it noted that a century earlier all boys had lived "close to nature." But since then an "unfortunate change" had led to industrialization and the rise of big cities, and so boys were cut off from access to the woods. The Scouting magazine, *Boys' Life,* began publishing in 1912 and preached the same message. It soon grew to become America's largest periodical for youth.

A young Teddy Roosevelt in the Badlands: no tolerance for "nature fakers."

The wilderness craze did wonders for not only respected naturalists like John Muir, but also for sentimental nature writers such as Ernest Thompson Seton, Charles G. D. Roberts, and William J. Long. Seton, never missing an opportunity for anthropomorphism, claimed that foxes would lure pursuing hounds onto railroad tracks so that they might be killed by passing trains. In their way, by ascribing higher purpose and complex thought to foxes, eagles, and wolves, the works of these writers helped Americans take a more humane approach to the animal kingdom, replacing the more utilitarian view that had prevailed in the nineteenth century. But they definitely took liberties with science.

Roberts, known as the father of Canadian poetry, wrote in the 1902 *Kindred of the Wild: A Book of Animal Life* that eagles are the kings in a well-established hierarchy of the air, and (shades of *The Lion King*) all lesser birds pay tribute with regular offerings. He has a panther roll a balled-up porcupine down a hill and into a river to force it to uncurl. He ascribes great powers to the mysterious lynx. The latter assertion set off Roosevelt, who damned Roberts with faint praise by calling him "a charming writer" of "fairy tales." Roberts's lynx takes on eight wolves with "savage exultation," but Roosevelt said that "The lynx . . . would stand no more chance than a house-cat in a fight with eight bull terriers."

Seton, whatever his failings as a writer, was also a Scouting pioneer of considerable importance. He shared the view that boys were being ruined by the urbanizing trend. For Seton, the cities were full of "money grubbing, machine politics, degrading sports, cigarettes, town life of the worst kind, false ideals, moral laxity and lessening church power. . . ." He concluded that "city rot" had "worked evil in this nation."

Seton based his woodcraft lessons on the traditions of Native Americans, and his 1906 scouting handbook (published four years before the Boy Scouts were founded in the United States) was called *Birch-Bark Roll of the Woodcraft Indians.* Knowles's book includes a chapter on the virtues of scouting and specifically lauds Seton's work, his only such acknowledgement.

Long, a Connecticut minister, wrote that red squirrels had cheek pockets that could hold six chestnuts (when they actually lack cheek pockets at all). His stories told of porcupines curling into a ball and rolling downhill for fun, of eagles dying in flight and gliding gracefully to earth, of kingfishers that caught fish to instruct their young and then released them.

Just a few years before Knowles donned his breechclout, from 1903 to 1907, a controversy raged about "nature fakery," with naturalist John Burroughs ("the dean of nature lovers," said the *New York Times*) and his friend President Theodore Roosevelt among the more prominent protagonists.

As Lutts writes in his useful study of the affair, the president and the naturalist were in many ways well positioned to take on the sentimental animal lovers. Burroughs, initially influenced by and in the shadow of Ralph Waldo Emerson, built a towering international reputation through more than two dozen books on natural themes. He was at the height of his influence at the turn of the century.

And Roosevelt was without a doubt the U.S. president most knowledgeable about, and protective of, the natural world, even rivaling Burroughs in his ability to identify and characterize flora and fauna. In 1888, he had co-founded the Boone and Crockett Club (hunters dedicated to protecting wildlife), and as its president helped develop and expand Yellowstone National Park and pass the Forest Reserve Act. But Roosevelt cared as much about taking animal life as he did preserving it, and he was firmly convinced that animals were motivated by very simple impulses and base instinct.

Burroughs took on Long and Seton in a famous 1903 essay in *Atlantic Monthly* titled "Real and Sham Natural History." He lamented that Long wrote like "a man who has really never been to the woods, but who sits in his study and cooks up these yarns from things he has read in *Forest and Stream,* or in other sporting journals." He asked, as Roosevelt did, "Why impute reason to an animal if its behavior can be explained on the theory of instinct?"

According to Lutts's account of the battle royal, Burroughs charged that Seton and "his awkward imitator" Long had repeatedly crossed "the line between fact and fiction." He called their work "yellow journalism of the woods." Seton, in *Wild Animals I Have Known,* opens with the line "These stories are true," fighting words for Burroughs. The naturalist suggested an alternate title for Seton's book, *Wild Animals I Alone Have Known,* taking particular umbrage at a description in the book of a fox that leaped upon a sheep and rode it for several hundred yards to throw pursuing dogs off the scent.

President Roosevelt was delighted with the *Atlantic Monthly* article, writing his friend Burroughs, "I have long wished that something of the kind should be written." He later joined Burroughs in excoriating Long for claiming that orioles had built an elaborate framed nest tied together with string (using "a reversed double-hitch"). "He might just as well say that Jenny Wren built herself a log cabin with a bark roof," the president said. Piling it on, Burroughs added that the nest was "so extraordinary that it can be accounted for only on the theory that there is a school of the woods, and that these two birds had been pupils there and had taken a course in strings."

Long, for his part, got in an effective jab. He chastised Roosevelt's well-known blood lust, questioned his love of nature, and compared his behavior to the game butcher who "hides behind a tree and kills three bull elks in succession, leaving their carcasses to rot in the woods . . . in itself . . . incomprehensible to sportsmen."

The "Nature Fakers" controversy had its amusing aspects; but for Seton, Long, and Roberts it was probably not much fun to be pilloried in public by such eminent men (though, initially at least, Roosevelt stayed in the background). As Lutts writes, many observers probably found the affair rather strange—"a bunch of grown men, prominent and respectable men at that, arguing over whether porcupines roll downhill or foxes ride across a field on a sheep's back."

Eventually, even *Call of the Wild* and *White Fang* author Jack London was drawn into the controversy. Roosevelt was upset at London's portrayal of wolf behavior, and was incensed that the author had depicted in *White Fang* a fighting bulldog defeating a wolf in pitched battle. "It is merely a statement of a difference of opinion," London wrote from Tahiti in 1908. "President Roosevelt does not think a bull-dog can lick a wolf-dog. I think a bull-dog can lick a wolf-dog. And there we are. . . . But what gets me is how difference of opinion regarding the relative fighting merits of a bull-dog and a wolf-dog make me a nature-faker and President Roosevelt a vindicated and triumphant scientist."

Burroughs and Roosevelt might have been more charitable had they acknowledged the profound role that amusing but undoubtedly apocryphal tall tales had in forming America's frontier story. The heartwarming (and often morally instructive) anthropomorphism of the "Nature Fakers" was a logical extension of the backwoods lore, traded around campfires, that had been common currency up to that time. The literal truth wasn't expected, and it was rarely offered.

The great showman Phineas Taylor Barnum, writing in 1865, declared firmly that "humbug is astonishingly widespread—in fact, almost universal. . . ." Though Barnum grew up in rural Bethel, Connecticut, far from the western frontier, he certainly recognized that something in the American character loved a good tale more than it did the literal truth, and was willing to pay to be entertained by the wildest tomfoolery.

It's also amazing how uncritically Barnum's claims were taken in the popular press of his time. When Barnum introduced Joice Heth in 1835 as the supposed wet nurse of George Washington, claiming she was 161 years old, most papers reported it as gospel truth. "From the bill of sale of the old lady from Gen. Washington's father, *we can have no doubt that she is 160 years of age* [emphasis in the original]," said the *New York Evening Star.*

Barnum cheerfully admitted as early as 1841 that Joice Heth was a fraud of no more than seventy-five years, but not before putting over another rich falsehood on James Gordon Bennett, Jr., publisher of the *New York Herald:* After Heth died and an autopsy revealed the impossibility of her advanced years, Barnum told Bennett that Heth was actually still alive and that the body autopsied was that of an unfortunate Harlem woman. Since this "scoop" gave Bennett a chance to snipe at his Heth-debunking rivals, it received banner headlines in the *Herald.* The public never did get the whole truth, but Barnum noted that "the joke

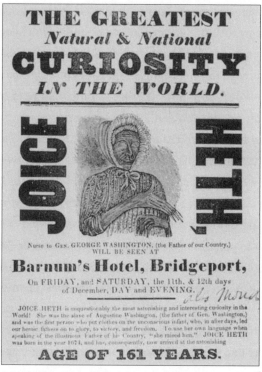

JOICE HETH WAS PROBABLY IN HER SEVENTIES, BUT A GULLIBLE
PUBLIC ACCEPTED BARNUM'S CLAIM THAT SHE WAS 161 YEARS OLD.

was considered a rich one," and that was far more important than
the sober facts. He was soon foisting the "Feejee Mermaid" on a
gullible public that had learned nothing from its previous encounters with the wily promoter.

The concept of the backwoodsman as unfettered natural man was
well established by Knowles's time. This figure had roots in the Enlightenment thinkers like Jean-Jacques Rousseau, who popularized
the idea that primitive man had noble instincts; but the backwoodsman was decidedly homegrown and always larger than life.

The quintessential exemplar of this tradition was Colonel Daniel Boone, whose exploits in the "howling wilderness" were first described in a fanciful 1784 book by John Filson. There are many legends about Boone, quite a few of them totally inaccurate, but he definitely led a colorful life that included more than one capture by Indians, land speculation, political service, and a lively career as a fur trader. It's instructive that Boone is best remembered for a statement he supposedly made about leaving civilization behind. When he was a venerable sixty-four years old, Boone pulled up stakes and moved west to Missouri. Asked why he was leaving his beloved Kentucky, he reportedly replied, "Too crowded—I want more elbow room." Boone was fleeing a population density of ten people to the square mile, or the same as South Dakota would have in the year 2000; Kentucky had 100 people per square mile in 2000.

By the time of J. B. Jones's 1841 adventure novel *Wild Western Scenes*, the image of Boone as restless westward force was widely disseminated. "But it was not in Boone's nature to be long at rest," the luridly illustrated book proclaims. "There were still boundless tracts of rich lands to be explored, so, shouldering his rifle, he once more bade adieu to civilization and plunged alone into the wilderness, to open new roads for the tide of emigration that was soon to follow."

But Boone wasn't always peripatetic; he was in fact a leading citizen of Kentucky, serving as sheriff of Fayette County and a lieutenant colonel in its militia, as well as an elected representative of the state legislature. And in fact, late in life he publicly disowned the notion that he had moved west merely to escape the sight of his neighbor's chimney fire. But even without Boone's active connivance the legend grew, spreading to Europe, where the

DANIEL BOONE: A RELENTLESS QUEST FOR WILDERNESS? ILLUSTRA-
TION FROM *HISTORY OF OUR WILD WEST* (1901) BY D. M. KELSEY

poet Lord Byron hoisted him aloft for living the free life "in wilds
of deepest maze."

Practically forgotten today is nineteenth-century legend Mike
Fink, one of the Mississippi River keelboatmen who used a combination of brawn and wits to manhandle a small craft and deliver
passengers through the river's treacherous currents. The six-foot-
three Fink, born sometime between 1770 and 1780, was the last
boatman on the Mississippi before steam made the profession re-
dundant, and that helped his legend take hold. Fink was a reck-
less daredevil, but his real life never matched the figure of legend

Mike Fink's Great Shot.

IN A NINETEENTH-CENTURY ILLUSTRATION, KEELBOAT LEGEND MIKE FINK SHOWS
OFF HIS SHOOTING PROWESS.

who rode a moose through the wilderness, held a she-wolf under-
water until she drowned, and scalped an Indian with a single
shot. The first published reference to Fink was in an 1821 farce
called *The Pedlar*—he appears as a boastful bully—but more
admirable traits were also ascribed to him.

Fink was a real person, but he became what author Constance
Rourke in her 1931 book *American Humor* called "a Mississippi

river-god, one of those minor deities whom men create in their own image and magnify to magnify themselves." Over time, she writes, he "grew supersized; he had eaten a buffalo robe, but New England rum had ruined his stomach. He became Mike Finch, Mike Finx, Mike Wing, in a hundred minor tales. Driven at last from the Mississippi, he moved into the unknown regions of the farther West, achieving the final glory of heroes, a death wrapped in mystery. . . ."

The 1847 "Death of Mike Fink" by Joseph M. Field reports that a half dozen different deaths were attributed to the boatman, and it attempts to clear the "mythic haze" by asserting that he breathed his last in 1823, killed in retaliation after accidentally shooting his best friend, a youth named Carpenter, in a drunken brawl.

Fink was often linked to the Tennessean Davy Crockett in early stories—and on television, too, in the 1950s where he became Fess Parker's foil in two Disney episodes. Crockett may have spent much time in cities, and even served, as his theme song goes, "a spell" in Congress, but he proved an even more durable basis for backwoods mythmaking and tall tales than Boone. Crockett was a legend while he was still alive, but his reputation really grew after his death at the Alamo in 1836. With the departure from the scene of this crack marksman, the alligators of the Mississippi were said to have grown fat and lazy, and there was reportedly "great rejoicin' among the bears of Kaintuck." The bears certainly had something to celebrate, because by his own 1834 account Crockett dispatched no less than 105 of their number in a year "while my competitor was in Congress." Some of Crockett's stories are astounding for the sheer amount of ursine dispatch.

What were the authentic voices of these sons of the soil? It depends on who you ask. According to John Filson's 1784 account (very popular in Europe), Daniel Boone said things like, "Thus situated, many hundreds of miles from our families in the howling wilderness, I believe few would have equally enjoyed the happiness we experienced. . . . [T]he beauties of nature I met with in this charming season, expelled every gloomy and vexatious thought." Boone's actual speech was probably much more plainspoken, and would sound archaic to later ears, hence the tendency of the popularizing biographer to modernize him. One example of Boone's actual writing was reportedly carved on an American beech tree in Tennessee. He supposedly wrote "D Boone cilled a bar on tree in year 1760."

Perhaps it was Crockett's voice that rang in Knowles's head as he stepped out onto the trail. At least according to *People* magazine, Crockett was "a flamboyant frontiersman who owed his reputation to his ability to tell tall tales." Crockett's folksy vernacular, preserved in his stump speeches and 1834 autobiography, comes down to us much more clearly than Boone's more distant voice. Knowles's folksy speaking and writing style owed quite a bit to Crockett's. Given a well-oiled audience, the Boston backwoodsman could embellish any tale with comic exaggeration. Crockett could grin a raccoon out of a tree, and Knowles could wrestle wild animals to the ground with his bare hands. They shared a fixation with taking down bears. Knowles would end up trapping one, but Crockett dispatched them with real gusto. "I . . . found my dogs had a two year-old bear down, a-wooling away on him," he wrote in his *Narrative of the Life of David Crockett of the State of Tennessee*. "So I just took out my big butcher, and went up and slap'd it into him, and killed him without shooting."

The stature of giants like Boone and Crockett was reinforced not only with lurid tales in the popular press, but also with relatively sober accounts written by respected biographers, including Teddy Roosevelt himself, who wrote, "With Boon[e], hunting and exploration were passions, and the lonely life of the wilderness, with its bold, wild freedom, the only existence for which he really cared." He could have been writing about Joseph Knowles.

Accurate scholarship about Daniel Boone and Davy Crockett in the nineteenth century was made more difficult by the widespread popularity of dime novels, which never let the truth get in the way of a good yarn. One of the acknowledged masters of the genre (his heyday was between 1860 and 1890) was the colorful Ned Buntline (real name Edward Zane Carroll Judson). His own life could have been the basis for one of his books: In 1846, when he was twenty-three, Buntline was allegedly tried for murder in Tennessee and lynched, but was cut down before the rope could finish the job. He was also known for getting drunk—after delivering temperance lectures, of all things—and for stirring up trouble as an anti-immigrant "nativist."

Buntline's major subject was not Boone or Crockett, but hunter and scout William "Buffalo Bill" Cody, whose legend he had helped manufacture in an 1869 dime novel. According to Cody's sister, Helen Cody Wetmore, in her 1899 account *Last of the Great Scouts,* Buntline was much impressed by Cody's potential as an actor "and was confident that a fortune awaited the scout if he would consent to enter the theatrical profession." To that end, Buntline in 1871 produced the pot-boiling drama *The Scouts of the Plains,* with Cody himself in a starring role. Cody's early stage career was also encouraged by James Gordon Bennett, Jr., the aforementioned editor and publisher of the *New York Herald.* Newspapers then and in Knowles's day knew the value of good publicity, and Bennett didn't mind injecting his own reporters into the story.

With the passing of the frontier into history, it's hardly surprising that it would live on in exaggerated, sentimentalized fashion on the late-nineteenth-century stage—or that it would soon become difficult to sort fact from fiction in Bill Cody's life. There are countless Cody biographies, many of them full of the most absurd nonsense. But Louis S. Warren's 2005 *Buffalo Bill's America: William Cody and the Wild West Show* does a fine job of paring away layers of myth about this "most famous American of his age."

In an interview with Powells.com, Warren makes a key point, noting that "the idea of having a public persona that takes over your entire life is no longer so strange as it was in Cody's day. In that sense, there's a little Buffalo Bill in all of us." And certainly in Joe Knowles, who learned by experience how to stay in character as the larger-than-life Nature Man. Richard Slotkin, in his book *Gunfighter Nation: The Myth of the Frontier in Twentieth Century America,* writes that Cody's frontier hero was full of self-reliance "and acquires scientific knowledge through the necessary operations of his native curiosity and engagement with nature." And that also fits as a description of Knowles's "experiment."

Cody did, in fact, win a Congressional Medal of Honor in 1872 for Indian fighting, but many other aspects of his biography—including pioneering rides for the Pony Express and a close relationship with George Armstrong Custer—are, Warren writes, to be approached with caution. Slotkin in *Gunfighter Nation* calls the pre–1869 Cody "a minor actor on the stage of western history." It was on America's literal stages that his name was writ large.

Though Cody's accounts of his Pony Express derring-do (and friendship with James Butler "Wild Bill" Hickok) in his autobiography and stage shows was accepted as accurate for decades, Warren unravels a far more mundane tale. Cody was a teamster

in Denver, but he likely never rode for the Pony Express during
its short eighteen-month existence. Instead, the fourteen- and
fifteen-year-old was probably still in school in Leavenworth,
Kansas at the time, where he was said to have been a determined
ballplayer.

Cody also claimed a close relationship to the man of Little Big
Horn that went back to 1867, when he supposedly guided the
"dashing and gallant Custer" between Fort Ellsworth and Fort
Larned. Later, after the brave general had fallen in 1876, Cody
went west to take the "first scalp for Custer." He staged this scene
many times in his Wild West shows, and it is graphically depicted in D. M. Kelsey's 1903 book *History of Our Wild West*. In
an account that mirrors Cody's own autobiography, the scout is seen
riding with the Fifth Cavalry immediately upon hearing the news
of the demise of Custer ("the flower of our knighthood") and encountering a huge party of 800 Cheyennes. In reality, writes Warren, Cody's celebrated encounter didn't take place until almost a
month after the Little Big Horn massacre. And it was a minor
skirmish, involving no more than thirty warriors, what Warren
calls "an encounter so small it could hardly be called a battle."
The Cheyenne who Cody killed was actually a "subchief" named
Yellow Hair.

In Kelsey's account, Yellow Hair is "decked in all the paint and
ornaments of a war chief." He calls out Cody in dramatic fashion, shouting, "I know you, Long-Hair; if you want to fight, come
and fight me." (Cody indeed rose to the challenge for one-on-one
combat; but since he didn't speak Cheyenne and Yellow Hair had
no command of English, the dramatic exchange itself is unlikely.)

In Kelsey's purple prose, Cody's aim is true and, as 200 warriors bear down on him, he steps over the "prostrate savage," and

"with one stroke of his knife severed the scalp-lock from the head, swung the reeking trophy and its gorgeous adornments in the air with the words: 'the first scalp for Custer!'" It was perhaps a minor detail that Custer was actually killed by the Sioux, not the Cheyenne, and this skirmish with the Cheyenne probably delayed pursuit of the responsible parties.

According to Cody's autobiography, Custer was so impressed with the scout's abilities that he promised to find him a job. But Warren demonstrates convincingly that Custer and Cody actually met fleetingly only once, at an opulent buffalo hunt staged for Russian Grand Duke Alexis in 1872. Cody lent the Grand Duke both his horse, "Buckskin Joe," and his rifle, and helped this son of Czar Alexander II kill a large bull buffalo.

It's likely that the Duke enjoyed himself thoroughly, because a sanitized version of the Wild West was then much in vogue in Europe. No less a personage than Mark Twain wrote to Cody in 1884: Twain proclaimed himself thoroughly entertained after having seen the Wild West show twice, and pointed out that the English had been complaining that our theatrical exports were not purely American. "If you will take the Wild West show over there, you can remove that reproach," Twain said.

There's no doubt that Cody's spectacular program was American, but painstakingly historical it was not. It made $1 million in 1893, the same year it wowed audiences at the World's Columbian Exhibition in Chicago. Whether Cody took time out to enjoy the groundbreaking lecture there by Frederick Jackson Turner is not known, but he certainly understood the significance of losing the frontier.

The public suspended its disbelief when it came to Buffalo Bill Cody, because he put on such a rip-roaring good show. Even those who knew the truth about his career, including Wild Bill Hickok, not only kept quiet about the particulars but took the showman's dollar for appearing on stage themselves. In some cases, they embroidered each other's legends, as was the case when U.S. Marshal Wyatt Earp took pen to paper for a (probably ghostwritten) 1896 article in William Randolph Hearst's *San Francisco Examiner* that paid tribute to his old friend, gunslinger John Henry "Doc" Holliday. Typically for a period that demanded sterling character from its heroes, this frontier dentist and key player in the gunfight at Tombstone, Arizona's OK Corral was described by Earp as a "mad, merry scamp with heart of gold and nerves of steel; who . . . stood at my elbow in many a battle to the death."

Hickok also chronically exaggerated the truth of his own illustrious career, and in fact was something of a model for Buffalo Bill in that regard. Both claimed, wrongly, to have ridden with the Pony Express. (At least Hickok, at twenty-three, was old enough to have theoretically done so.) Enhancing, and entwining, the legends of these two historical bit players was to their mutual advantage. And the making of outlandish claims was almost expected of them. As Louis Warren writes in *Buffalo Bill's America*, "By the 1860s, no region could match the West as a venue for the staging of attractions and the invention of personas that appealed to popular desires and begged audiences to separate them from reality." Hickok's major problem was his inability to be that larger-than-life character on stage. He was fired from the Wild West show, after a short term in residence, for getting into brawls in billiard rooms and antagonizing other members of the company.

Similarly given to tall tales (and also claiming falsely to have ridden with the Pony Express) was Martha Jane Cannary-Burke, better known as Calamity Jane. Though she did meet Hickok in his later years, she never married him as she claimed, and their supposed love child was probably fictitious. Like Cody, she also falsely claimed to have scouted for George Armstrong Custer. None of this affected her standing with the Wild West show, which hired her sporadically, though like Hickok she had a considerable drinking problem.

At the Palace Museum in Minneapolis in 1896, she was billed as "the heroine of a thousand thrilling adventures," "the terror of evildoers in the Black Hills," and "the comrade of Buffalo Bill and Wild Bill Hickok." But it's unlikely that those Western evildoers cared one way or the other when she moved east, where the interest in the Wild West seemed insatiable. At the Pan-American Exposition in Buffalo in 1901, Calamity Jane rode horses in buckskins, sold copies of her fanciful autobiography, and got in trouble with the police for excessive drinking. Buffalo Bill, who provided her with money to get out of town, proclaimed, "I expect she was no more tired of Buffalo than the Buffalo police were of her, for her sorrows seemed to need a good deal of drowning, and she got into lots of trouble. Well, of course she was one of the pioneers."

In calling Joseph Knowles the "Dr. Cook of the North Woods," the *Boston American* knew it was launching a barb that would hit home. Dr. Frederick Albert Cook, M.D., was justly famous as an explorer, having laid claim in 1906 to being the first person to have climbed America's highest peak, Mount McKinley. But in 1908 he made a much more controversial claim. Was Dr. Cook the first to reach the North Pole (along with two Inuit guides), as he claimed, or was that honor due to Robert Peary, who traveled there in 1909?

Dr. Cook could not produce detailed records to validate his claim, but he insisted that such documents had existed and charged that Peary had had a hand in ensuring that they were lost to posterity. As with Knowles's claims about what he did in the woods, charges and countercharges were flung. In a 1911 book, Cook wrote: "As to the relative merits of my claim, and Mr. Peary's, place the two records side by side. Compare them. I shall be satisfied with your decision."

It's quite possible that neither Peary nor Cook actually reached the North Pole, but it's Cook's reputation that suffered. After his North Pole achievements were questioned, it wasn't long before detractors went after the Mount McKinley claim too. Modern climbers continue to dispute his accounts, pointing out that his description of the summit diverges considerably from the wind-swept reality.

Cook fell even further after Knowles's time, and was convicted of stock fraud in 1923 and imprisoned. Today he's held in somewhat higher esteem (a Frederick A. Cook Society continues to flourish), but in 1913 being called "the Dr. Cook of the North Woods" was clearly no compliment.

Knowles never toured Europe, but he might have done very well there. The affection with which Europeans held the Wild West, no matter how outlandishly depicted, has already been noted. In 1903, Buffalo Bill's Wild West show toured England and visited the seaside resort of Hastings. In the audience was an imaginative fourteen-year-old boy named Archibald Stansfeld Belaney, known as Archie. Young Archie may have been middle-class and English, but he was nicknamed "Squaw Man" by his schoolmates for organizing gangs of "Red Indians" to raid enemies and plan scalping parties for parents. And this was *before* he saw the Wild West show.

As Jane Billinghurst writes in her book *Grey Owl: The Many Faces of Archie Belaney,* the young man had long had dreams about the American West, and wanted something more out of life than "a desk job in a sleepy seaside town." In 1906, he made those dreams real by boarding the SS *Canada* for Halifax, Nova Scotia. He worked briefly selling men's furnishings in a Toronto department store, but within a few months he was in northern Ontario, beginning his journey to a more elemental way of life.

By the summer of 1910, Billinghurst writes, "Archie was 21 years old, and he had found the Indians he had been looking for." They were Ojibways, and Belaney later described a colorful induction circle, complete with medicine men and dancing to reed pipes around an open fire. To a background of simulated owl hoots, he was given his new Indian name, Ko-homsee, "Little Owl," which he was later to amend. He married into the tribe, and his new wife taught him the Indian way of setting traps and making fish nets.

It's interesting to note that Knowles claimed similar tutelage among Sioux and Chippewa Indians in South Dakota, and that this contributed greatly to his woodcrafting knowledge. But Knowles never claimed to actually *be* Native American. Belaney did. As early as 1908, he began telling anyone who would listen that he was a half-Apache who had been born in Mexico, spent his youth in the Southwest, and had even traveled with Buffalo Bill's Wild West show. He explained his English accent by claiming that his father was a Scot, and that while traveling overseas with Buffalo Bill he had been dropped off in the south of England for a proper education.

The man we will now call Grey Owl left a messy wake behind him. He abandoned his Indian wife and child, abandoned another pregnant girlfriend, and then became a bigamist by marry-

GREY OWL: UNDER THE INDIAN COSTUME WAS BRITISH-BORN
ARCHIE BELANEY. COURTESY OF THE ARCHIVES OF ONTARIO

ing again in England after his service in World War I. None of this
prevented him from returning to Canada and marrying, for the third
time, a beautiful Iroquois woman named Pony, who he named
Anahareo. Like Knowles, Grey Owl hired himself out as a hunting guide, supplementing his income with a growing career as a
magazine writer.

The trapper's evolution into a pioneering conservationist began
in 1928, when he and Anahareo took in a pair of beaver kittens
that had been orphaned by the fur trade. Soon he and his beavers
were starring in films made for the National Parks Board of
Canada. By 1930, this child of the English seaside was signing
his letters "Grey Owl."

Soon this pretend-Indian, who in more than a decade in the bush had now weathered to look the part, was appearing in full-feathered regalia for public appearances. In a close parallel to Knowles, he talked about the value of wilderness and the Indian way of life, and he showed nature films. Grey Owl's first book, *Men of the Frontier* (he'd wanted to call it *The Vanishing Frontier*), was published to an appreciative audience in England, to which he soon repaired for a four-month lecture tour.

Buffalo Bill had paved the way, and Grey Owl (in a beaded buckskin costume that might have come from a Hollywood fitting room, but was instead made by Anahareo) was a huge hit in Europe. According to Billinghurst, he spoke to half a million people and attended 200 meetings. A rapturous reporter wrote that Grey Owl "steps right out of the pages of James Fenimore Cooper." With no conscious irony, he added, "He looks too good to be true to life." On a second trip to England, in 1937, he gave a command performance at Buckingham Palace for King George VI (who he lectured on conservation) and Queen Elizabeth.

Grey Owl was a gifted writer. The Native American, he said, was in tune with his or her surroundings and could detect the slightest change in the environment. "[A] movement where all should be still; a disturbance of the colour scheme; a disarrangement in the set of the leaves; the frayed end of a newly-broken stick, speak loud to the Indian's eye."

Grey Owl fought for preservation of the Canadian wilderness, which, he wrote, is "a living, breathing reality, and has a soul that must be understood. . . ." He built a huge reputation as a speaker and conservationist, though on visits to Toronto he was terrified of being recognized and exposed by people who had known him in his former life. But those who did know the truth, including at least one newspaper, kept the story to themselves. Grey Owl spoke to 1,700 people at Canada's first book fair, and hundreds were turned away from his lectures.

He died in 1938, after which his secret was soon revealed. According to Billinghurst, a media furor ensued, and Grey Owl's dedication to conservation was hotly debated. "If he were an impostor, could his words be sincere?" she wrote.

When Knowles was questioned by the *Boston American,* the debate went in a different direction. It wasn't his commitment to conservation that was in question, but his accomplishments in the woods. For Knowles, preserving wilderness was always part of the message, but not the core of it. As we've noted, he wasn't an eloquent speaker; and though his book did offer much commentary on the salutary effects of living wild, it was probably ghostwritten.

The riddle of Joe Knowles focused on whether he really had gone into the woods naked and alone and lived off its bounty. It was a test of human ability, man against nature. The Maine affair had ended ambiguously, but he was soon to get an unprecedented second opportunity to prove himself.

——— •◆• ———

FIVE

Knowles
Makes
Headlines
out West

JOSEPH KNOWLES'S ADVENTURES IN THE MAINE WOODS HAD BEEN followed with interest around the country through syndication. When Hearst's *Boston American* exposed the Nature Man, abbreviated versions of the exposé ran in the chain's holdings across the country.

On June 21, 1914, the *San Francisco Examiner* ran a lengthy, bemused account that actually added a few details to its sister paper's version. Knowles's half-Indian accomplice, Joe St. Ober (misidentified as "Joe Sober") was now said to have personally made the Nature Man's bark pack, his bow and arrows, his chaps, and his deerhide sandals. The celebrated bullet holes in the bearskin were said to have been "skillfully scraped and sewed." The book *Alone in the Wilderness* was attributed by the *Examiner* to "a reporter friend." The account also said that the *American*'s reporter, Bert Ford, had been harassed by game wardens in the pay of Knowles, had his telegrams stolen, and was threatened with "death and violence."

The tone was condescending. Under a subhead proclaiming "But He Got Too Fat," the story said that Knowles "lived so high and got so fat that it was thought well to take the hike of forty miles to Quebec to reduce weight."

This was probably the low point in the saga of Joseph Knowles. In just a few months, the hero of the Boston streets and best-selling author had been reduced to a risible footnote to history. Though the *New Yorker* reported that he had made $3,000 from his stage appearances, the vaudeville star was running out of bookings. The plans to establish a school of the woods so that others could get educated in the science of woodcraft and firemaking had also failed to materialize.

According to a dubious 1976 column in the *Bangor Daily News*, Knowles's departure from Boston was hastened when an unnamed newspaper (probably the *American*), suffering heavy circulation losses, threatened a lawsuit, presumably either for libel or for defamation of character against reporter Bert Ford. "Joe escaped the slammer when the threatened lawsuits never came off," wrote Bud Leavitt in the 1976 column. "He quietly drifted off into the setting sun, settling down, finally, somewhere in California [*sic*]."

Knowles tried to put the best possible face on the adventure. The *American* may have threatened a lawsuit against the *Post*, but Knowles really *did* file one against the *American*, for $50,000. He claimed that the *American* was so embarrassed by its role in attempting to smear him that it had quietly dismissed seven employees for their roles in the affair.

What followed was one of the great turnabouts in American journalism. Very quickly, Hearst's attitude toward Knowles changed for the better. The first peace offering came from *Hearst's International,* a monthly magazine, which suddenly opined that Knowles's experiment was "a noble piece of poetry. A naked man against the tooth and claw of nature, and coming out victor— clothed, fed, healthy; it is a deal more comforting to our proper human pride than the erection of a Woolworth Building."

But Knowles's full rehabilitation—and second nature trip— would come about through the good offices of the *Examiner,* the flagship paper that miner's son William Randolph Hearst (the model for Charles Foster Kane in Orson Welles's *Citizen Kane*) had inherited from his father in 1887, when he was only twenty-four.

As Welles portrayed him, and as he was in real life, Hearst loved sensational journalism, and he loved bare-knuckled newspaper wars. In 1896, he stole away the entire Sunday staff of bitter rival Joseph Pulitzer's highly successful New York paper, the *World,* and in the process acquired for his own *New York Journal* Richard Felton Outcault's "The Yellow Kid"—the wildly popular comic strip that gave yellow journalism its name. (For a time, the strip ran in both papers, drawn by different artists.) It was at the *World,* in 1905, that Hearst is said to have created the first early-morning "bulldog" edition, based on his exhortation to his staff to create journalism that would "bite the public like a bulldog."

Among Hearst's greatest newspaper stunts was the "Evangelina Affair." Though Hearst probably doesn't deserve credit for starting the Spanish–American War, he certainly fanned the flames. When tales of Spanish perfidy in Cuba fell from the front pages in April of 1897, Hearst found a way to bring the story to life

again by focusing on the plight of the young and beauteous Evangelina Cisneros, the imprisoned daughter of an anti-Spanish in-
surgent. In Hearst headlines, Cisneros, a "Cuban Joan of Arc,"
fought to protect her chastity against the unwelcome advances of
her lustful jailer, a Spanish colonel.

Hearst pulled every stop to get Cisneros freed, including getting signatures on a petition signed by many prominent women,
including Julia Ward Howe (author of "The Battle Hymn of the Republic"); the mother of President William McKinley; and the widow
of Jefferson Davis. When that campaign failed, he actually sent
a reporter to Havana to break Cisneros out of jail. This effort
proved successful, amazingly enough, and Cisneros was freed in
October of 1897 and smuggled aboard the *Seneca,* bound for New
York. The *Journal* lauded its own efforts as "the greatest journalistic coup of the age," and gave Cisneros a Knowles-like parade
through the streets, followed by a rally at Madison Square Garden. She later met President McKinley at the White House, and
the Spanish were properly embarrassed.

The *Examiner* was close to Hearst's heart, because it was in
its city room that he had first proved his worth as a newspaperman of genius. Hearst himself had written the headlines for an
1887 story about a hotel fire in Monterey: "Hungry Frantic
Flames," read the banner. The subhead was "Leaping Higher,
Higher, Higher, with Desperate Desire," followed by "Rushing
in upon the Trembling Guests with Savage Fury!" If Hearst thought
the contents of his papers insufficiently sensational, he would
proclaim to the editor or writer in question: "This is like reading the telephone directory." He was competitive to a fault, and
he didn't hesitate to use the clout of his father—who was not
only immensely wealthy but also, after 1886, a U.S. senator—to

gain an advantage for the *Examiner* over his hated rival, the *Chronicle*.

Hearst had long since ceded day-to-day control of the *Examiner* by 1914. He was at the time distracted by his foray into movies, including the creation of the twenty-episode *Perils of Pauline* serial. But he still kept a proprietary watch over his first paper, and there's little doubt that he would have loved the Joseph Knowles story, both the exposé in the *American* and the Nature Man's subsequent rehabilitation on San Francisco's front page.

The details of how Knowles signed on with the *Examiner* are murky, but a deal appears to have been struck while the Nature Man was still on the road. In the spring of 1914, he had set out on a long lecture tour that was to culminate on the West Coast. In mid-June, Knowles was in Kansas City and slowly making his way west. This "square-built bulk of a man, deep-chested, strong-faced, two-handed," visited the office of the *Star* on June 19 and regaled the wide-eyed editors with tales of his adventures in the woods, and at sea "on every rig of ship under the sun and on all the seven seas: bark, brig, brigantine, barkentine, and three-masted schooner." He told the staff he was on his way to San Francisco for a second nature experiment, and in the California woods he would make his own writing paper—because there were no birch trees as there had been in Maine. He promised to create a full-color picture using natural pigments from berries and tree stains, which turned out to be a promise he kept.

The *Examiner* picked up the story June 22, reporting with a Denver dateline that the "Nature Man Exposed as Faker" was on his way out to San Francisco, and that he planned to once again plunge into the wilderness (for a month this time). The paper was still somewhat bemused by the whole thing. "In the light of his Maine woods adventures, when he grew fat comfortably, it is not expected his exploitation of the primitive will cause him any real privation," the short account said.

The report was datelined Denver because, the *Examiner* said, he had gone to Colorado to "try and find a natural wilderness in which to make his second experiment." Alas, "he could find nothing in the Rockies. The hand of man had encroached too far." Considering how much unspoiled land existed in Colorado in 1913, it's actually more likely that he couldn't find a newspaper sponsor there.

By July 11, the *Examiner*'s outlook on Joseph Knowles had brightened considerably and the jokes were stowed away. Now, with Knowles having signed a Hearst contract, the paper was "handling this experiment with an open mind, seeking only to give Knowles a fair chance to prove his case."

Knowles continued west to San Francisco, which was more hospitable than Denver had been. He noted that he'd been on the road for a month before reaching the Golden Gate, so there might have been other ports of call too. It is likely that between the *Examiner*'s scoffing story of June 22 and its admiring one of July 11, a deal had been struck. A 1991 story in the *Cowlitz Historical Quarterly* suggests that Hearst had agreed to take part "with the proviso that Joe enter a forest completely unknown to him." The paper would become Knowles's benefactor, but under very different conditions than had existed in Maine. He would not be "alone in the wilderness," but would go in with a virtual team.

In addition to staff reporter Phillip H. Kinsley (a stylist like Boston's Paul Waitt), this expedition would be overseen by "special commissioner" Professor Thomas Talbot Waterman of the department of anthropology at the University of California at Berkeley.

The *Examiner* ran a bylined story by Waterman proclaiming, like Harvard's Dudley Sargent before him, that Knowles's experiment was "certainly one of great general interest." He seemed enthusiastic, though somewhat skeptical. "Whether Mr. Knowles actually 'knows the ropes' remains to be seen," he wrote, adding that perhaps the Nature Man had evolved an ability to live on his "bodily strength" for limited periods.

Professor Waterman was in a good position to serve as Knowles's judge and jury. In 1911, he had been one of the first anthropologists on the scene when Ishi, the man known as "the last wild Indian," was discovered still living a primitive life in northern California.

Waterman had been first dispatched to the region by his department head, the leading anthropologist Alfred Kroeber, in 1908 to look for surviving tribal members. As reported in Orin Starn's fascinating *Ishi's Brain*, Waterman had turned up only a scrap of rabbit-skin blanket. But in 1911, Ishi wandered out of the back country near Oroville and was cornered—wearing only a shirt— in a slaughterhouse. He was believed to be the last of the Mill Creek band, known later as the Yahi, who had been mercilessly persecuted by settlers in the previous century.

Waterman went to Oroville immediately upon seeing the news in the *Examiner* that "a savage of the most primitive type" had been discovered. It was Waterman who broke the linguistic barrier (Spanish, Chinese, and the Indian language Maidu had been tried) with a dialect of the Yana language. And it was Waterman who escorted Ishi by train to his new home in the University of

ISHI IN 1914. COURTESY OF THE UNIVERSITY OF CALIFORNIA
AT BERKELEY

California anthropology museum in Berkeley. In residence as a
kind of living exhibit, he became a much-studied celebrity until
his death from tuberculosis just five years later. In an interesting
twist, the museum's major benefactor was Phoebe Apperson
Hearst, William Randolph Hearst's mother. Small wonder, then,
that the *Examiner* got the inside track with Ishi.

Now, three years later, with Ishi still at the museum, Waterman
was preparing to accompany Knowles into the woods. The destination was the Siskiyou Mountains in northernmost California

and southern Oregon. Once again, Knowles went through a complete physical examination (by Dr. A. H. Meads of the University of California). It was duly reported that he now weighed 193.7 pounds (about the same as when he went into the woods the first time) and had "the blood pressure of a man under 30."

The "New Adam" was once again confident of success, secure in the Indian lore he had learned from his mother. "I think I have a great mission," he said, "one that will lead the people choked in city smoke back to a saner life." He was still talking about creating schools of nature in the woods. And like Charles Kellogg, the "Nature Singer," he said he could sit down under a tree and within an hour "birds will come and chipper beside me and let me stroke them." Among the other blarney in the early stories was the notion that he had never worn shoes until he was fourteen—an unlikely story for a boy raised in the wintry blasts of Wilton, Maine, home of the famous Bass boots.

According to the *Examiner*, Knowles was to set off on July 11 to "look around for a proper wilderness in which to wander. He will then establish camp with his companions for a few days, taking short excursions into the woods to get into training, talking to trappers and woodsmen on the nature of the trees and animals and herbs of the Sierras. Then, on an announced day, with fullest publicity, he will strip to Nature's clothing and plunge into the new experiment." Among other things, Knowles needed to know which Californian trees were best for creating his "fire sticks" and bark paper.

This time, there was no thought that Knowles would be in familiar territory. He had, in fact, never been on the Pacific Coast before, and it's unlikely there would be friendly hunting guides lurking in the forest glades.

By July 12, Knowles was en route by train to Grants Pass, Oregon, savoring some precious store-bought food and smoking some of the last cigarettes before the woods became his larder and tobacconist. Back in San Francisco, the paper was bannering his story across the entire second section. Contradicting one of the key points in *Alone in the Wilderness,* Knowles was now saying that he never felt lonely in the woods, because "he feels at home there, as though he were on his mother's breast."

Professor Waterman, in another bylined article, compared Knowles to the California Indians he had studied at length, and wondered if this Easterner would instinctively use their methods for making fire and finding local food plants (they knew some 250 of them). Would he use wooden tools, or stone? Would he be able to catch fish without hooks, as the Native Americans did?

"Knowles's methods will be watched and compared with the methods of the primitive peoples," Waterman said. "He should open up a fund of wood lore that will be of interest to scientists as well as to the average man who loves the woods. . . ."

On the train to Oregon, Knowles and Waterman got on the subject of Ishi. Knowles said he shared Ishi's prowess with the bow and arrow and, indeed, knew "as many of the secrets of the woods as the Indian." Even better, his "superior intelligence" gave him an advantage in food gathering and building a shelter over the last of the Deer Creek Indians. Waterman's reaction to this bit of racism is unrecorded, but he himself always spoke of Ishi with respect.

"I suppose they call Ishi a faker too," Knowles added, though the Native American's credentials had never actually been questioned. Even if he had acquired English proficiency, it's unlikely

Ishi would ever have been as boastful as Joseph Knowles with an audience around him. "Well, boys," Knowles said, gazing out the window of his Pullman coach, "I will soon be out there in those wild, wet woods, walking by my wild lone." He told his wide-eyed listeners that he would handle California's mountain lions with the same panache he'd used on Maine's bears. He told Waterman that he could sail from the East Coast to any port in the West Indies with "common sense and a compass."

Among Knowles's interlocutors on the train was Silas Christofferson, the Oregon-based aviator, who told Knowles that he'd rather "fly to the gates of the nearest star" than go naked in the woods. Knowles replied that he'd rather live in a cave with a grizzly bear than "risk his neck in the air." They appear to have been evenly matched. Christofferson is best remembered for setting a world altitude record and taking off from the roof of the Multnomah Hotel during the 1912 Portland Rose Festival. He landed safely at Pearson Field, but died in an air crash a few years later. Christofferson was never able to fulfill his promise to give Knowles his first airplane ride.

After a train trip of twenty-two hours, Knowles wrote from Grants Pass on July 13 to say that he had found some "virgin territory" at the northern tip of California that "has never been explored to any extent by white man." The *Cowlitz Historical Quarterly* adds a perhaps apocryphal but intriguing insight into the location. "By now," it said, "Joe had become friends with a kindred spirit, [*Call of the Wild* author] Jack London. Although the *Examiner* favored either the Rockies or the redwoods, London persuaded [Knowles] that neither of these locations would provide enough food. At London's suggestion Joe chose the Siskiyous in Oregon." But if London had been involved, wouldn't the

Examiner have exploited that fact? After all, the paper played Knowles's encounter with Silas Christofferson for all it was worth, and gave a few paragraphs to a brief sparring match with boxer Carl Manley (in training in the woods).

The *Quarterly* also says that the same dynamic duo later planned a trip around the world for the Hearst papers, with London doing the travel writing and Knowles the art work. But London died in 1916, before the trip could occur. A 1997 *Washington Post* story about Knowles adds the detail that Hearst actually hired Knowles for the trip. The Knowles–London connection proved difficult to verify, but it's entirely feasible that they would have had at least an amiable correspondence.

Biographer Alex Kershaw, author of *Jack London: A Life,* was unaware of a friendship with Knowles, but he says such an acquaintance was "plausible," given London's interests at the time. "That's different than saying it actually happened, though," Kershaw added.

The *Examiner* didn't seem to be in a huge hurry to get Knowles into the woods. There were several days of preparation and regular reporting on the Nature Man's prowess. He ran into a miner (gold had been discovered in the region in 1852) who told him he'd seen a huge she-wolf a few days before, trailed by five or six little ones. Knowles says he was "tickled" by the knowledge, since he "would like nothing better than to get that wolf. If I could, I would have a coat made that would rival anything I know of."

There were bears in the woods too, and Knowles said he'd be disappointed if he didn't bring out the skin of at least one. He was looking forward to sending some mountain lions to their "last sleep" too. "Their skins will ornament my body as coat or trousers," he declared. Knowles was not all talk; he impressed Waterman and Kinsley on July 15 by diving into the Rogue River and coming up with a three-pound salmon in his bare hands. The performance, Kinsley noted, "should settle the old controversy over whether or not he can catch fish without hook and line . . . Knowles is as much at home in the water as he is on land."

Knowles, having seen satisfying signs of wildlife and ample water resources, was finally ready to go into the woods by July 16. He was given a proper sendoff by the awestruck residents of Grants Pass, including Mayor E. T. McKinstry. He was once again the modern Crusoe, saying goodbye to the outside world. "I expect to come out of the woods in 30 days, well-fed and with more clothes on than when I go in," he told the crowd gathered in front of the Oxford Hotel. "I expect to find fat living in the California mountains, but if I do not I will take off my hat to nature and say it has beaten me."

Knowles warned any idlers who might want to come into the woods to see the Nature Man that they'd be in danger of being caught (and "jerked into eternity") by a snare he set out for the mountain lions. But his attitude—and the whole nature of the new experiment—was markedly different than it had been in Maine. Where he had been (at least theoretically) alone, now he was taking a reporter and a professor with him. And though idle hangers-on were discouraged, he welcomed any scientific investigator who might want to stop by his camp in the woods.

Further, a second man of science had been added, Professor Charles Lincoln Edwards, head of the nature study department in the Los Angeles school system. The prodigiously bearded Edwards was said to be an expert on California Indian life, and at home on the Oregon-California border.

Amazingly enough, with Edwards on his way, Waterman took time out to comment on the "nature fakers" controversy of just a few years before. He noted how much natural history literature had recently accumulated. "There has been such a fad for this sort of thing that everybody seems to be trying his hand at it," he wrote. "Some of the worst of the 'nature fakers' have been amply exposed by responsible observers such as Mr. Roosevelt and the staffs of our various scientific institutions."

Notwithstanding the fact that Knowles had been accused of being a "nature faker" himself, Waterman turned to him for expert guidance on the ways of animals. With the Nature Man's counsel, he concluded that the popular notion that animals are cunning—a regular feature of "nature faker" material by Ernest Thompson Seton and others—was based on myth. "If what Mr. Knowles says is true, wild animals are for the most part distressingly stupid," Waterman wrote. "It is amazing how easy it is to outwit them and what silly things they do."

From Knowles, Waterman gathered some bits of wildlife lore every bit as questionable as what flowed from the pens of the nature fakers. For instance, Knowles said that if a person were to catch a fawn and rub its nose and blow in its nostril, it would follow him or her for miles. Bear cubs, he said, will run up to humans and suck their thumbs. He told Waterman he would come out of the woods with various wild beasts in tow.

Knowles's great scientific experiment seemed to be degenerating into proving that he was smarter than the wild animals he encountered. He wanted a bear and a mountain lion to "show that the wits of men are far and away greater than those of the beasts of the forests." Surely that fact had already been established, but Knowles was echoing the broad outline of Burroughs and Roosevelt.

Reporter Kinsley wasn't above a bit of nature fakery himself. To heighten the drama of Knowles's situation, he played up the danger of lion attacks. Gangs of three or four of these animals would stalk humans all day, he said, then at night drop down from trees for the kill. In fact, however, the shy and elusive cats were usually the loser in encounters with humans. And there were isolated fatal mountain lion attacks in California in 1890 and 1909, but no further ones for seventy-seven years, until 1986.

If all this wasn't funny enough, the *Examiner* began running a humor column about one "Knoseph Joles," who came out of the woods in "the garb of Nature" and proposed a different kind of experiment: He would enter the depths of the city of San Francisco for a month and emerge without being "pinched, held up, buncoed or run over." It's plain the paper wasn't taking its "scientific" nature experiment too seriously.

By July 19, Knowles was said to be "chafing at the bit" and eager to go into the woods the next day. As Kinsley put it, "He will go fast and far when the last goodbyes are said and his hairy legs have rustled out of sight in the dim forest isles." Reports indicated that the mountains were experiencing some cold and damp nights, so Knowles would have to work fast to build his snug lean-to.

The arrangements were far more complex—and compromised— than the Maine experiment had been. Instead of avoiding all contact with his fellow humans while behind his leafy curtain in the Klamath National Forest, he would go out and catch his bear or other big game, then haul it into camp "by appointment." Knowles, having again taken a vow of silence (but not one of solitude this time), would then give a non-verbal demonstration of his skinning and fire-making skills for the assembled professors. A horse would be kept on hand for Waterman or Edwards to carry Knowles's dispatches (again written with charcoal) to Grants Pass and the outside world.

There was evidence that the ambiguous ending to the Maine adventure was still raising questions. But Kinsley had answers. "It is safe to say that Knowles has no confederates in the woods," he wrote. "There is no one living there for miles and miles on all sides." But actually the countryside turned out to be teeming with people.

Finally the great day came, with Knowles once more holding forth at Grants Pass to an assembled crowd of mountaineers, cowboys, miners, businessmen, and, of course, reporters. As Professor Edwards described it, "The warning honk of our machine has sounded. . . . This becomes a test of modern man. Is he a real man, quick witted and resourceful under conditions where grim death may lurk in the shadows of the forests?" Edwards professed his neutrality on the subject, though like Waterman he was an obvious partisan of Knowles and his experiment.

One onlooker asked for a lock of Knowles's hair, in case he "came back in a pine box." Knowles good-naturedly complied, telling his admirer that he'd come out "fatter than when I went in. You boys know the woods and you know I can do these things."

With his incessant boasting, Knowles had rather painted himself into a corner. He would have to do more than merely survive in the woods: He would have to thrive on the fat of the land. He had told the crowds that he was more comfortable sleeping on pine boughs in the woods than on feather pillows in the finest

KNOWLES AND SUPPORTERS JUST BEFORE THE CALIFORNIA EXPEDITION BEGAN. FROM LEFT:
UNIVERSITY OF CALIFORNIA ANTHROPOLOGIST THOMAS TALBOT WATERMAN, KNOWLES, *EXAMINER*
REPORTER PHILLIP KINSLEY, AND CHARLES LINCOLN EDWARDS OF THE LOS ANGELES SCHOOL
SYSTEM. COURTESY OF THE ILWACO HERITAGE MUSEUM

hotel in San Francisco. He said he would make his own tobacco,
and a suit of clothes (including a hat) fit for a king. He would paint
a refined work of art with animal-fur brushes and colors sourced
from nature.

Knowles added that he would build a serviceable table among
the trees and as his sojourn was ending he'd set upon it a magnificent feast for his observers, made from the bounty around him.
"There will be roots and berries, bread [made from acorns] and
meat, and maybe I shall have a dessert." It was to be "a repast
unlike in every respect anything they have ever seen." On his
menu was everything from fern tops and dandelions to trout, wild
hog, and venison.

But the first disappointment came almost immediately. Knowles had said he was going into the woods on Monday, July 20, but the long hike to his jumping-off point along blind Siskiyou mountain trails had exhausted his much-reduced party, and the big event was postponed for a day. Knowles's highly confident small group had set out and then got lost in a swamp, "out of which we finally struggled late at night." He added, perhaps unnecessarily, "If ever there was a wilderness, this is it."

Waterman admitted to a "strenuous time" in getting to the would-be base camp at Indian Creek in the Klamath National Forest, and concurred that an extra day's rest was needed. He noted that the only sign of animal life they'd seen was a "super-annuated deer track." The lake they'd been told was a game and fish paradise turned out to contain only salamanders. A forest ranger urged the party to shift its base into the Preston peaks in Del Norte county, but that was thirty miles to the west and Knowles worried it would put him too far from civilization and a supply line for his regular dispatches.

Finally, on July 21, clad only in "an Indian loin cloth," Knowles bid farewell to a small party that included Waterman, Edwards, Kinsley, and photographer Bert Lambert (himself a former Maine guide). A priceless Lambert photo, which ran in the *Examiner* July 25, captures the moment: Edwards is shaking Knowles's hand, while the latter stands near-naked behind some strategic shrubbery. With his gold tooth glinting in the sun, Knowles gave a final grin. "Goodbye, boys, I will make good," he said to the group. "Don't have any fear for me." In a final dispatch to readers of the *Examiner*, he told them that by the time they read the story he'd be in the wilds, sleeping on a bed of moss. He admitted to a bit of loneliness as he closed with "*Au revoir* for a while!" The end of the experiment had been set at August 20, so he was facing a full month in the woods.

On July 22, the *Examiner*'s Knoseph Joles caught his first wild game in San Francisco—a wharf rat. But of Joseph Knowles there had been no sign. The professors sat shivering in their sleeping bags, wondering how the Nature Man was getting on. Waterman, still sending daily reports to the newspaper, let his admiration of Knowles run riot, comparing him to Renaissance author and sculptor Benvenuto Cellini as a man of many natural gifts. "Like Benvenuto he can turn his hand effectively to anything, from a work of art to a homicide," wrote Waterman, who had obviously read Cellini's *Autobiography* (in which he contemplates a satisfying murder).

For the big Sunday edition of July 26, the *Examiner* had its first word of Knowles's progress—he'd been spotted on a wilderness trail by a trio of prospectors. He was still mostly naked, though he had made some rough shoes out of cedar bark, with wooden soles. The group had no trouble recognizing the famous Nature Man, but he refused to answer their greetings. Nonetheless, they concluded he wasn't doing too badly because he carried a small string of fish. In lieu of an answer to their question as to his welfare, Knowles waved his fish and disappeared into the underbrush.

The fact that Knowles appeared to be thriving should have been front-page news, but it was relegated to an inside section. A glance at that day's headlines left no doubt as to the reason: The armies of Austria, Russia, and Serbia (called "Servia") were being mobilized, and it appeared that a European war was likely to start "at an instant's notice." Austrian Archduke Francis Ferdinand had been assassinated in Sarajevo less than a month before, and Serbia had rejected a long list of Austro-Hungarian demands that it considered humiliating. In Berlin, wild mobs supporting the Austrian position were surrounding the embassy of Serbian ally Russia and calling for war.

Poor Joe Knowles had told his handlers that he wanted no news from the outside world, adding that he wanted to go about his work even if his saintly mother died in the interim. On July 27, Knowles finally sent out his first message, though it was rather perfunctory in contrast to the flowing prose he'd posted in Maine. Writing with charcoal on separate pieces of dry-rotted white fir, he offered the following terse comments: "Slept before open fire first night. Ten miles of Indian Creek, Country full of miners. They are fishing or hunting all the time. If I can avoid the prospectors and get a living I will do well. I have seen five prospectors and one has seen me. This will be very hardest week. You will hear from me Saturday." It was signed "JOE."

The area chosen for its "primeval" forest was proving more populated than had been originally thought. In addition to the many prospectors scaring away game, Knowles had to contend with an Indian cattle herder who drove a hundred head right through his prime hunting ground. Waterman opined, with echoes of Daniel Boone, "California is getting too settled up for a real wild man. When you see five men and two cabins in 40 miles of territory it is time for those who like the real woods to go farther north."

Nonetheless, Waterman saw deer and a 400-pound bear, indicating that game was still extant. A worried Waterman speculated that Knowles might find the animals harder to come upon than in his native Maine, where the omnipresent mosquitoes and gnats sent them for relief to streams and lakes.

On July 28, Austria-Hungary declared war on Serbia, sent in 400,000 troops, and began shelling Belgrade. Great Britain and France sided with Russia, though they temporarily held their forces in abeyance. Rather less momentously, Knowles was having a hard time of it in the woods of California. His legs were scratched by the sharp underbrush he compared to the quills on a porcupine's back, and continuing cold nights limited his movements. Hunting season was set to open, and Knowles's path was repeatedly crossed by hunters and prospectors. "My fourth day—I have done nothing so far but exist," he said in his second dispatch. He had made some crude leggings from woven bark, and was living mostly on fish he caught with a willow bark net.

The same front page that proclaimed war also contained the news that New York opera impresario Oscar Hammerstein's son, Lieutenant Harry Hammerstein, had died of a diabetes attack while stationed on Fisher's Island in Long Island Sound. The news would not have meant much to Knowles at the time, but within two years, he would have a dramatic encounter with young Harry's cousin Elaine Hammerstein.

Edwards told the *Examiner*'s readers on July 31 that Knowles's feet were painfully swollen and he was having trouble walking. As evidence of his ingenuity, the Nature Man left his well-worn first pair of shoes for the professors to find; they were made from white fir sticks and woven grass, held in place by slender strips that fit into a groove at the bottom. In his third dispatch, Knowles said he had seen a bear and several deer, but had succeeded in catching only fish and a few squirrels. He was weaving a grass blanket, which he hoped would allow him to let his fire go out at night and still remain warm.

Meanwhile, things were growing darker in Europe. On July 31, the Austro-Hungarian Empire's ally, Germany, issued an ultimatum to Russia demanding that it stop the mobilization of its troops. When those demands expired without answer on August 1, Germany declared war on Russia. The next day, neutral Belgium received a similar ultimatum from Germany, demanding safe passage through its territory to attack France. It refused, and Germany promptly marched its troops through the practically defenseless Belgium on their way to Paris. This violation of Belgium's sovereignty immediately drew Great Britain into the war.

The timing was unfortunate not only for peace in Europe, but for Joe Knowles in the woods. He was apparently getting more confident of his abilities, and he invited professors Waterman and Edwards to a fish dinner as soon as it could be arranged. Knowles was feeling so good that, as in Maine, his thoughts moved beyond mere survival to creating what Kinsley described as "a large water color picture of animal life," using natural pigments gathered from the forest floor. Perhaps a spectacular portrait would compensate for the failure to capture any big game.

On August 4, the *Examiner* bannered the news of war between France and Germany, and Great Britain's growing involvement, across the front page. Knowles was relegated to a back corner, next to an ad for Castoria, a digestive medicine for children (with three percent alcohol). Knowles did have some news to share: He had found the body of a deer slain by a mountain lion, and was able to use strips of its hide to make a set of leg-covering chaps. His feet, which he'd been packing with black mud, were healing too.

By now, two weeks had passed. Waterman was ready to call the experiment a success. Knowles had shown that he could live on his own in the woods, even if they were unfamiliar to him. The professor thought prospectors, fur hunters and other modern-day frequenters of "uninhabited places" could learn from the Nature Man's example. "Mr. Knowles is merely beginning back where our earliest ancestors began," he wrote in the August 5 edition of the paper. "To say that it can't be done is like saying that a man cannot harvest without a mowing machine or till the soil without a plow."

A face-to-face visit was next on the agenda. F. L. Brown of Hartford, Connecticut, working in that city's then-burgeoning automobile industry, told of a visit to Knowles's camp around this time in a September 1914 *Hartford Courant* story. Although Knowles had supposedly taken a vow of silence, it had now gone by the wayside. He met Brown, Edwards, and Waterman at a pre-arranged spot in the woods on August 7 and thrust out his hand, saying, "Hello, won't you speak to a fellow?"

Though Brown describes him as browned to copper by the sun, with legs torn by brush, swollen feet, and hands black with crusted dirt, Knowles was reportedly in great spirits. "Never felt better in my life," he said. "I am stronger than when I went into the woods. I have the wind of a horse. My paunch is gone and lots of extra fat, but what is left is clean."

According to Kinsley in a separate *Examiner* account of the meeting, Knowles was wearing a grass-and-bark hat and wooden-soled shoes, but not much else. A girdle of matted witchgrass was around his waist, and to deter flies a collar of the same material was around his neck. He looked "like the Fiji Islander of pictorial fame."

Knowles said he had breakfasted on smoked fish, and showed Brown, Edwards, and Waterman a fish hook made from the breast-bone of a woodpecker, adorned with partridge feathers. "You

A BARELY CLOTHED KNOWLES GOES FISHING IN CALIFORNIA. COURTESY OF THE ILWACO HERITAGE MUSEUM

cannot starve me in the woods," Knowles said. "I have snared a few birds and I can kill squirrels with rocks. I am a dead shot. Then there are berries and green acorn nuts and roots and fish."

A few days later Edwards stumbled across Knowles's camp while on an owl-shooting exhibition. In fact, much to the professor's chagrin, he nearly plugged Knowles with an errant shot. Knowles showed Edwards around his camp, where he had dug out a depression and covered it with slabs of bark. He slept on fir boughs in a sheltered bedroom windbreak, with a fireplace at one end and a loom for making grass clothing on the other.

Waterman was brought in to see for himself, and declared that this abode was built according to "correct scientific principle." Native hunters and explorers in the Arctic slept the same way, he said. Knowles was still living mainly on fish and berries, but was in excellent spirits and opined, according to Kinsley, that "for a man run down by drink and dissipation, he would prescribe a month naked in the woods."

It was a convincing demonstration, but could Knowles be faking his test in the California woods, as he probably had in Maine? The question was definitely raised. U.S. Surveyor Fred W. Rodolf heard a rumor in San Francisco that Knowles was really living in a comfortable cabin on Green's Creek (a fork of Indian Creek) and had been supplied with all the necessities of life. In a bylined August 7 article in the *Examiner,* Rodolf wrote that he decided to investigate for himself, found the cabin in question, and satisfied himself that the rumors were false. The test, he wrote, "is as honest and as reliable as it is possible to be."

But Rodolf appears to have done no more than ask some men in the area if they'd seen Knowles at the cabin. Their denials were apparently enough for him, but hardly constitute proof that Knowles was conducting an honest test. Since no other newspaper took up the hue and cry, the rumors went nowhere. Rodolf also visited with Professor Edwards (who was scientifically labeling a gray-whiskered rat at the time) and came away convinced that the men watching over Knowles were serious about keeping him away from comfortable cabins and featherbeds.

Knowles undoubtedly appreciated Rodolf's gesture. In later years, he retyped a newspaper account that mentions the surveyor, and wrote a note by hand at the bottom of the page: "After 24 years, Rodolf visits my studio in 1938." The newspaper account, from the *New York American* on September 24, 1916, as Knowles was headed into the woods for the third time, quotes Rodolf as saying, "It just happens that I and two of my men had been occupying that shack [the cabin on Green's Creek] for a month." But that's not what he said in 1914.

On August 13, three weeks into the test, a dispatch from Knowles carried the exciting news that he had succeeded in rop-ing a deer and now had the makings of deerskin clothing. The rope was made of cedar bark looped in cowboy fashion and hung on the deer trail at night. When the deer's head poked through, a hidden Knowles had closed his lasso; in the ensuing "struggle be-tween man and beast," he won out. Though the news was sensa-tional, it was told in three paragraphs on an inside page. San Francisco's attention was undoubtedly wavering.

Knowles was now in his final week, and doing well. He had a fully stocked larder of venison and fish, and had even discovered a honeybee hive to provide him with dessert. He was working busily on a suit of clothing to wear to his reunion with civiliza-tion, and on a full-color nature painting. He was also looking for-ward to the experiment's end, when he would be reprising his role in the woods for a motion picture company commissioned for the purpose.

Knowles told Edwards during a meeting on August 15 that the California air and sun provided a perpetual tonic for him. Knowles complained only of being bitten by a particularly nasty species of fly. "It seems so strange to talk to you after weeks of silence," he told Edwards. But Knowles doesn't seem to have been all that quiet; compared to his sojourn in Maine, the California woods were alive with visitors.

By August 18, the experiment was winding down. The talk of getting a bear and a mountain lion had subsided, and he was now concentrating on his nature picture. "I can paint a picture in full color from the materials around me, and I will have a finished prod-

uct to prove it when I return to you Wednesday next," he said in
his last dispatch from the woods. Kinsley reported that he was set
to emerge "strong in body, clear in mind, clothed, and with one
of civilization's highest refinements—a picture—tucked under
his arm."

On August 19, President Woodrow Wilson proclaimed U.S.
neutrality in the emerging European war "in fact, as well as in
name"; if Knowles knew about it, this stance probably gave him
hope that the conflict would now be relegated to the back pages.
But meanwhile the Germans were marching to Brussels.

It was a very strange-looking character who finally emerged
from the woods on August 20 at Waterman and Edward's camp.
In Kinsley's telling, he was "a bronzed, soot-blackened figure,
clothed in deer skin, his flesh scarred, his hair matted, his beard
half grown, his eyes dazed, his legs almost too weary to carry him
another step." He lurched for the water pail, but was soon well
enough to call each man there by name. With renewed vigor he
chopped wood, tossed a 150-pound man over his head, played a
racist minstrel ditty named "Zip Coon" on the fiddle no one in
later years remembered him possessing, and wrote a bylined story
for the *Examiner.*

Knowles was pleased with what he had accomplished. "I am
prouder of my achievement than I would be of a million dollars,"
he said, adding that he did not leave his friendly campfire and
crude shelter without some misgivings. Once again, he expressed
regret at having had to kill game (including the deer) to survive.

The next day, Knowles and party rode out of the mountains to
the small hamlet of Holland, where a large group of miners and
"men of the hills" had gathered in welcome at the local hotel.
Knowles led the procession, riding a self-willed mule named

Maudie, who at the last minute pulled him away to go investigate a stable. The local gentry set the dogs on poor Maudie and threw stones, finally persuading her to get back in line. But Kinsley writes that "the dignity of the procession was sadly marred."

The Oregonians took Knowles very seriously indeed, and he was accorded the honor of being the very first passenger on the California and Oregon Coast train. To the disappointment of some, however, he appeared in front of the assembled crowd in his civilian clothing, and the crowd made its displeasure known. A quick change back into his wilderness attire saved the day, and Knowles was paraded through town several times in the best automobile that could be found.

The Nature Man returned to the wild with the miners and a visiting film crew to give them a tour of his forest domain, showing off such highlights as his lean-to on a mountainside beside a clear stream. Though he failed to keep his promise of a banquet laid out on a custom-made table, there was jerked venison, smoked fish, and berries in his larder, and a huge, flat-topped stone for cooking in his fireplace. For his audience and the moving picture cameras, he cut bark from a tree with a rock and wrote a message on it in charcoal. He boiled water in bark dishes; he speared fish with a trident and cooked them in his stone fireplace.

While Knowles didn't have a bearskin to show off, he did tell a story of having had his deer carcass dragged off by "Mr. Bear." And he bragged that he could have trapped that bear easily with a deadfall, as he had done in Maine, but was too preoccupied with making his full-color nature picture.

The picture, a forest scene, was made with fir-tree bark as canvas and a chewed stick as brush. The broad outlines were done in charcoal, and colors were created from leaves, dead wood, and moss. It was hung in the lobby of the Oxford Hotel in Grants Pass; hundreds crowded in to see the picture and also to see Knowles, who made a speech there.

Waterman and Edwards judged the experiment a resounding success, and the latter went somewhat overboard in describing Knowles as having "the grit and steel muscles of a champion boxer, the resourcefulness of a sailor, the craft and endurance of a guide and trapper." His long-ago time among the Chippewa Indians had now grown, in Edwards's telling, into a full year under their tutelage.

Edwards and Waterman served more as cheerleaders for Knowles than as his harsh and exacting scientific judges. They were unabashed nature boosters, and they saw Knowles's "experiment" as unparalleled publicity for the cause. No doubt they would have screamed foul had they seen their quarry with his feet up at a cozy cabin, but they were not likely to go looking for violations. Besides, they were having too much fun themselves to want to take a chance of spoiling the party.

Joe Knowles was a big hit in Oregon. A few days after he reentered civilization, a tremendous reception was held in Portland, including a free talk for schoolchildren and an "illustrated lecture" at the Hellig Theater. "Joe Knowles saw downtown Portland and downtown Portland saw Joe Knowles," proclaimed the *Morning Oregonian.* The city "shouted a cordial greeting and Knowles waved a long brown arm, muscled to the wrist and tattooed like a South Sea Islander—a memento of the days when, in Knowles's words, he was 'a fool kid in the Navy.'"

The paper added that the Nature Man may have been in a brief costume of skins, but "it would have made several copious wardrobes for Isadora Duncan, Lady Constance Richardson and other dancers of the ultra-modern school." But another critic, a cop, looked askance at Knowles's outfit and said, "We got several fellers down in the jail who have more on than you have. It wouldn't take more'n two minutes to get the wagon."

"How's life in the woods?" yelled a bold newsboy as Knowles's motorcade wound slowly through thronged streets. "I might want to go out sometime myself."

"Fine, my boy, fine," Knowles replied. "I'll tell you all about it tomorrow." And, said the paper, it was "Hello, Joe" all over town, and among those exchanging pleasantries were Portland Mayor H. R. Albee and several commissioners.

By the first of September, the whole party was back in San Francisco, among the tall buildings, trolley cars, and what Knowles called in an *Examiner* article "the mighty hum of human life." The Nature Man, who for a month had seen nothing taller than a miner's cabin, supposedly got a stiff neck from craning his view upward. Despite having been kicked off the front page, he did not return to the big city in disgrace. As Kinsley put it, "He did everything that he said he would do and more," including building a shelter, storing preserved food, and clothing himself in animal skins. What's more, he'd created that color picture from nature's discards, dead leaves and old bark.

Many, if not most, of the more recent Knowles articles make this second trip into the woods appear a failure because World War I torpedoed interest. "It was a hell of a note for Joe Knowles," wrote Stewart H. Holbrook in the *American Mercury* in 1936. "The Naked Thoreau news went into the back pages next to the classified ads, and many a Californian doesn't know to this day whether Joe Knowles *ever* got out of the woods." In *American Her-*

itage in 1981, Gerald Carson said that the experiment "quietly expired." In *Wilderness and the American Mind*, Roderick Nash says Knowles attempted to repeat his Maine triumph "without success."

The *New Yorker* account of 1938 even quotes a bitter Knowles as having proclaimed back then, "What does the public care about a naked man in the wilderness when Belgian babies are having their hands cut off?" Some even say the experiment was cut short (but the fact of the matter is that it did last the full month).

Knowles was undoubtedly dismayed by the breakout of the war, and the paper did indeed take the coverage off the front page, but the experiment was reported vigorously right to the end. Kinsley had almost daily bylines, and Waterman, Edwards, and Knowles himself were given regular columns. The paper went all-out when Knowles walked out of the forest in his skins. And the *Examiner,* without taking its attention off the war news from Europe, had prepared a warm welcome in San Francisco.

SIX

— ◆ —

Ishi and
the Native
Tradition

To celebrate Knowles's return, the *Examiner* arranged
a rather special public demonstration. An invitation went out to
the schoolchildren of San Francisco, inviting them to the Cort
Theatre for an afternoon event that included not only Knowles
and his nature films, but the celebrated Native American Ishi as
well. Given Waterman's role in Ishi's stay at the University of California museum, this addition to the bill was probably easy to
arrange. There was also the plain fact that the museum's principal benefactor was Phoebe Apperson Hearst, mother of the *Examiner*'s owner. The museum had originally been created to house
her collection, from ancient Egypt, Greece, Rome, and Peru. In
fact, she showed a Citizen Kane–like zeal for amassing these
possessions.

The native Californian and the Nature Man from Maine were living exhibits. With great cross-promotion, they were to work in tandem making fire. "Ishi and Joe Knowles on the same stage make a programme of remarkable interest," wrote the newspaper. And how!

Knowles was said to be anxious to meet Ishi and study his methods not only for fire-making, but also bow-and-arrow shooting, clothes-making, and other arts. But while Ishi was said to be free from ego, the same could not be said for the "civilized" Knowles. One imagines that this more recent denizen of the haunts that had been Ishi's for forty years was wary about being upstaged.

Knowles often said that he'd learned his survival techniques during his time in Michigan, where he became acquainted with tribes of Sioux and Chippewah Indians around the Great Lakes. "I gave up the sailing and went among them," he had written, adding that he had learned their techniques for hunting and trapping. In a 1921 interview, Knowles mentioned that he had "a strain of Indian blood" on his father's side, and that it might explain "the lure of the far horizon" that was constantly with him.

Idealized portraits of Native Americans were a major theme in Knowles's art. In fact, *Alone in the Wilderness* was packaged with a ready-for-framing painting called "The Indian," showing a young warrior with bow and arrow by a stream as twilight illuminated the scene. It is the book's only color illustration. Many of Knowles's etchings, and the paintings he did for the Monticello Hotel in Longview, Washington (described in Chapter 8), featured Native American subjects. It was well known that he created such works using the faces of local and decidedly non-Indian friends. One such acquaintance, Ivy Purdin, was so indignant at her portrayal as an Indian princess that for many years she hid the painting Knowles had given her behind her wood stove. Knowles had intended to produce a book of his Native American etchings, but he got no further than mocking up the cover (which is now on display in a Klipsan Beach, Washington antique store).

He had expounded at some length about Native Americans shortly after coming out of the Maine woods in 1913, just after a visit to what was then a rapidly dwindling band of Penobscots in Old Town, near Bangor. According to the *Bangor Daily News*, Knowles said that visiting the Penobscots was one of the greatest pleasures he'd had since coming back to civilization. "In contrast to their white brothers, none of these Red Men were curious to know any details in regard to my methods of living while in the forest alone," he said. "They seem to feel that it could be done, a feeling that perhaps was inherited from their forefathers, who had lived closer to nature and to the wild life than any white man."

Knowles said he met the Indian governor and the tribal chiefs and spent time with the children too. He shook hands with famous marathon runner Andrew Sockalexis, a Penobscot who had placed second in the Boston Marathons of 1912 and 1913 and had competed in the 1912 Stockholm Olympics. "No white man could show more hospitality than these men and women of Indian blood," he said. "My experience among these people has led me to believe they are more sensitive than any white man."

Knowles's interest in Indian subjects for his art fit in with public tastes, and his portraits of brave warriors and equestrian chiefs were among his most popular etchings. "We have enjoyed the heads—particularly the Sioux and the Blackfeet," San Francisco art dealer Philippine Schmidt Rettenmayer wrote to him in 1931. Not all markets were equally enamored: The Detroit-based Himelhoch Brothers and Company told him in 1931 that his Indian subjects weren't selling, even for $1 or $2.

The Native American's status as holder of ancient wisdom was on the rise, even as his hegemony over the land was eclipsed. The midwife of that transformation was in part Ernest Thompson Seton, the same writer and scouting pioneer who became embroiled in the "nature fakers" controversy. An Englishman, Seton had migrated with his family to northern Ontario as a young boy in 1866 and there became absorbed by Native American traditions and respect for nature.

Determined to pass along these "woodcraft" lessons to his own tribe, he published the appallingly titled but nonetheless respectful *How to Play Injun* as a guide for boys in 1903. Its ideas (among them teepee making, fire starting, and using "wampum" as currency) were incorporated into Seton's very successful *Birch-Bark Roll of the Woodcraft Indians* in 1906. Seton (known by the Indian name "Black Wolf") shared his teachings with General Robert Baden-Powell at a meeting in London that same year, and many were incorporated into the first editions of the latter's *Scouting for Boys*.

Seton's Woodcraft Indians quickly gained young "braves," and by 1910 it had an estimated 200,000 active members and alumni. But the fledgling group was quickly eclipsed by and absorbed into Baden-Powell's Boy Scouts, which continued to advance many of the Native American themes Seton had introduced. The stage was thus set for lifelong bitterness between the pair, because Seton was convinced that Baden-Powell had failed to credit him properly.

Despite these origins, the wisdom of the Native American as advanced in Seton's "Gospel of the Red Man" remained at the forefront of wilderness lore. Knowles claims in *Alone in the Wilderness* that he never read a single book on "the primitive life," but his philosophy closely follows that of the well-meaning but occasionally naïve Seton, who declared that "No man owns the woods of the forest, or the water of the rivers, or the soil of the earth."

Knowles pays tribute to Seton in the only literary reference in *Alone in the Wilderness.* "It is useless for me to tell the Boy Scouts how to build a fire without any matches," he wrote. "They know already. To the boy just beginning, the chapter on woodcraft by Ernest Thompson Seton in the *Boy Scouts' Handbook* will explain all that very quickly."

There's no doubt that Knowles had a healthy respect for Native wilderness skills, though he could be patronizing at times to actual Indians. In this, he was a child of his times. "Nature Singer" Charles Kellogg was a sincere naturalist, but in his autobiography he can't resist referring to the "Digger" Indians of California's Sierra Mountains (who had taught him his first woodcraft lessons) as a "lazy, happy-go-lucky lot." In one scene, he teaches a Nova Scotia Ojibway who speaks in pidgin English how to make fire, as their tribe seems to have forgotten the art.

Ishi knew how to make fire. Though he was effectively on stage for museum visitors, Ishi could not have fully understood the vaudeville conventions that Knowles (and Kellogg, for that matter) took to so easily. But he was learning. In a remarkable bit of serendipity, Ishi's doctor, Saxton Pope, had taken him to see Buffalo Bill's Wild West show when it came to San Francisco. Orin

Starn's *Ishi's Brain* relates that both Ishi and Pope enjoyed this carnival of cowboys, Indians, sharpshooters, and daredevil riders. Starn relates:

> There Ishi met a Sioux chief, doubtless decked out in his war-bonnet and face paint for the performance. The chief examined Ishi from head to toe and fingered a strand of his long hair. Whether in jest or not, he announced that Ishi was "a very high grade of Indian." Ishi took no offense. He enjoyed the show and later described the Sioux to Pope as [what he understood to be] a "big chiep."

Ishi also met some Blackfeet performers from a traveling revue, and a photo survives of the group posing stiffly together, as Ishi hands his fellow Indians a bow and arrows he had made.

At the San Francisco school event in the Cort Theater, Ishi appeared in a suit and Knowles in his skins, making a neat role reversal. A photo shows them shaking hands, framing their distinguished presenters: Waterman, San Francisco Mayor James "Sunny Jim" Rolph, Jr., and Waterman's boss at the University of California, Professor Alfred Kroeber, founder of the department and one of the country's leading anthropologists. Kroeber had gone searching for remnant Mill Creek Indian bands in 1908, but found only a few forlorn relics. The appearance of Ishi had been like manna from heaven for him.

Starn says that Kroeber saw Ishi as a kind of "living fossil," with firsthand knowledge of the ancestral language and culture that the anthropologist was studying. In fact, the information Kroeber gathered from Ishi became part of his *Handbook of the Indians of California*. It's not all that surprising to learn that Kroeber was

PROFESSOR ALFRED KROEBER (CENTER) WITH ISHI (RIGHT) AND YAHI TRANSLATOR SAM BATWAI. COURTESY OF THE UNIVERSITY OF CALIFORNIA, SAN FRANCISCO SCHOOL OF MEDICINE

the father of visionary science fiction author Ursula K. Le Guin, because her work frequently reflects both anthropological and environmental themes, and is laced with Indian lore.

Instead of accepting the offer he had in hand from a vaudeville promoter to take Ishi on the road, Kroeber kept him in and studied him. Ishi lived for the most part quietly in a cabin on the museum grounds, though on Sunday afternoons he was put on display, making arrowheads, fire drills, and bows to the delight of what were sometimes large crowds. He cleaned up afterward, receiving a janitor's salary of $25 a month.

The idea of this last survivor of a once-proud race being made to sweep floors seems outrageous today, but the folklorist John Lomax, who discovered the singer Leadbelly in 1933, also employed the latter as a chauffeur at the Lomax home in Wilton, Connecticut. And Ishi was certainly treated much better than Ota Benga, a Pygmy purchased in the Belgian Congo in 1903 by a contractor for the St. Louis World's Fair. When the fair was over, Benga found a new home—in the monkey house at the Bronx Zoo. He shared his cage with an orangutan. "We are taking excellent care of the little fellow," proclaimed the zoo's director when the Colored Baptist Ministers' Conference objected. "He has one of the best rooms in the primate house."

According to *Ishi in Two Worlds*, the celebrated 1967 standard text on Ishi by Kroeber's wife Theodora, Ishi was quiet and painfully shy, though he also possessed great natural curiosity and enjoyed learning new things. Alfred Kroeber described him as "the most patient man I ever knew."

Waterman was Ishi's first friend, Theodora Kroeber writes. "The two men liked and understood one another, a warm relation of equals developed from the acquaintance between an old man, as Ishi seemed to Waterman, and a brash but lovable young man, as Waterman seemed to Ishi." Waterman was the first white person to converse with Ishi, and his home was the first to which Ishi was invited as a dinner guest. He even lived with the Watermans for a time.

In 1914, the museum arrangement was three years old and Ishi was relatively comfortable with crowds. He was well equipped to handle the 1,500 children who were generating "a howling bedlam of shrill boyish noise" before the curtain rose at the Cort Theatre. He stepped forward when introduced by Waterman as "a primitive man who has become thoroughly civilized," but for many years "lived the primitive life because he could not help himself."

It was Ishi who made fire for the kids in just two minutes, using a fire drill made from buckeye sourced in Golden Gate Park. A newspaper account says he put on "a remarkable exhibition of fire-making by the friction method of the Indian." Knowles—introduced as the civilized man who had become primitive—was to have rubbed sticks, too, but "found at the last moment that he had left his materials in a trunk which had not reached San Francisco." Some time later, Knowles produced a sensitive pencil sketch of Ishi, subtitled "The Last of the Yana." It shows him with a smile on his face working his fire drill, as a wisp of smoke curdles skyward.

The San Francisco kids, who appear to have been exclusively male, had to settle for some of Knowles's nature films, which at least showed him making fire. He told his youthful audience that the great book of Mother Nature had been sorely neglected, and that he intended to remedy this with an unspecified "campaign of education."

Knowles and Ishi appeared to get along well during their brief encounter, but the Nature Man's comments on the train to Grants Pass show that his undoubtedly admiring attitude toward Native Americans was flavored with more than a little condescension.

Knowles's ideas never evolved much. In 1938, he sent a letter to the CBS radio network commenting on an Edwin Hill "Human

Side of Life" broadcast on archery. He agreed with Hill that Ishi "wasn't much with the bow and arrow." According to Knowles, "I out-shot him with his own outfit, which is nothing to brag about, and I wasn't much of a bowman, either."

It's unclear when this archery contest took place, but Knowles—in a fit of honesty—admits in the letter that Ishi got the better of him in the quest for fire. "He bested me in a primitive fire-making contest at the Court [*sic*] Theatre before 5,000 [*sic*] school children," Knowles wrote. "Mayor Rolfe [*sic*] of San Francisco and Professor Kroeber of the University of California were the judges."

Hill's report appears to have been rather fanciful, for it said that Knowles came out of the woods of Maine riding a wild moose and dragging along a bear. Knowles said he didn't recall doing that, but it "made a good story and brought many letters from old-time friends." By that time, he was wondering if anyone remembered his exploits.

Knowles and Ishi never met again, but they remained on parallel tracks. In May 1914, a few months before the event at the Cort Theatre, a group consisting of Kroeber, Waterman, Saxton Pope, and Pope's young son accompanied Ishi back to the northern California woods where he had been found, with the stated purpose of studying his pre-civilized behavior. But, of course, turning back the clock at that point was very difficult, just as it was for Knowles to transform himself into a real cave man. Kroeber put Ishi in a loincloth for the trip to Deer Creek, though he clearly preferred a suit and tie by then, and the Yahi never wore loincloths anyway. Ishi was photographed making arrowheads from flaked obsidian, constructing a spear for salmon fishing, and performing other "primitive" tasks. He guided the group to some of his favorite former haunts and sang Yahi songs. Pope responded by playing "Gunga Din" and "Mandalay," reportedly Ishi favorites, on his ukelele. The dinner fare included ginger snaps and oxtail soup; no attempt was made to actually live the primitive life *a la* Knowles.

According to *Ishi: The Last of His People,* Kroeber and Waterman watched carefully and recorded "how Ishi cupped water in his hands to drink, how he inspected soil, and how he stared at the moon." If this was really the last of the Yahi Indians, the professor wanted to record as much as possible of how they lived, from an unimpeachable source. But was Ishi truly a Yahi? Could he, in fact, have been on one level as much of a fraud as Joseph Knowles? While he was undoubtedly 100 percent California Indian, recent research at the University of California at Berkeley's Phoebe Apperson Hearst Museum of Anthropology (Ishi's alma mater, as it were) concluded that he may not have been the last full-blooded Yahi, after all.

According to Steven Shackley, a research archaeologist there, the arrowpoints Ishi made more closely resemble those found at historic sites of the Nomlaki or Wintu tribes, which were historically the Yahi's enemies. Shackley says Ishi's points have long blades with concave bases and side notches, but known Yahi blades in the museum's collection are short and squat, with contracting stems and basal notches.

From this, Shackley concludes that one of Ishi's parents may have been from one of those two tribes. "This makes Ishi's story even more romantic and sad," Shackley said in a university press release. "Being of mixed blood, he is an example of the cultural pressure the Anglos placed on the dwindling number of Indians in the mid-to-late 1800s to marry their enemies." Shackley calls Theodora Kroeber's book "simplistic."

Whoever he really was, Ishi was still a figure of considerable interest. Pope had brought his camera and amply documented the trip. The resulting pictures make a nice criss-cross with similar shots of Knowles. As Waterman pointed out, the primitive man had become civilized, and the civilized man primitive, but the field of study was similar.

And Ishi went before the movie cameras too. As Theodora Kroeber's book reveals, some 1,500 feet of film (the same amount shot for Knowles's first movie) were exposed by the California Motion Picture Corporation. Ishi was shown making fire, fashioning arrow points, and stringing a bow and aiming it. He was also shown going about his janitorial duties and working a multigraph machine, though these scenes presumably had less anthropological interest. Unfortunately, the film was badly stored and melted into what Kroeber called a "single glutinous mass." (Joseph Knowles's nature films are missing too, though they may yet turn up.)

Another thing that went missing was Ishi's brain. Ishi's time in the spotlight was short-lived; he died an untimely death of tuberculosis in 1916. Like Einstein's later did, Ishi's brain (removed in a dissection that Kroeber protested, saying "science can go to hell") went on a cross-country odyssey and ended up in Washington, D.C., early the next year.

But if the brain was out, it might as well go to a good home. At Kroeber's suggestion, the Smithsonian's National Museum took possession and was glad to get this interesting specimen because brain study was quite in vogue at that time. Men of science said they could tell a person's future by feeling the bumps on his or her head, or intelligence by measuring the size of the skull. As

Orin Starn related in an interview, one of the points of these "bad sciences," known as phrenology and craniometry, was to show the superiority of the white brain (an argument with which Knowles was obviously in concurrence). The explorer John Wesley Powell gave advance permission for his brain to be removed after death, and in fact it ended up being stored by the Smithsonian next to Ishi's.

Amazingly enough, as Starn relates in *Ishi's Brain*, Kroeber was also involved in another celebrated Native American dissection. Both Waterman and Kroeber had studied under the man who founded Columbia University's anthropology department, the German-born Franz Boas, who was also an assistant curator at the American Museum of Natural History. At Boas's urging, Admiral Robert Peary had brought six Inuit from Qaanaaq, Greenland, back from his Arctic trip in 1897. Boas had been chief assistant in anthropology at the World's Columbian Exhibition in Chicago (also featuring Buffalo Bill and Frederick Jackson Turner). Many Eskimos had been exhibited there, and many died of modern diseases for which they were woefully unprepared, but Boas apparently learned little from that tragic experience.

The Eskimos Peary brought back ended up in the care of Boas and Kroeber, who at the time was Boas's assistant, in New York. As with Ishi, tuberculosis took its toll, and in February 1898, four of them, including a shaman named Qisuk, were among the dead. As described in Kenn Harper's book *Give Me My Father's Body*, Qisuk's eight-year-old son, Minik, went to the museum demanding his father's corpse for burial. "He was dearer to me than anything else in the world," Minik later wrote, "especially when we were brought to New York, strangers in a strange land."

But Minik's very reasonable request put the scientists in a quandary: If they buried Qisuk, how could they study and exhibit his remains? Kroeber had some knowledge of Inuit funeral arrangements and so, Harper writes, "the scientists at the Museum of Natural History decided to duplicate the primitive funeral as best they could on the [Bellevue Hospital] grounds [where he had died]"—but without Qisuk's body.

According to museum building superintendent William Wallace (who later adopted Minik), the co-conspirators "got an old log about the length of a human corpse. This was wrapped in cloth, a mask attached to one end of it and all was in readiness." Proceeding at dusk, when they were less apt to attract attention, the funeral was duly held. "While Minik stood sobbing by, the museum men lingered around watching the proceedings," relates Wallace. "The thing worked well. The boy never suspected. . . ."

Boas had Qisuk's bones boiled down to preserve his skeleton for the museum's collection. Much later, Minik learned the truth when he saw what was left of his father on display at the museum as a "curiosity." The "scientific" study of the six Eskimos had apparently yielded little. According to Harper, Boas published only this: "Many things heretofore unknown have been learned regarding their language, their traditions and their personal characteristics. Casts of their heads have been made for the museum."

Minik tried unsuccessfully to repatriate his father's remains, and he himself ended up caught between two cultures—at home neither in the United States nor in Greenland. Minik died in the great influenza outbreak of 1918. Qisuk's remains did finally return to Greenland in 1993. And after some resistance (and denials that it even had the organ), the Smithsonian finally relinquished Ishi's brain, and in 2000 it was repatriated and laid to rest with his ashes in a Native American ceremony in northern California.

SEVEN

———•◆•———

Dawn Man
Meets
Dawn Woman

ONE OF THE FIRST THINGS KNOWLES SEEMS TO HAVE DONE AFTER
the festivities in San Francisco were over was to get married for the
second time. Public records in Pierce County, Washington, show
that he married the former Marion Louise Humphrey of Dedham,
Massachusetts, in Tacoma on November 13, 1914. At least one
source describes her as a former *Boston Post* illustrator who worked
alongside Knowles, and that's possible: A lovely watercolor still
life of what looks like a European scene, signed by her and dated
1907, is among the huge inventory of the Knowles estate.

According to her obituary in 1947, Marion (born in 1886) was
the great-great-granddaughter of Roger Sherman, a signer of the
Declaration of Independence and delegate to the Continental
Congress; and a great-great-great-granddaughter of Captain John

McIntosh, a leader in the preliminary riots leading up the Boston Tea Party. A copy of a letter from George Washington to Mc-Intosh, dated October 21, 1776, was among the papers found in Knowles's studio.

As we shall see, Knowles's love life was rather tangled, and unraveling it was complicated by the fact that he rarely referred to women at all in his voluminous writing. In fact, he wrote almost nothing about his personal life (except for his youth and his time spent in the woods), and hardly anything about his two marriages. Even his exact age is in some doubt. According to research by genealogist Hazel M. Standeven and Sandra Tellvik of the Ilwaco Heritage Museum, the 1900 census of Eustis, in Franklin County, Maine, shows Joseph E. Knowles as having been born in 1866, not the 1869 on his tombstone. By 1910, when census records show him as the owner of an artist's studio in Boston, he was listed as thirty-eight years old, which would place his birth in 1872.

The issue of Knowles's exact birth date will probably never be fully satisfied. Knowles's obituary in the *Chinook Observer* in 1942 reveals that the actual natal date is unknown because it was kept in a family Bible that burned up. "Joe had given his birth year as 1869," it said, "but of late years relatives stated he was not born until some 10 years later." Further complicating the issue is a birth registration book kept by the town of Wilton (started in 1795). It lists Joe Knowles's birthdate as August 13, 1867, also crediting the information to a family Bible.

One bit of Knowles folklore actually has him and Marion Louise getting married on stage in the aftermath of the Maine trip, perhaps a year earlier than stated above; that makes a good story but appears to be incorrect. Because the new Mrs. Knowles was from the East Coast, she may have accompanied Knowles on his slow trek west to California. Perhaps because they weren't yet married, decorum kept her out of the news columns.

Even though Knowles rarely wrote anything about affairs of the heart, and nothing akin to a love letter from him is extant, the fact is that he had many female admirers. One of these, identified only as "Florence," wrote him a series of smoldering letters from the Hotel Manx in San Francisco while he was on the road, expressing the profound hope that they would be together again soon, though she feared they were parting forever. "Good morning, dear boy," she wrote. "I *want* you so [emphasis in the original]. . . . I feel like a bird shut away in a cage far away from the sunshine and air." She was moved to quote from a song "that must have been written under very similar circumstances." It began, "Sweetheart, our day is over / And the dream done / You must go back to your life / I must go back to mine."

Another admirer from afar was Katherine Baker, who wrote him often from her summerhouse in Bradford, Vermont (where Knowles had a studio during his Boston years), sometimes enclosing snapshots. "The letter that I should like to write you is very different from the objective one I am sending you tonight, but the other must wait," she wrote, still carrying the torch aloft in 1930. "It is difficult for me, anyway, to express what my heart feels, for words speak less truly than thoughts. . . . Do write to me, dear Joe."

Knowles had had a very good experience making his first nature films in the fall of 1913. And while he remained in San Francisco for some months after his second woods experiment, he agreed to make another one, *Alone in the Wilderness* (the same title as his book), this time in the Feather River Canyon country of northern California. The location was just thirty miles north of Oroville, where Ishi had been found in 1911.

A playbill for the film relates that even though the story is set in Canada, it was actually filmed in northern California and shows "some of the wildest and most extraordinarily beautiful bits of scenery in the state."

This wild scenery almost proved his undoing. In May 1915, the *Examiner* carried the news that Knowles had fallen into the river during the filming and was "dashed from rock to rock." According to the paper, "He was so badly battered and cut by the rocks that his life was at first despaired of. Reports from Belden, tonight, however, were that he was still alive."

Indeed he was. The playbill adds the detail that "Knowles was almost drowned and his horse actually killed." *Alone in the Wilderness* is a dramatic film, involving some flimsy business with Knowles being accused by the North West Mounted Police of killing his former partner, who had "really" been shot accidentally. This miscarriage of justice gets him out in the woods, fleeing pursuers with the aid of his daughter, who is played, the flyer says, by the "prominent Bluebird star" Evelyn Selbie. As she weakens, he braves snowdrifts and raging torrents to get her to safety. The drama "shows some action which any but a seasoned woodsman could hardly survive," the California playbill notes.

Appropriately, Selbie had been a sidesaddle rider in her youth and had appeared in many Westerns, including Cecil B. Demille's first Hollywood film, *The Squaw Man*, and was the screen partner of "Broncho" Billy Anderson. She even made it into the Marx Brothers' 1935 film *A Night at the Opera* as an (uncredited) singer.

KNOWLES IN A DRAMATIC FILM STILL FROM *ALONE IN THE WILDERNESS*, WITH EVELYN SELBIE. COURTESY OF KAYE MULVEY-COWAN

The flyer for *Alone in the Wilderness* (which may have had the alternate title *The End of the Trail*) indulges in some considerable hype, when it notes that "Perhaps no unofficial figure stands more prominently in the public eye than Joseph Knowles. . . . Long before he attempted the mastery of Nature, he was recognized as the greatest American painter of outdoor life, his paintings adorning the galleries of some our best art salons. Now for the first time, Knowles presents himself as a bona-fide actor of the movies to wrest the laurels from Broncho Billy, Billy Hart, Bill Farnum and other Bills who attempt to portray the wild and wooly character of the borderlands."

An accounting sent to Knowles indicates that more than 10,000 feet of film was exposed, and that he and Selbie were paid $50 a week each for their work.

Even though *Alone in the Wilderness* featured Selbie, a recognizable star of the period, and was released by Bluebird (a subsidiary of what is now Universal Studios), it is still impossible to find these days. Thousands of silent movies are lost, a product of both indifference and combustible film stock. As we will see, much of the silent work of Elaine Hammerstein, Knowles's future partner in the woods, is similarly lost or missing.

The comprehensive Internet Movie Database at IMDb.com lists only *The Nature Man* among Knowles's credits, and misidentifies the lead player as "John Knowles." It includes a comprehensive filmography for Evelyn Selbie, but does not include *Alone in the Wilderness* among her credits.

The film titled *The Nature Man* appears to have been a documentary, also released by Universal and edited together from both the 1913 footage Knowles used on the vaudeville circuit and scenes he shot later in California. The film was still being shown in 1916, when the *Atlanta Constitution* advertised local showings and called it "the biggest novelty of this or many seasons." The management of the Savoy Theater there was treated to a special private showing and called it "the most gripping and intensely interesting picture you will ever have the pleasure to witness." An ad for the five-act film that appeared in *The News* of Frederick, Maryland, that same year further noted that Knowles "tackles fierce animals without weapons and makes clothing from their skins." This was not entertainment for the faint of heart.

One of Knowles's many side trips was to Los Angeles, where he saw the sights for the first time and delivered a lecture. Hollywood as we know it today was in its infancy in 1915, but Knowles may have caught a glimpse of the emerging film industry on his visit.

On September 21, he was introduced by Professor Edwards to a gathering at Manual Arts High School. When he wasn't making fire on stage (it took three tries), he told the schoolchildren that he had gotten attached to the West. "The men out here shake hands like real men," he said. "I am impressed with the hundreds and hundreds of thousands of acres of forest and mountain wild you have. It is your opportunity to get lessons from nature in a lore you cannot get from books." Knowles's picture in he-man pose made the local papers along with some starlets of the day, in a montage captioned "Some stars of the theatrical firmament."

A poster from his California tour indicates that Knowles was accompanied by a wrestling bear, which may have been the property of his friend, Hollywood animal trainer Bud White (who counted Mary Pickford and Buster Keaton as clients). The bruin was named John Brown. "He likes to wrestle as much as ever," White wrote to Knowles in 1923.

This brief taste of Hollywood seems to have gone to Knowles's head. While still in San Francisco in November 1915, he wrote to S. Lesser of the Golden Gate Film Company proposing a new nature film, which would combine a melodramatic story (a man shipwrecked on a South Seas island) with a real-life survival experiment. While the shipwreck itself would be staged, the essence of the film would be a documentary of Knowles on an isolated island off the Mexican coastal city of Mazatlán (in Sinaloa state). Knowles had already made arrangements with the island's owners.

He planned "to leave San Francisco at an early date with cameraman [it was to be George Lawrence, who had shot the Feather River pictures] and complete outfit for moving pictures, and on reaching Mazatlán make final preparations before starting on my

test, which will consist of getting a general line on the island conditions, meeting officials and delivering a lecture to the public just before starting on my trip."

The cameraman would accompany him to the island, where it would be his job "to watch my stunt in the interest of science and record it as an educational moving picture." Knowles would arrive by boat, and while it was anchored off the island he would "strip myself of everything, dive overboard and swim to the island. . . . I shall start with absolutely nothing, kindle my fire by friction, clothe and feed myself and build a boat from the natural recourses [*sic*] of the island without aid or suggestion from anybody. I shall capture one or more specimens of the animals, birds and fishes and within 30 days sail back to the mainland in the boat. . . ."

He would even arrange his own publicity, sending full accounts of his proposed trip to all the leading newspapers, "giving them liberty to publish a story covering my experiences as they did during my recent experiment in the California mountains."

Knowles was supremely confident that he could pull off this third trip. With Lawrence's experience as a cameraman "and mine as a 'Nature Man,' we should be able to produce the desired results," he wrote.

With no intention of leaving his creative fate in the hands of a Hollywood scriptwriter, Knowles penned his own screenplay, entitled *A Modern Robinson Cruso* [*sic*]. Though he would later become a prolific writer, most of his output is short stories and reminiscences. But all of it is full of life, amusing, disjointed in one way or another, full of misspellings, and fatally lacking in structure. His short stories often start strongly, announce their intentions, and then fail to fulfill them as their writer wanders off on tangents.

A Modern Robinson Cruso is better organized than most of Knowles's stories, and probably would have made a perfectly credible silent film. As Knowles described to the film mogul, it stars Knowles as himself—"'The Nature Man' and conqueror of the wilderness"—along with a big cast of "wild animals, birds, reptiles and fishes."

The story is a hoot. It starts out with Knowles shaking hands with the "governor and other officials" for some reason, then cuts to a terrific shipwreck, with him as its sole survivor. Wandering the beach, he finds and captures a turtle, sees wildcats fighting, locates edible fruits and vegetables, makes a fire, and roasts that turtle.

Knowles supposedly sailed the world in his youth, and often spoke of time spent in the South Seas. Yet his knowledge of the flora and fauna that inhabits Pacific islands seems a bit off. The monkeys in the trees (who perform many amusing antics, including throwing coconuts, and who eventually become companions) are debatable; but what's with those deer breaking out of a thicket? An encounter with coyotes seems a stretch, as does Knowles's fight with an alligator. And who knows where the rabbits, which appear regularly, came from?

In the end, Knowles builds his boat (a process that is lovingly described), and with monkeys as his passengers sails back to the mainland, where his old friend the governor is waiting with outstretched arms. The End.

Knowles definitely saw the educational value of his work as paramount. Kids would take in the enlightening details, such as: "Showing use of sea shells and sharp stones, how clay pottery is made, rope making, making fish nets and cloth, making use of the coconut husk, drawing on bark with charcoal [and] making cigarettes from wild tobacco." Knowles was perhaps ahead of his time in specifying, "No killing of animals or birds in the picture." But for this to be credible, we have to give him points for dispatching the poor turtle offscreen.

The Golden Gate Film Company and its Mr. Lesser seem to have vanished into the mists of history. San Francisco did not end up the film capital of the United States, and Joseph Knowles was destined never to be marooned on a desert island with some very displaced flora and fauna.

This was just one of the disappointments for Knowles in this period. With his second trip into the woods ending in obscurity— through no fault of his own—he seemed to be casting about for something else to do. He had a young wife to support; but because he'd fallen in love with the West, it seemed unlikely that he'd go back to just getting by with freelance art in Boston. He was now the nationally known Nature Man, with a reputation to uphold.

He was still lecturing, but bookings were beginning to get a bit thin. He was hoping to start his forest school, but he had concepts rather than concrete plans. Knowles had earlier talked about the Canadian Northwest as a possible location for his forest school, but now his attention was firmly placed somewhere in the West. And he was beginning to think about the curriculum. The pupils appeared eager to take the courses.

"Boys should be taken into the woods by men schooled in woodcraft and taught self-reliance there," Knowles told his enthralled high school audience in Los Angeles. "Each to make his own lean-to, to get fire by friction, to find berries and roots to eat, to trap and snare game as needed for food." What red-blooded American boy (no girls need apply, apparently) of 1914 wouldn't jump at the chance? When Knowles spoke to a crowd of kids in

Victoria, British Columbia, the local paper wrote that "a pin could have been heard dropping" as he described his adventures.

Knowles probably did not have the discipline or the organizational skills to put together a nature school on his own. He preferred to be an actor in a play that was staged for him. Without any immediate offers, he languished in San Francisco. As 1915 faded into 1916, the war was deepening, and the British and Australian disaster at Gallipoli increased the pessimism. Though the United States was not yet at war itself, President Woodrow Wilson and his military commanders were making preparations. The new year brought the grim battle of the Somme, in which the British Expeditionary Force suffered an incredible 420,000 casualties. With this somber backdrop, there was less time for the call of nature, and Knowles grew increasingly worried about what would come next.

In May 1916, Knowles wrote to the newly elected mayor of Chicago, William Hale "Big Bill" Thompson, offering to accompany his honor into the woods of northern Wisconsin. Thompson had been born in Boston, so perhaps there was a connection there. And Big Bill certainly had an adventurous streak. After two terms, he left office, telling his former constituents that he was off to the South Seas islands on an expedition to find tree-climbing fish and capture them on movie film.

"I have strong reason to believe that there are fish that come out of the water, can live on land, will jump three feet to catch a grasshopper, and will actually climb trees," said Thompson at the time. His yacht *Big Bill* made it as far south as New Orleans, but by that time the mayor was no longer a passenger. *Time* noted in 1924 the "derisive amusement" among the know-it-alls at this announcement, but pointed out that *Anabas scandens,* a six-inch-long fish known as the "climbing perch," actually can live out of water and travel on land. The only problem is that it's a resident of India and its environs, nowhere else. "The ex-Mayor has science on his side, though his geography may not be infallible," *Time* said. The magazine's headline, interestingly enough, was "Nature Faking?"

In 1916, Thompson was amused enough to write Knowles back, even if weighty matters kept him at his desk. "The prospect of my being able to get away for a month is as vague as it is exulting," Thompson said. "I am afraid that there is no chance of my being able to avail myself of the opportunity."

Just when things began to look dark for Knowles—would he have to go back to guiding hunters in Maine?—salvation arrived from a familiar quarter. The Hearst newspapers, it seems, weren't quite finished with him. Joseph Knowles, the man of the wilderness, was now to be reborn, with his story enlivening the hothouse that was big-time New York City journalism. And to give this aging story a new twist, something new and exciting was to be added: a naked woman to accompany the naked man. Adam was to get his Eve.

The news came in July 1916 from the *New York American* and its sister paper, the *Evening Journal,* which were later to merge as the *Journal-American* in 1937. The competition for circulation wasn't quite as fierce and bare-fisted as it had been in the 1890s and the first decade of the 1900s, the heyday of yellow journalism. Joseph Pulitzer had died in 1911, and his less-competent son, Joseph Pulitzer II, was in charge at the *New York World.*

But the Hearst papers still knew a good story when they saw it, and they had gotten quite a bit of mileage out of Knowles before the war broke out. This new thirty-day experiment was to be conducted by the papers with the help of Hearst's International Film Service (IFS), which planned weekly news reports for the silent screen. IFS had been launched by Hearst in 1915 as a way of creating cartoon versions of his newspaper funny papers. The staff included noted animator Walter Lantz (later the creator of *Woody Woodpecker*).

These short silent films were attached to the newsreels produced by Hearst's International News Service. It's interesting that the task of documenting the Dawn Man and Dawn Woman (as they were to be called) went to the company whose more usual fare was *Krazy Kat, Maude the Mule,* and *Bringing Up Father.*

The experiment was launched in mid-September, very late in the season. The location was already chosen: the Adirondacks, with the town of Old Forge, two hours northwest of Albany and 100 miles north of Syracuse, as the jumping-off point. Daytime temperatures in the region (as recorded at Fort Drum) average in the low fifties at that time of year, and it gets much colder at night. Near-freezing evening temperatures as early as late August are not uncommon. The lowest-ever temperature in the state, negative 52 degrees Fahrenheit, was recorded in Old Forge in 1979.

Old Forge itself is a lovely place, located in the town of Webb (New York's largest township) in the central Adirondacks. In Knowles's time, the area was a popular getaway, having been opened up by the Mohawk and Malone Railroad coming through in 1892. Tourists traveled by steamboat to the many new hotels on the 200 lakes and ponds around Webb.

The cool climate and clean mountain air were thought to provide a good escape from the pestilence of the festering cities. In 1887, *Treasure Island* author Robert Louis Stevenson made his way to nearby Saranac Lake, where he battled tuberculosis. He was much remarked upon locally for his fondness for playing the pennywhistle. According to a 1912 account by fellow Scotsman Stephen Chalmers, "He did not fish. He did not hunt. He lacked the principal virtue of a man in the wilderness—physical strength; and for a living he seemed only to tootle upon a pennywhistle and cut a fantastic figure on skates on the lake behind the cottage where he lived."

It was also to the neighboring Adirondacks that hermit Noah John Rondeau had fled in 1914, two years before Knowles arrived. Rondeau settled into the Cold River country in the High Peaks Wilderness. "Man is forever a stranger and alone," the solitary Rondeau once said, adding that he liked crowds "going the other way." Still, in 1947 he allowed the Conservation Department to pick him up by helicopter and fly him to a sportsmen's show in New York, where he chatted with interviewers, appeared on a popular radio show, and was filmed for newsreels. After a storm knocked down his woodland in 1950, when he was sixty-seven, Rondeau finally quit the woods for a sedentary life in Saranac Lake.

Knowles must have cut nearly as fantastic a figure as Rondeau and Stevenson, especially in his woodland costume. But from the beginning, the press that swarmed over the Dawn Man and Dawn Woman experiment had eyes only for the female of the pair. She was the young (just twenty at the time) and beautiful actress Elaine Hammerstein, who, according to the *American*, had been selected from among forty contenders for the honor of going into the woods with Joe Knowles.

The idea of a single Dawn Woman seems to have grown out of an earlier plan for a larger, group effort. The *New York Sunday World* wrote on June 25 that the experiment was to start sometime the next month, and that it was to include "two back-to-back nature squads—one of men and the other of women—and each squad will surround itself with different sections of the Adirondacks."

That plan was operational for at least several weeks. The *Washington Post,* in a bemused account that July headlined "Six Eves to One Adam," announced that a group of six "corsetless, un-hairpinned and non-mirrored" young women—led by one Emily Davis, whose husband had been killed on the front in northern France—would receive preliminary training from Knowles in finding edible roots and making snares, then would disrobe and make their way to a "secret camp in the Adirondacks." After a month, Knowles (who was soon to go off on "another of his famous back-to-nature jamborees," wrapped in nothing but "an expression") would have the enviable task of retrieving them.

At Knowles lectures around this time, the Nature Man was co-billed with Miss Mary Louise Hescock, who according to posters of the period "has arranged with the *New York* and *Chicago American* to make the test of woman against nature in the Adirondacks under the direction of Mr. Knowles and under the observation of Columbia University."

All of this planning occurred despite the fact that Knowles himself was rather dismissive of female independence. "The trouble with women," he told the *New York Sunday World,* "is they are the only females dependent on the males in all the world. Among the animal species, the females are the real fighters and the food getters. . . . Over-civilization has by slow degrees brought women to the position of being—no, I will not say parasite, for that is a bit harsh—but dependent fits all right." He concluded by noting that if a party of female volunteers would go into the

Adirondacks (under his personal direction, obviously) and "turn themselves loose" for thirty days it would make an "interesting and instructive" experiment.

But the party of women became instead a single Eve. Elaine Hammerstein had an impeccable theatrical pedigree. She was the granddaughter of the opera impresario Oscar Hammerstein, and the only daughter of composer and Broadway producer Arthur Hammerstein. (Among many other things, her father wrote "Because of You," which became Tony Bennett's first hit in 1951.) Her uncle Willie was a flamboyant vaudeville producer, of whom no less a personage than Will Rogers proclaimed, "We have never produced another showman like Willie Hammerstein." Her first cousin, lyricist Oscar Hammerstein II, was to co-write *Show Boat* with Jerome Kern. His output with Richard Rodgers included such classics as *Oklahoma!, Carousel, South Pacific, The King and I, Flower Drum Song,* and *The Sound of Music.*

The Hammersteins were one of America's first families of the stage, and their natural habitat was New York theater in both its high and low varieties—about as far from the woods as it was possible to get. And far from being a renegade tomboy in that theatrical world, Elaine Hammerstein was deeply of it.

The Hammerstein story starts with Oscar I, eldest son in a large middle-class family of German Jews. After early musical studies, Oscar Hammerstein ran away to America at fifteen, arriving in New York during the Civil War in 1864. Finding menial work sweeping up in a cigar factory, he soon turned his newfound skill to his advantage. He held forty-four patents in cigar manufacture, and founded a successful tobacco journal (while serving as a theater manager in his limited spare time).

Hammerstein built his first theater, the Harlem Opera House, in 1889. It became the showplace for popular actors including Georgie Drew Barrymore, Lillian Russell, and Edwin Booth (brother of Lincoln assassin John Wilkes Booth). Opera was Oscar's passion and also his undoing. Though he built ten theaters in the United States and staged many triumphantly successful productions, dominating the grand opera world and developing Times Square in the process, Oscar also overspent himself into near-bankruptcy. Accepting a $1.2 million payout (negotiated by his son Arthur) from the Metropolitan Opera to stay away from New York productions for ten years, Oscar promptly spent all his money opening a financially unsuccessful theater in London.

Oscar's other son, Willie, had a genius for giving audiences what they actually wanted: the popular entertainment known as vaudeville. Brilliantly manipulating the competing scandal sheets of the period (Hearst's *Evening Journal* and Pulitzer's *New York World*), Willie kept his productions in the public eye.

In his amusing book on vaudeville, *No Applause, Just Throw Money,* author Travis Stewart credits Willie Hammerstein with inventing "the freak act, which comprised not only obvious sideshow fare like Rahja the snake charmer from Coney Island, but a whole succession of tabloid headline acts as well, such as Nan Patterson 'the Singing Murderess,' and 'Shooting Stars' Ethel Conrad and Lillian Graham, so called because together they'd shot up a dude named Web Stokes. In 1913 he booked Evelyn Nesbitt Thaw, one of the original Floradora girls, whose jealous husband, Harry K. Thaw, had shot and killed the famous architect Stanford White, throwing both press and public into an uproar." Thaw's dramatic escape to Canada for that murder had, of course, competed with Knowles's Maine foray for the headlines in late 1913.

Willie's vision had many modern echoes, one of them being his habit of booking acts simply because they were famous. Thus not only singers and actors trod his boards, but also such "celebrities" as boxer Jack Johnson, baseball player Babe Ruth, explorer Captain Cook, P. T. Barnum midgets Tom Thumb and Lavinia Warren, and even Helen Keller (who told the story of her life with the aid of a sign-language interpreter).

It is tempting to conclude that Elaine Hammerstein's selection above forty other aspirants for the Dawn Woman title might have been more because of her theatrical connections than her large, melting, and luminous eyes. But that conclusion is undone by timing. Willie Hammerstein had died in 1914, aged just forty-two, and the family's vaudeville holdings were in total eclipse. Elaine's father, Arthur, had in fact tried to rescue Willie's empire, but he did not have his brother's flair for the medium. Their theater, the Victoria, closed in 1915. Meanwhile, Oscar I had sold the family's vaudeville production rights in New York to entrepreneur B. F. Keith, whose theaters around the country had welcomed Knowles.

Elaine Hammerstein's transition to film may have been in part propelled by these events. In mid-1916, the young actress was not yet a movie star, though she was well on her way to becoming one. She was a few months out of her second Broadway play, *The Trap*, at the Booth Theater. Hammerstein "acquits herself very credibly," said the *New York Times*, but the show ran for only twenty-seven performances. Her first play, *High Jinks*, which was seen at the Casino and Lyric Theaters, had been more successful, running for 213 performances at the end of 1913 and into early 1914. The plays had something in common: Both were produced by her father.

But Hammerstein's *All About Eve* moment came sooner rather than later. Despite growing up in the theater, she abandoned both it and her father's enveloping cocoon very early on. Even before she met Joe Knowles, this slim, dark-eyed beauty with something of Claudette Colbert's cupid-lipped appeal was making movies. Her first was *The Moonstone,* based on the story of a cursed gem by the pioneering British novelist Wilkie Collins. (Even in 1915, Hammerstein's version was the third film take on this popular and very early detective novel of 1868; there had been French and American silent versions in 1909 and 1911.)

Also in 1915, she'd appeared in *The Face in the Moonlight,* a filmed version of the play, and the interesting fifteen-episode serial *Beatrice Fairfax,* which was shot (as were many other films of the period) in Ithaca, New York. Hammerstein was not the star of the latter (Grace Darling, a former Hearst reporter, portrayed Beatrice Fairfax in this suspense series, which also featured the screen debut of the troubled and tragically short-lived Olive Thomas). But Hammerstein's career was definitely rising.

As a character, the newspaper advice columnist Beatrice Fairfax has an interesting genesis. Beatrice was the pen name writers Marie Manning and Lilian Lauferty used when writing advice columns for Hearst's *Evening Journal* in New York. The premise of the series was that Beatrice would go on adventures solving mysteries suggested by letter-writers to her column. Hearst himself produced the Beatrice serial, with guidance from one of his former magazine editors.

This was a continuation of the work that Hearst had begun with the very successful 1914 *Perils of Pauline* (which, by the way, originated the cliché of tying a heroine to the railroad tracks). As Hearst biographer David Nasaw explained to an interviewer from the *NewsHour with Jim Lehrer* in 2000, "[I]n the 1910s, [Hearst] realized that the film industry was not going to go anywhere without the newspapers, that the newspapers created the stars, created the buzz about the movies, and published the schedules of where the movies were playing. So he figured he would get into the business."

Nasaw adds that Hearst was one of the first to see the possibilities of "synergy" between his different media platforms. On Sunday, his papers would run copious advertising, with stills and plot synopses from the serials. On Monday, the films were in theaters. In 1916, Hearst instructed the editors of his magazines to buy only short stories that could be turned into films, with Hearst holding the option.

Both *Beatrice* and *Perils* were made by the Wharton brothers, Ted and Leopold, who built their Wharton Studios in Ithaca in 1914 with financing from Hearst. One reason for the location, in addition to low-cost filmmaking, was the region's many gorges and cliffs that lent themselves well to "cliffhanger" endings.

Ted Wharton was something of a self-promoter, describing himself as "directly responsible for the creation and success of a vast number of Motion Picture Stars who are numbered among the headliners in the industry"; but he backed it up by churning out well-made and frequently successful serials and features. And they did indeed have Hollywood royalty in them, including Francis X. Bushman, Lionel Barrymore, Oliver Hardy, Irene Castle, and (the future Charlie Chan) Warner Oland.

Wharton did his best to re-create Hollywood on the Cayuga. The actors stayed at the Ithaca Hotel or rented cottages along the lake, and there were frequent parties. Ithaca was dry and Prohibition loomed, but bootleggers kept the moonshine flowing.

Terry Harbin, whose day job is with the county library in Ithaca, is the ranking expert on silent filmmaking in that city. "They said all the footage had been dumped in the lake," he told me, "but I found thirteen to fourteen hours of it, including six hours of *Beatrice Fairfax*."

In addition to producing a documentary about the Wharton brothers' work, Harbin has supervised a restoration and release on DVD of a nearly complete *Beatrice Fairfax*. It is enhanced with an original score and is missing only its first episode, appropriately titled "The Missing Watchman." Mysteriously, that lost episode includes a cameo from Hearst himself, as well as the *Evening Journal*'s publisher, Arthur Brisbane.

The first episode may also contain the bulk of Elaine Hammerstein's work on the series. Hearst's concept was to have major stars of his International Film Service—including Mae Hopkins, Nigel Barrie, Lionel Barrymore, and Olive Thomas—"guest star" to add box-office appeal (and cross-promote his other films). A 1915 visitor to the Wharton set in Ithaca found guest star Barrymore involved in some elaborate business with firearms and "secret panels." Hammerstein (who was prominently billed in the series at the time) may have been in the first episode only, because Harbin has been unable to identify her in subsequent installments.

The fate of the absent footage is unknown, but Hearst had a major rift during the filming process with the Whartons about the direction that the *Beatrice Fairfax* material was taking. (He later resolved to remake the whole series with his muse, Marion Davies, in the title role.) It is possible that he suppressed the first episode because it included his image and associated him with a production he no longer supported. But many other explanations are equally plausible.

Hearst was very "hands-on" with his film properties, stemming from his love of theater—and of the actresses who appeared in the plays. The biography *Citizen Hearst* says the mogul believed in fidelity only in the abstract; he had, the book says, "affairs of the moment that for one reason or another did not satisfy him." Hearst's son, Bill, Jr., described him as a perennial "stage-door Johnny" who never missed the latest plays. He was said to buy a seat at the *Follies* just for his hat. As Nasaw writes in *The Chief*, he was also "something of an authority on chorus girls," and his newspapers were filled with "photographs of actresses and chorus girls, puff pieces on their careers and friendly reviews." Editors were admonished that negative reviews were unnecessary.

When Hearst took up with chorus girl Marion Davies around 1917, she received wide and extravagant coverage in his newspapers. He also signed her to a $500-a-week movie contract and made sure she was favorably featured in the gossip columns. She was the centerpiece of his new feature production company, Cosmopolitan Pictures.

Hearst's directors were bombarded with notes and suggestions on casting and story line, which made some top talent reluctant to work on his productions. The set designer of one of Hearst's Ithaca films, the sensational and racist *Patria* (which baited the Japanese and angered the Wilson administration), was instructed by the boss, "We must have variety and individual thrills. . . . Every thriller must really *thrill* [emphasis in the original]. . . . The few close ups which must be faked should be convincingly faked."

Given all this, it's not hard to imagine that Hearst got a good look at the smoldering beauty that was a still-teenaged Elaine Hammerstein and decided that she was ready for a starring role—

though not necessarily in a dramatic movie. Richard O. Boyer, in his 1938 *New Yorker* profile, suggests that the idea of a woman in the woods with Knowles was the brainchild of an executive at the New York *Evening Journal,* but it may have been Hearst himself who picked the leading lady. He could have seen her on the set during one of his occasional visits to Ithaca, or in the footage sent to New York for his perusal.

Another possibility is that Hammerstein was in Ithaca *because* of Hearst. Since he haunted the city's stage doors, he might have seen her in one of her Broadway appearances earlier that year and foisted her on the Whartons. In an e-mail exchange with me, Nasaw said he considers some version of these events to be plausible. "Sounds to me like you're absolutely on target," he wrote. Harbin concurs. "I agree," he said. "Hearst had the hots for Irene Castle, too, and the Whartons had to keep him away from her during the filming of *Patria.*"

The timing is instructive. According to film historian Harbin, work on *Beatrice Fairfax* began in May and June 1916 and continued until October. A possible explanation for the late start of the "experiment" in the nearby woods is that Hammerstein was tied up in filmmaking until then. It's clear that this third woodland sojourn was to be another of Hearst's multimedia extravaganzas. His International Film Service was given a starring role in setting up the project for the *Evening Journal* and *American* and received photo credit on the provocative images used in the layouts. If all went well in the woods, it had the makings of another sensational journalistic coup for William Randolph Hearst.

Oscar Hammerstein III agreed to meet me for coffee at a Connecticut Starbucks and help explain the world his family inhabited.

ELAINE HAMMERSTEIN: A SOPHISTICATED CITY GIRL IN THE WILDERNESS. COURTESY OF
THE LIBRARY OF CONGRESS

Better known as Andy, he is an accomplished artist and also the
family historian, lecturing on that subject at Columbia University.

In person, he lived up to the family name, exhibiting a breezy
insouciance. When not bantering with the *barrista,* he said that
Elaine Hammerstein is "an odd one" in the family because she
escaped their insular, Broadway-centered theater world.

"I'd like to have known her," he said. "She's interesting because she got away from the theater and most of the family never did. Oscar I, for instance, lived right above the theater and never stopped producing." It might have been better if he had, because Hammerstein says his great-grandfather's refusal to call it a day after he took that $1.2 million payoff ruined the family fortune. "He pretty much emptied out the bank accounts before he died in 1919," Hammerstein said. "If Oscar had not been crazy for opera, we would own half of Times Square now."

Peerless lyricist Oscar II, the son of vaudeville genius Willie, and Elaine, daughter of Arthur, were first cousins. Family historian Oscar III says he "can't put them in the same room together," but it's likely they knew each other well.

The *Evening Journal* described Elaine Hammerstein as "a girl who has been reared in the warmth of luxury; a girl city born and bred, with the ideals and the mind of a child of creature comfort." She was "the pretty, softly cultivated daughter of Arthur Hammerstein of New York."

The paper gave Elaine's address as 216 West 99th Street in Manhattan. According to his biographer, Oscar Hammerstein II lived first on 135th Street and then, when he was four, moved to 125th Street. The cousins, just two years apart in age, were within walking distance of each other, and when Oscar went to Columbia University they were even closer still.

But they had other reasons besides proximity to be close. Oscar Hammerstein II's mother died in 1910 and his father in 1914, leaving him an orphan. He was basically taken in and nurtured by Elaine's father, Arthur, who became his protector and the champion of his first works for the theater.

Oscar III describes Arthur Hammerstein as "a warm, generous, salty, foul-mouthed philanderer and tail chaser." He did indeed earn that reputation. A lurid 1922 feature in the *Indianapolis Sunday Star* quotes him as saying, "A wife is like a derby hat. When a man gets a new derby he may think it is a fine derby. But he doesn't fancy he must wear that particular derby until he dies."

Arthur Hammerstein married Jean Allison, mother of Elaine, in 1895 when she was just seventeen. But Arthur was named as a co-respondent in a divorce case in 1906, and the Hammersteins divorced when Elaine was ten, in 1907. Unusually, Allison did not ask for permanent custody of Elaine, but gave her daughter the opportunity to choose which parent to live with. Arthur went on to marry several other famous beauties and leading ladies (rejecting one candidate because "she thinks in seven figures"). He squired around the much-married actress Peggy Hopkins Joyce, and was thought to be the leading candidate to take her to the altar again. But during his "single" period in 1922, he told the *Star*, "I may not marry at all. I'm more interested in my daughter's career right now than I am in my own."

When he wasn't philandering, Arthur Hammerstein took his nephew Oscar on the road and started him on his career by producing his first plays. Oscar's on-the-job training started in 1916 with work as assistant and full stage manager on several productions. Then Arthur volunteered to mount a New York production if Oscar could come up with something serviceable. The result, a tragedy named *The Light,* failed in New Haven after only five performances. "He always referred to it as *The Light that Failed,*" said his son, William Hammerstein, much later. "After the first act, Dad knew he had a flop."

But *The Light* was to mark the start of a long collaboration. "Much of what they did together flopped," Oscar III says, "but Arthur kept producing Oscar's shows." After three straight disasters, the pair (with creative input from Otto Harbach and Herbert Stothart) finally had a hit with *Wildflower* in 1923.

Arthur Hammerstein also promoted his talented daughter and turned her into a leading lady. The proud papa was the impresario for *High Jinks* on Broadway. A photo from that 1913 musical comedy production, which also starred Snitz Edwards, shows an amused-looking Elaine dressed as a nurse with supporting actor Burrell Barbaretto (wearing an evening coat and top hat). Did Elaine sing in the show? It seems likely. The co-author of *High Jinks* was Oscar II's frequent collaborator Otto Harbach, and the score was written by operetta composer Rudolf Friml, later to work with Oscar II on the big worldwide hit *Rose-Marie*. So it must have been a tight-knit crew working on these productions.

A second, non-musical father–daughter collaboration, *The Trap* in early 1915, was not very successful, and perhaps it soured Elaine on Broadway. After making her first film, she never returned to the theater.

The Elaine who Hammerstein recruited to become a Nature Girl was without doubt an urban sophisticate. According to the biography that appeared in the 1923 *Blue Book of the Screen,* she graduated from Armitage College in Pennsylvania at a young age. There seems to be no record of such a college, however. Other sources credit her with graduating from Bryn Mawr at just seventeen years old, which would make her something of a prodigy. But the college alumni office at Bryn Mawr has no record of her attendance there.

Hammerstein in 1922, under contract to Lewis J.
Selznick.

Hammerstein was a novice in the woods, but her 1923 biography describes her as "a vigorous outdoor girl at all times," fill-
ing every minute of her spare time with "tennis, golf, canoeing,
riding her spirited horses or driving a powerful automobile." She
was said to be a student of "good literature" who could—no as-
set, unfortunately, in silent films—"converse in several languages."

The *Blue Book of the Screen* also describes the young Elaine
as something of a rebel. "Born with a decided theatrical 'pull,' the
young lady refused to use it, preferring to make her own way up
the ladder of fame. . . . Instead of relying upon her influential relatives, Miss Hammerstein applied to a motion picture company
as any other girl might have done. Her beauty and charming per-
sonality won for her a small part in a film."

Presumably the reference is to *The Moonstone* or *The Face in the Moonlight,* both made in 1915. Hammerstein didn't really establish herself in films until *The Argyle Case* in 1917. This, curiously, was not only a Lewis J. Selznick picture, heralding that Hammerstein had signed a lucrative deal, but it was directed by the very successful Ralph Ince.

The name Ince doesn't mean all that much today, but it was the stuff of tabloid headlines in 1924, when pioneering filmmaker Thomas H. Ince (Ralph's brother, one of three who made movies) was taken off William Randolph Hearst's yacht, *Oneida,* in stricken condition, apparently after suffering a heart attack. Ince's subsequent death made big headlines, but only the *New York Daily News* said he'd been on Hearst's yacht, and this information made only early editions of the paper.

The Hearst organization evidently did a poor job of handling the affair, leading to much speculation about what had actually happened. A popular theory at the time was that Hearst himself shot Ince with a bullet meant for Charlie Chaplin, who couldn't keep his hands off Marion Davies. *Vanity Fair,* in 1997, ran a story speculating that Hearst had run Ince through with one of Davies's hatpins. For keeping quiet, eyewitness Louella Parsons supposedly won a lifetime contract as Hearst's Hollywood columnist. This angle takes center stage in Peter Bogdanovich's 2001 film *The Cat's Meow,* with a perfectly cast Edward Hermann as Hearst.

Given Hearst's enormous power in the early 1920s, it's not surprising that questions about a cover-up arose, though David Nasaw in *The Chief* concludes that "there is still no credible evidence that [Ince] was murdered or that Hearst was involved in any foul play." Even so, filmmaker D. W. Griffith, who had partnered with Ince and Mack Sennett to form the Triangle Motion Picture Company in 1915, later commented, "All you have to do to make Hearst turn white as a ghost is mention Ince's name."

Hearst, of course, had only to say the word in 1916, and his New York newspapers would find an unknown city-born actress as the best candidate for Dawn Woman, beating out forty other contestants (if they even existed). And so, incongruous as it might have been, this scion of a glittering Broadway family ended up in Old Forge.

From the beginning, there was a lot of heavy breathing. "Hammerstein's slight, dark-haired and piquant good looks attracted much attention on the train and at the Old Forge Hotel, and curiosity as to her purpose here is already deepening," the *Evening Journal* wrote from its base in the Adirondacks. "Dawn Woman is enthusiastic over the prospect before her, and plans to make a beautiful and acceptable Minnehaha." The news that her mother, Jean Allison, was along to act as chaperone might have spoiled the fun for some of her fans. Allison was said to be confident of her daughter's success, though "naturally concerned with the difficulties of the experiment."

Dispatches to the *Evening Journal* from the camp in the woods at Fourth Lake followed a circuitous and watery route in 1916. Fourth Lake is one of eight Fulton Chain Lakes, and navigating them, then as well as now, makes a good alternative to overland travel. This canoe route was popularized by the nineteenth-century outdoor enthusiast George Washington Sears, also known by the Indian name "Nessmuk" in his many letters to *Field and Stream* magazine. Sears, author of the book *Woodcraft,* pioneered the use of lightweight canoes to portage through the Adirondack wilderness. Sears had learned his outdoors skills from a Narragansett Indian as a youth, so he would have undoubtedly gotten along well with Knowles (if he hadn't died in 1890).

There were steamboats on the lakes then, to carry passengers and the mail. The *Evening Journal* carried ads for steamship excursions on pages opposite its Dawn Girl stories; a day's outing with dancing and outdoor sports at Bear Mountain (forty miles up the Hudson from Manhattan) cost just fifty cents. There were also small branch railroads that helped make travel easier in a time when there were few roads (and not many private cars either). The camp near Fourth Lake was not completely isolated, but it was fair to call it wilderness.

So far from Manhattan and sleeping in a cold tent, Elaine Hammerstein pronounced herself satisfied. "I really am making my threat good," she said in the *Journal* of September 21. "After dancing every night for a week at a college prom following a whole winter of nothing but good times, I told a friend I was tired, tired of New York and its gayeties. I wanted to run wild, see if I could enjoy my own company far away from everyone and everything, and get rest and enjoyment out of what nature offers."

In the *American,* she declared that the challenge of living by the sunrise and sunset would "seem a blessed relief after hundreds of nights of sauntering on the Great White Way." The woods had given her "a new grip on life," and she would emerge with a natural "gospel" to preach to her bored urban friends. The woods were waiting for every woman, she said.

Dawn Woman was caught up in the excitement of starting on her own shelter, also known as a "house of boughs," and a photogenic grass skirt to replace her store-bought clothes. "Mr. Knowles, a real subject of Mother Nature, will teach me how to get everything necessary from nature itself," she said, "my tooth brush, comb, fire, food, shelter and clothing." It was a little over-whelming for the former denizen of the urban canyons. "This really seems too wonderful to believe," she said, "but it is possible[,] for it all has been explained to me."

If he even saw the papers, Knowles might have been a bit miffed by the emphasis on Dawn Woman over Dawn Man. He had been the star of the two previous outings. Fortunately, he was busy scouting the territory with a local, Ollie Tuttle, who owned a lumber camp in the area. Knowles covered ten miles of densely wooded trails through mountains and swamps south of Third Lake. The two explorers saw plentiful signs of deer, rebounding populations of beaver (protected in the Adirondacks since 1908, after being nearly exterminated for the hat trade), raspberry patches, trout spawning in the streams—and even another Knowles delicacy, hedgehogs.

The weather was fine, consisting of a string of Indian summer days, though there was the ominous sign of the maple, birch, and poplar leaves starting to turn color.

The next day, Hammerstein found herself worked to near exhaustion building the shelter, her hands a "sight" with their thick smears of dirt and pitch. But the shelter, placed next to a sweet coldwater spring in a leafy glade not far from a beaver pond, was done. It had been carefully angled to catch the sun during the day and avoid the northerly winds.

Under Knowles's direction, Hammerstein built a framework with birch and maple wood, then she made moosewood cross-pieces and covered the whole thing in downed limbs to serve as rafters. Early tests showed it was not fully rainproof, so teacher and student put in a few more hours with fir branches and strips of bark to tighten the roof.

The floor was covered with evergreen boughs to make a bed "as warm as a fur rug." It was not yet known if Hammerstein could be comfortable there, so she made plans to stay only a few hours the first night, with a cheerful fire burning on her hearth. But there was no doubt that she looked the part. "Framed in the rude doorway of her cabin, with her cheeks ruddied by the autumn sun, the 'nature girl' fitted the surroundings to perfection," said the *Evening Journal.*

There was even more of this kind of thing the next day, September 23, when, to the gratification of the *Journal*'s reporters, Hammerstein donned the grass dress Knowles had made for her. The reporters were not the only onlookers—a colony of beavers was also on hand. According to the *Evening Journal,* the beavers

saw a sight which they can hand down to their descendants as the most surprising thing that ever happened in their family history. A beautiful, brown-haired, blue-eyed young girl, clad in a gown of plaited grass with buskins [leg coverings] of the same material, marched out upon their structure of logs and sticks and mud. She was trying to find a way across where the rushing water, brown from the tamarack swamp, poured over the logs. Her bare shoulders gleamed in the Autumn sun and her bare knees peeped through the crevices in her skirt of sword-grass and blue-flag. The beavers certainly never saw a sight like this.

The unidentified reporter was inspired to near-poetry by the sight of this "forest maid," this "exquisite, white-skinned Pocahontas." With her skirts bouffant from the stiff grass blades, she melted into the greenery along the path and was like "some new and beautiful orchid growing out of the leaf mould." Unfortunately, immediately afterward, this "Pocahontas" of the mountains stubbed her toe on the beaver dam, sank into the mud, and lost one of her grass buskins.

Hammerstein's enthusiasm for the enterprise would seem to have been even then on the wane. The water was swift, the logs slippery, and she was sunk in mud halfway to her knees. "She gave it up to seek another crossing," the report continued, "and droopingly retraced her way back across the dam to the shore," all to the evident amusement of the beavers.

Given all this, it's hardly surprising that the story by Joe Knowles was relegated to the bottom of the page. He called on his readers to get back to the woods, to "discard all uncomfortable clothing and let Nature feed your starving body with the fragrance of her wild trees and flowers." Given the prospects for an encounter with the grass-skirted Hammerstein, some of his readers might have been inclined to take his advice.

Recalling his 1913 adventures with Dr. Sargent at Harvard University, Knowles said outdoor exposure would toughen the skin so it would serve as nature's perfect overcoat. And he told an amusing story designed to shrug off the coming cold weather: A white trapper met an Indian dressed only in a breechclout on a game trail in October, and asked if he was cold. The Indian replied, "Is your face cold?" The shivering trapper said it wasn't. "Injun all face," said the Indian.

To the newspaper readers snug in their warm homes, he asked a rhetorical question. "Why do I go in the woods and live like this?" And his answer was simple: "To prove that it can be done by the man of today—to show that centuries of civilization have not robbed us of the resourcefulness of our forefathers."

Knowles said he was proud of his pupil, a "slip of a girl" who he was confident would succeed in "a test which has never been attempted by civilized women."

The previous two expeditions had had scientific oversight, and this one was no exception. The appointed academic dons (or "savants," in the language of the day) were professors Rudolf M. Binder of New York University and Dr. Woods Hutchinson. They didn't get a chance to do much observing, but they were an interesting pair.

Hutchinson was a British-born physician who before 1900 had taught anatomy and comparative pathology at the University of Buffalo and Iowa State. More recently he had been the Oregon State Health Officer and was at the time of the experiment professor of clinical medicine at the New York Polyclinic. A prolific writer and Hearst health columnist with millions of readers, he was also the author of such books as *Exercise and Health* (1911) and *The Child's Day* (1912). The latter, quite sensibly for its time, is a book-length paean to the values of fresh air, exercise, sunlight, and outdoor play.

But Hutchinson had another side to him. He was a committed eugenicist, later to serve as an advisory council member of the American Eugenics Society. Eugenics, though couched in scientific terms, was a deeply racist social philosophy that held that heredity could be improved by human intervention. Eugenicists believed that the "feeble minded" (a category that included many non-whites and immigrants) should be discouraged from breeding, because their offspring were prone to crime and degeneracy. According to a Society exhibit, "Very few *normal* persons ever go to jail" [emphasis in the original].

Teddy Roosevelt, a proponent of eugenics when he wasn't exposing nature fakers, advanced the theory that America was in danger because the solid white European stock that had founded the country wasn't breeding fast enough. The country could be overtaken by a horde of Asian immigrants, he warned, saying "the prime duty . . . of the good citizen of the right type is to leave his or her blood behind him in the world; and that we have no business to permit the perpetuation of citizens of the wrong type."

Binder held similar views. He taught seniors and graduate students a "general course in anthropology and ethnology." He was a regular lecturer on the subject of eugenics, something that would hardly get through the door at New York University today. But belief in eugenics was surprisingly common and respectable at the time. It was an outgrowth of the "nativist" movement, particularly favored by wealthy Americans of Mayflower stock. Both Alexander Graham Bell, the inventor of the telephone, and agricultural scientist Luther Burbank flirted with eugenics. Margaret Sanger, the well-known birth control pioneer, had less-than-benign reasons for wanting to limit certain population groups: "More children from the fit, less from the unfit—that is the chief issue of birth control," she said.

The Cold Spring Harbor Eugenics Record Office was founded by the Carnegie Institute in 1910, and its first director was a Harvard zoologist who was twice president of the American Association for the Advancement of Science. Binder, it seems, was an enthusiastic teacher of eugenics. He was the author of the book *Eugenics and Religion* and wrote articles on "Germany's Population Policy" for the *Eugenical News*. (The latter published the translation of Germany's compulsory sterilization orders in 1933.

"From a legal point of view, nothing more could be desired," the publication said.)

Especially in Germany but also in the United States, the eugenicists considered the Jews a race to guard against, so it's unclear whether Binder was aware that Elaine Hammerstein was Jewish.

In the end, none of this mattered, because the professors were never put to the test. Their names were not mentioned again after they were introduced as scientific consultants to the experiment. Did the eugenicists have an ally in William Randolph Hearst? Hearst does not appear to have been directly involved in eugenics organizations, but he was without doubt a fellow traveler for a time. The Whartons made the infamous film *The Black Stork*, which was firmly pro-eugenics, with Hearst's backing in 1916. The film's philosophy would seem to coincide with Hearst's actively hostile views toward the Japanese and Mexicans, on full display in his film *Patria* (shot around the same time as *The Black Stork*, and using many of the same actors).

The Black Stork—a particularly repellent piece of work—stars the real-life Dr. Harry J. Haiselden, a Chicago physician who in November 1915 refused to assist an impaired baby, instead choosing to deliberately let it die. Dr. Haiselden then contacted Jack Lait, a columnist at Hearst's *Chicago American*, and told him what he had done. Louis Pizzitola's *Hearst Over Hollywood* says that Dr. Haiselden was "widely promoted in the Hearst press for his advocacy of a perfect race." Among the applauding voices was that of Dr. Woods Hutchinson, who declared the doctor's actions to demonstrate that "the world is becoming rational at last, thanks to science."

The case was then dramatized by the Wharton brothers as *The Black Stork*, written by Hearst columnist Lait. *The Black Stork* (only fragments of which still exist, according to the Library of Congress) shows the doctor's refusal to act, and the poor handicapped baby (who is seen in a fantasy sequence as doomed to a life of degeneracy, fathering other such creatures) being mercifully delivered to the waiting arms of Jesus.

Ads for the film quoted Dr. August Forel, a Swiss psychiatrist, as stating that "the law of heredity winds like a red thread through the family history of every criminal, of every epileptic, eccentric and insane person." The full details of Hearst's involvement in *The Black Stork* are not known, but according to Martin S. Pernick, author of a book on the film, Hearst visited the Whartons' Ithaca studio while it was being edited.

Hearst was enthusiastically pro-German in the lead-in to both world wars, met with Hitler in the 1930s, and signed both the Führer and Mussolini to write articles for his publications. But there's no evidence that he was actively anti-Semitic (though he certainly skirted it at times).

The *Sunday American* gave the experiment a huge spread on Sunday, September 24, with big, splashy photographs of Dawn Woman, the first in film-star mode and the second, looking "just as dainty," in a full-length grass skirt. She had walked the "wonderful" woods, had a lesson in making fire, and collaborated on her costume, which she said was "of tall grass, held by a very artistic belt of braided grass."

She would wear this outfit until, of course, she killed a deer. "Then I will have a winter dress from its skin, or if bearskin be more becoming, I must kill a bear, which will be more difficult. . . ." Hammerstein had so far seen the whole thing as no more taxing than a stroll up Fifth Avenue. But she was soon to be disabused of this notion.

There were lengthy trial runs to get ready for the day when the experiment would begin in earnest. Hammerstein was trying to get used to the outdoor life, without the rigors of actually being alone in the wilderness. The experiment would start when Knowles deemed his pupil ready, but it was slow going. The would-be Nature Girl, it turns out, made a dozen attempts to start a fire without avail, finally achieving a bright flame on the thirteenth try under "Joe's anxious direction." One can imagine her reaction when Knowles told her that the pickings were a bit thinner here than they had been in the Siskiyous, and that rabbit and deer were out because of the game laws. Instead, she could feast on the abundant frogs.

Hammerstein reacted with horror to the news that she was expected to actually kill wild animals. She had apparently expected Mother Nature to set a more genteel table. "Why, you don't mean that I will have to get my hands all bloody, do you?" she said with what the *American* called a wail of despair. "I never thought of being frightened about the wild animals I should meet, but killing them is another matter. Joe Knowles said something the other day about my hitting them on the head with a stone after I had trapped them, and I forgot all about skinning them."

By the next day, Knowles was sounding a bit defensive about the choice of Elaine Hammerstein for the nature test. He didn't claim to have had a hand in choosing her, but he wrote in a by-lined article that he had welcomed the idea of working with "a girl of exceptionally dainty and luxurious tastes, who has never tramped with the 'back to nature' faddists, nor exerted much more energy than is necessary to keep a rocking chair in gentle motion."

Knowles had made a point of telling the *American* before the experiment began that his nature girl did not have to come from "a Wild West show, a circus, a ranch or even a farm." If she had ordinary, sound health, she could come straight from Fifth Avenue.

Knowles added that he had initially seen Hammerstein as "pretty near an ideal figure for my mental conception of the Dawn Woman." Why? Because training such a "delicately raised" specimen to eventual success in the woods would be a "triumph." Had Knowles read or seen a production of George Bernard Shaw's 1912 *Pygmalion,* in which Professor Higgins accepts the challenge of transforming a mere flower girl, Eliza Doolittle, into a lady of quality? "I shall make a duchess of this draggle-tailed guttersnipe," Higgins declares.

Knowles was clearly a man of his time in declaring that he was aware of the limitations of his female subject. "I'm not saying that a girl with a limited experience in woods life can do all that a man can do," he said, "but I do say that if she will faithfully follow my instructions she can live for thirty days or even longer on the resources of this country."

But was she willing? "She must first understand that what she is undertaking is worthwhile," Knowles wrote in a bylined article that appeared in the newspaper of Monday, September 25. "Next, she must have confidence in her ability to make good, and she must put her whole time and attention on the task she has set for herself."

Eliza Doolittle wanted to rise above her station, so she put up with the professor's torturous linguistic lessons. But Elaine Hammerstein, much to Knowles's evident exasperation, was apparently not so malleable.

"I think she is beginning to have doubts," said Knowles in a remarkably candid admission. "I'm beginning to have doubts myself." The September 25 article seems to have been written to try to goad the increasingly reluctant young woman into action. He had sternly instructed her that she'd never make it without rigorous training, but it seems that she wasn't paying attention. "In Miss Hammerstein's case," he wrote, "I am beginning to fear that the will and the endurance are not sufficient to harden her against the hardships."

Knowles's new choice for an ideal female back-to-nature candidate was, not surprisingly, his own mother, who had been compelled by poverty to live close to nature. But it's doubtful that the newspaper-reading public would have been transfixed by a nature test starring Joe Knowles's aged mother.

The trip to the woodshed was unavailing, because Hammerstein quit the nature test a mere two days after Knowles's story appeared, on September 27. "I decided today that I cannot undertake the primitive back-to-nature experiment as Joe Knowles meant to start it this week," she admitted to the *Evening Journal*. "I am not a 'quitter,' either. My week's preparation has simply shown me that I have not got the physical fitness necessary to make the test. It is more of physical endurance test than I imagined it would be at first."

She pointed out the obvious: The season was late, it was getting too cold in the mountains to parade around in a grass costume, and the prospect of living on a "monotonous" diet of berries and wild cucumbers was not appealing. Cooking your food in a birchbark pan, over a fire you started by rubbing sticks together, was "infinitely more difficult than preparing a chafing dish spread or a gas stove dinner at home." No more attractive was the idea of killing a wild animal and getting her hands "all covered with blood." She added, "No man seems to think this a matter of any importance, but girls do not always see these things as a man does."

Still, Hammerstein tried to go out on a high note, declaring a new love for nature and the deep and magisterial forest. "Tango teas, Broadway and matinees are a far cry from the absolute silences of these woods," she said. While she was the wrong girl for the job, she thought that there must be plenty of others who could do the job successfully. The trick for a nature girl was facing the facts of nature, she said, and not relying on "beautiful theories she has gleaned from her piazza reading of John Burroughs or Thoreau."

According to Stewart H. Holbrook in the *American Mercury*, Knowles's only comment on Hammerstein's defection was "She just couldn't take it." For once, he was left without anything more to say. Holbrook added, "With the Dawn Woman back in her sissy boudoir, there wasn't any use of sticking around, so Joe came out of the woods himself and put on his pants." The third and final nature test was over.

Knowles never saw Elaine Hammerstein again; and if he had, he probably would have walked across the street to avoid having to say hello to her. They were from two irreconcilable worlds.

In his voluminous writings after the Adirondacks trip (most of it unpublished), Knowles refers to Hammerstein hardly at all. But he may have taken some consolation from a letter he received just after emerging from the woods. Elsie Frick of 148th Street in New York City wrote to him offering her services as a nature girl, if a replacement was needed. "If you decide to continue your experiment," she wrote, "you will find me your obedient servant. I am city bred, tall and healthy."

EIGHT

The Artist
out of
the Woods

I{\sc n his chapter on the} B{\sc oy} S{\sc couts in} *A{\sc lone in the} W{\sc ilderness}*, Knowles lamented the fate of the average youth of 1913. While the boy of the nineteenth century had lived close to nature, he said, the modern boy was coddled, with his every whim catered to by parents who refused to give him any responsibility. "Today, all kinds of luxury surround the average boy," he wrote. "Even the sons and daughters of the very poor have their clubs, and[,] having them, enjoy more privileges than the boy of means years ago."

Even his toys are bought for him, said Knowles, who, as mentioned above, was so poor as a child that his only toys were ones he made himself. He remembered fondly the delight he took in a bow and arrow he fashioned out of scrap materials. It was all part of a deep education in self-reliance, forged mainly in the pristine woods of Maine.

"I realize only too well that the average Boy Scout will not go into the depths of the woods as I did," Knowles wrote. "However, I feel that the average American boy of reasonably good health, and with a reasonable amount of resourcefulness, could accomplish things in the forest that he and his parents would never dream of."

Knowles considered it the duty of parents to add to the rolls of what were then two million American Boy Scouts, and he made clear his approval of the Girl Scouts too. "Boys and girls," he said, "the responsibility of the future lies upon your shoulders. Study nature at every opportunity, for the more you know of nature the more you will know of true living."

The Boy Scouts of America did not ignore Knowles's kind words. They issued a special edition of *Alone in the Wilderness* in 1939 and began to consider him the ideal model of a Boy Scout leader. Perhaps this established route could be the fulfillment of the "school of the woods" that Knowles was always talking about.

By the spring of 1917, Knowles was in Portland, Oregon, where he had washed up after a final round of appearances on the Pacific Coast's Orpheum circuit. He was thus perfectly situated for an opportunity that came his way and, in the course of things, changed his life.

"Be Prepared." It is the Boy Scout motto, and also the heading on a flyer that went out in the early summer of 1917, announcing a Scout summer camp to be held at North Beach, near Ilwaco, Washington, between July 16 and August 15. The flyer doesn't mention it, but the camp director was Joe Knowles. If he had not necessarily found a calling, he at least had found something to do after the fiasco in the Adirondacks.

Knowles had not given up on his dreams of glory on the silver screen either. On July 5, he wrote to the Pathé Exchange production company to tell them he'd been appointed to the camp director job and that he was "anxious to have certain events on the trip pictured in the weekly [newsreels]."

He was probably thinking of the ambitious plans he had for the summer camp. According to the *San Francisco Examiner,* Knowles would supervise 400 Scouts, but 16 "striplings" would be selected for a special experiment in woodcraft, living on their wits "without tent, kit or provender." Tryouts for these coveted slots were held in San Francisco, Los Angeles, and other cities. The boys were to get one suit of clothing, two changes of underwear, and one double blanket. Everything else in terms of food, fire, and shelter would have to be sourced in the woods. It's unclear how this novel twist on Knowles's wilderness jaunts worked out, but the Scouts continued to hire him.

On July 17, after arriving in Ilwaco, he wrote to a newspaper correspondent in San Francisco, announcing that he'd arrived and was getting ready to produce some first-rate material for the papers. He had already made arrangements with J. G. Sill of Portland to shoot motion picture film, in case he could get that placed. "There won't be anything very thrilling at first, but what I want is to get the papers to run something in the daily so as to keep the stunt before the public. I am sending out an information column, illustrating and describing our daily work, which will give the public a chance to ask questions. . . ."

He was looking in a different direction a month later. The month in the woods had been a tonic to him, and Knowles was now trying to get backing for his school of the wilderness from the owner of the Ilwaco camp, E. E. Merges. "If we are surely going ahead with our nature school, I should like to close the deal before turning down any other offer," he wrote on August 21 from Seaview, just up the peninsula from Ilwaco.

Knowles was clearly anxious for Merges to come through with a contract, because he dangled the possibility that if the money wasn't forthcoming, he might have to take another offer. "I ask that you give this your immediate attention, as I am just now in receipt of an offer from Jake Subert to play the part of the nature man in his new production, 'The Show of Wonders.'"

In the end, nothing seems to have come of any of these possibilities, though Knowles did acquire his much-beloved "singing" dog Wolf (half husky and half timber wolf) from Merges. There were to be no more nature-man films, and the school of the woods was never opened. (However, Knowles did continue sporadically as a Boy Scout leader, attending Camp Clelland, operated by the Tumwater Council, B.S.A., in the Olympic National Forest as late as 1930. The boys were reportedly "overjoyed" to learn he was coming.)

"Jake Subert" was actually Jacob J. Shubert, who with his brothers built an enormous theatrical empire (including the Shubert and Winter Garden theaters in New York City). They were already leading theater powers in 1917. "The Show of Wonders" was an original musical revue that ran from October 1916 to April 1917, so it was already closed down when Knowles mentioned it in his letter.

Might the production have gone on the road after it closed at the Winter Garden in Manhattan, or was Knowles dangling an offer that had already expired? The role of "Hermit Joe," which possibly would have gone to Knowles, was in fact played by Ed-

ward Mulcahy. It would be fun to hear the song "Back to Nature," sung by Iona Richley and the Back-to-Nature Girls, today.

For whatever reason, Knowles did not launch a new career on
Broadway, and his first visit to Ilwaco did not produce any new
and lucrative ventures. But it did help him find a place to put down
roots. As he told the *Raymond Herald,* when the Boy Scout trip
ended he stayed behind to record on canvas some of the "beauty
spots" he'd seen while hiking around the area. "The colorful sun-
sets were most alluring," he said. He fell in love with the narrow,
thirty-mile-long Long Beach Peninsula, which boasts of one of the
longest continuous stretches of sand on the Pacific Coast. The
peninsula points north like a finger from the Oregon border and
is not far from the turbulent spot where the mighty Columbia
River meets the Pacific Ocean. The peripatetic wanderer and ad-
venturer built a home in Seaview and never left.

When Lewis and Clark's "Corps of Discovery" reached Pillar
Rock on the north shore of the Columbia on November 7, 1805,
William Clark wrote in his journal, "Great joy in camp we are in
View of the Ocian, this great Pacific Octean which we been So
long anxious to See." They were constantly wet from the damp climate and their clothes were rotting off their backs, but the end
of their westward journey was in sight—or so they thought.

At Pillar Rock, the Columbia widens and becomes an estuary.
For the first time in their journey of more than 4,000 miles, the
group could look west and see nothing but an unbroken expanse
of water. In reality, though, they were still eighteen miles from the
Pacific. They didn't reach the actual coast until November 18, at
the stormy point that had been aptly named Cape Disappointment by the English explorer Captain John Meares in 1788. Lewis

and Clark found the Long Beach Peninsula so rainy and foggy that they chose to winter on the other side of the river.

At the Columbia River Maritime Museum in Astoria, Oregon, amid heroic dioramas of Coast Guard rescue ships listing on fiberglass waves, a plaque tells the rather grim story: "Since 1792," it says, "approximately 2,000 vessels, including 200 large ships, have sunk at the Columbia River bar, and more than 700 people have lost their lives. . . . " The perfect storm is created by high seas and fast currents meeting a wild but shallow river at a place where shifting sands can catch unwary working traffic. It richly earns the title "Graveyard of the Pacific."

In Lewis and Clark's day, the peninsula was home to the Chinook Indians, whose sage navigation of the river's dangerous shoals and currents in seagoing canoes came through long experience. The Hudson's Bay Company appointed Chief Comcomly as its head river pilot.

Ilwaco was first settled in the 1840s, and the area initially supported small populations of oyster fishermen and cranberry pickers. A huge oyster boom (fueled by the California gold rush) enriched many residents in the mid-nineteenth century, but overly enthusiastic harvesting caused the lucrative seafood that gave Oysterville its name to play out by the 1880s. The trade was gradually rebuilt with farmed oysters.

But, fortunately for Ilwaco, commercial salmon fishing emerged to replace the oysters. The fish that Lewis and Clark became heartily sick of eating helped save the peninsula. The first salmon-packing company arrived in the mid-1850s, and by 1882 fishermen had successfully adapted trapping methods from the Great Lakes. Ilwaco's population swelled to 300.

A Finn named B. A. Seaborg opened a cannery in Ilwaco in 1880 and later started up a sawmill. He provided work for other Finns, and soon Finnish was more commonly heard in the area than English. Today, the saunas attached to some of the weatherbeaten homes in Ilwaco seem incongruous until you learn the history.

When Knowles first saw Ilwaco, it was still recovering from twenty-eight years of open warfare between gillnet fishermen and salmon trappers. The groups sabotaged each other's operations, eventually resulting in the National Guard being called in.

In 1917, the year Knowles arrived, both the *Lenore,* a fishing boat, and the *Captain James Fornace,* a steamship, were lost on the Columbia River bar. The next year, the loss of the *Americana,* a schooner, would drown thirteen people. Knowles would have first-hand exposure to many shipwrecks as he built his home in Seaview right on the beach.

The water was always rough, the currents treacherous. Adele Beechey of Ocean Park, who is now eighty-eight, has one clear firsthand memory of Joseph Knowles, and it's from the 1930s. "People would get caught in the waves and drown," she said. "I remember being down on the beach one time and seeing a man lying on the beach, with Joe and another man standing over him. They were arguing about the best way to resuscitate him. Joe said to turn him on his stomach and the other man said to turn him on his back, but it didn't matter because the poor fellow was already dead." Theresa Potter of Seaview, eighty-two, remembers Knowles as a pudgy "W. C. Fields type of character" with a "disreputable hat and sloppy pants," whose dogs killed the neighbors' chickens. She says he picked up paper from the wreck of the steamship *Iowa* (which went down in 1936 with a loss of thirty-four lives) and used it for etchings that he would sell to tourists for $3 each.

"Mother Ocean supplies all my wants," the *New Yorker* of 1938 quoted him as saying. "All I have to do is sit and wait, and she throws up what I need at my door. She gave me driftwood for my house. The other day she gave me a can of kerosene for light. She gives me clams and fish and crabs. The pancakes I had for breakfast this morning were made out of flour from a wrecked ship." And he confirmed Potter's memory: "One time last summer Mother Ocean brought me in some of the finest etching paper I have ever used."

The home Knowles built in Seaview (some say the second of two) was constructed at least partially of driftwood found on the beach, and that's the way Knowles himself usually described it. But, while it lacked interior plumbing and at least initially electric lighting, it was more than just a shack. Photographs show a naturally shingled cottage on stilts with a handsome dormer window. Inside was a skinny but sturdy iron stove Knowles had bought for $1.50, a daybed, a crudely built table and buffet, and a sparse arrangement of driftwood chairs. Peggy Lucas, a freelance writer in Astoria, Oregon, wrote a lengthy obituary of Knowles and seems to have known the artist well. She said that Knowles's three-room house was decorated in a style that could be described as "early American flotsam," but she added that it was "as comfortable as an old shoe." Above the door, a sign said "Welcome Stranger." Another sign on the corner of the house said "Joe Knowles the Nature Man, ETCHINGS, OILS=WATER COLORS."

Rodney Williams, who still lives in Long Beach, says that in the 1930s his family owned (and still owns) a home in Seaview only a few blocks from where Knowles lived. "[Knowles's] house is now long gone and sat on a short bend in the Seaview drainage creek (locally pronounced 'crick') that still serves that purpose," Williams said in a letter. "It stops flowing in the summer but runs briskly during wintertime. In the 1930s the house was probably within 1,000 feet of the ocean and on at least once [*sic*] occasion the house took a log through the front door caused by a storm surge up the creek. Further to the east, perhaps another 1,000 feet or so, lay the ruins of another house which I'm told was the original Knowles house when they first moved to the Peninsula." But Williams couldn't vouch for the authenticity of that story about the first house, and other memories of it are hazy also.

There was a garage next to the house, with Knowles's art studio above it. An outhouse with an excellent view of the beach completed the Knowles estate, and when it was in use the artist was rumored to have left the door open so as better to observe the passing scene.

In his 1938 *New Yorker* piece, Richard O. Boyer says that Knowles's "crazily angled" house was "lapped on three sides by the Pacific." The description got Knowles's dander up, since he was very proud of his work. "Strange as it may seem, I have no recollection of having ever met the gentleman or even heard of him," he wrote in the *Chinook Observer* some months after the magazine story appeared. "I did not mind the personal cracks but when he called my home a 'crazily angled shack with a meaningless sign of welcome over the door,' I failed to see any humor in that remark."

There's no evidence that Boyer and Knowles ever did meet, but Knowles was still alive and living in Seaview in 1938, so it's possible. What's more likely is that Boyer relied on the telephone on his New York desk, and talked to a few local residents (and possibly Knowles himself).

As soon as the house was built, Knowles sent for his wife, Marion Louise, who was still in San Francisco. He and Marion made good the promise to welcome strangers at their home built of flotsam. He proved himself a congenial host and a good friend. Theresa Potter says Marion Knowles was "a very nice person" who shared Knowles's love of company.

Letters to Knowles are full of references to warm-hearted evenings spent in his company, and the wish that they could be repeated at the earliest opportunity. Ross Carpenter, an artist friend from Los Angeles who was also trying to make a go of selling short stories, wrote Knowles in 1931, "I often envy you in your picturesque surroundings, your cozy housing and especially in your chance to do what you like to do in your art work and writing."

Many older residents of the peninsula say they were warmly received by Joe Knowles and his household when they were children. Some even got their portraits painted. Emery Neale, who later became a director of the Ilwaco Heritage Museum and donated considerable Knowles memorabilia to it, sat for the artist when he was twelve. Edna May Lidin of Kelso told the *Cowlitz Historical Quarterly* that she met Knowles when she was a teenager, and was fascinated by his big nose. "She recalls listening fascinated as he told stories," the *Quarterly* said.

Virginia Williams Jones, a Portland, Oregon artist and a first cousin to Rodney Williams, also has very fond memories of the Knowles family's hospitality. When she was a newlywed in Ilwaco in 1938, she and her policeman husband were feted by Joe and Marion Knowles at their home. Jones remembers the Knowles beach house as a "flimsy" affair, with the wood stove in the kitchen "sitting mostly on sand." Still, Marion produced an excellent welsh rarebit for the company.

The best part of that long-ago evening, Jones says, was the colorful anecdotes from one and all. "Everyone there was a big storyteller in his own right, but Joe held forth to top all," she said. "It was his show and he regaled us with many a story. He would get so excited and laughing that he would practically spit all over the place getting it out—red-faced to tell all!"

Mary Jane "Fuzzy" Walker, so named for her big head of frizzy hair, is a descendant of an old pioneer family in Ilwaco, and she and her dog still live there in a weatherbeaten home (with a Finnish sauna out back). In the 1930s, her family and Joe and Marion were neighbors. "I knew Joe Knowles forever," she said in an interview. "I used to spend all my time there as a little girl. Because he never had children, I was like the next best thing and his door was always open to me. He would tell sea stories, about people he met who wore bones through their noses, and I would just be sitting there with my mouth open. Maybe he was making some of those stories up on the spot, but they were great. My grandmother got mad at me for not coming home when I was supposed to. Joe even painted a picture of me by a big log there on the beach. I'd love to see that portrait again."

Walker describes Ilwaco as a good place to grow up despite the Depression, because even without money the ocean provided plenty of oysters, salmon, clams, and crabs. And the restless sea also provided bounty in the form of cargo from the wrecked ships that the kids also played on and around: Walker remembers cases

MARY JANE "FUZZY" WALKER AT HOME IN ILWACO. JIM MOTAVALLI PHOTO

of oranges, hams, and flour (the same stuff Knowles used to make his pancakes).

To wait out the Depression, Knowles was probably better off on the Washington coast than he would have been in Maine. In 1932, his niece Clara wrote to say "the Depression is terrible here in the east. . . . The woolen mill here closed January 1 indefinitely.

There isn't another thing do in the whole town, so it's awful on the laboring class." Clara's husband did find work on a farm—unpaid, but at least he was able to help himself to farm produce.

Despite inveighing against the evils of demon rum in *Alone* ("I don't even have to mention liquor to a Boy Scout, for he well knows its evils"), Knowles was a legendary drinker. "He certainly didn't turn them down," says Walker. "It was mostly home brew in those days [especially with Prohibition in place from 1920 to 1933], and after he'd gotten into the jugs of white lightning he would start on his writing." When he wasn't drinking, he was chewing tobacco and spitting the juice and remnants into a coffee can. Marion Louise Knowles rolled the homemade cigarettes the pair smoked.

Walker's parents frequently got "soused" with Knowles, and there were illustrious visitors as well. Though she didn't personally meet the great man (dead since 1916), Walker says Knowles often talked about time spent with Jack London and their adventures together—which supposedly included many boat trips. Walker says that one story involved a pair of pet monkeys. When they'd swab the decks of London's boat, the monkeys would, according to the tale, assist with toothbrushes.

Walker did meet the famous actor Edward Everett Horton, a great friend of Knowles and a frequent summer visitor to the peninsula. Knowles was commissioned to paint Horton's portrait, but it's uncertain whether the work was actually done.

"He used to come visit all the time, and I got to know him very well," Walker says. Perhaps Knowles saw a kindred spirit in Horton, who started out playing small parts in Broadway plays and touring in vaudeville. Horton was born in Brooklyn, the son of a *New York Times* proofreader and the grandson of Edward Everett

Hale, the abolitionist and short-story writer ("The Man Without a Country").

A onetime Columbia University student, Horton moved to Los Angeles in 1919 and began getting better roles in Hollywood films, including a lead in the 1922 comedy *Too Much Business*. Horton is best known as a character actor, a fussbudget who did a mean double-take, and he successfully transitioned into sound films. A frequent foil for Fred Astaire and Ginger Rogers, he can be seen in *The Front Page, Alice in Wonderland, The Merry Widow, The Gay Divorcee, Arsenic and Old Lace,* and many more—100 films in all, all the way up to *Sex and the Single Girl* in 1964 (and, amusingly enough, a remake of *The Perils of Pauline* in 1967). Despite all this, Horton is probably best remembered today as the narrator of the cartoon *Fractured Fairy Tales,* which debuted in 1959 as part of the series *Rocky and His Friends.*

During his time on the peninsula, Horton stayed in a rental cottage, rode horses on the beach, and was, like Knowles, a frequenter of the Ilwaco Theater (where several Knowles paintings were on display). On one occasion, theater owner Charles Strauhal scheduled Horton's 1923 film *To the Ladies,* based on a George S. Kaufman play, to coincide with the actor's visit, and he made a personal appearance. It's possible that Knowles and Horton met through that popular theater (which was later knocked down to make way for the Sea Hag bar).

It's fun to imagine the suave Hollywood insider—who was often mistaken for an Englishman—using Knowles's outhouse, smoking his smelly cigars, and sharing his homemade moonshine. It's entirely possible that Horton had known Elaine Hammerstein during his New York days, or later in Los Angeles, and perhaps a discussion of her enlivened one of their beach evenings.

Knowles had certain obsessions and definitely some frustrations, but he also knew how to relax with good friends around him. "Avast there, Sailor Knowles!" wrote Portland attorney U. T. DeMartini in 1935. "I hope I may assume from your steady-handed autograph that your liver is now hitting on all eight cylinders, and that you are pleasantly sitting up there in your citadel beside a cheerful fire and your devoted Mukaluks [the second of two doted-upon dogs], puffing a fragrant stogie and expectorating into one of those handy tin spitkids. . . . When I think of the vigorous and independent life you have led, I cannot help feeling that the rest of us are only monkeys in a cage—with nowhere to go and nothing to do but snatch for peanuts and scratch our genitals while the world of wonders goes by without our knowing it."

But Knowles couldn't just lie back and enjoy his ease. The nature experiments and films, as splashy as they may have been, paid him very little money. And his efforts to secure a new booking in that line had not proven fruitful. But could lightning strike a fourth time?

In late 1917, when Knowles was still a new arrival, the *Ilwaco Tribune* carried a story suggesting that he might have another trip lined up. "It is reported that Joe Knowles, the famous 'nature man,' will pull off some of the stunts that brought him national notoriety in the Maine woods," the story said, "by going into the Bear River Mountains [part of the Wasatch Range in northeastern Utah and southeastern Idaho] bare handed, bare footed and rather generally bare everything else, providing himself with clothing, food and other comfort by the exercise of his knowledge of woodcraft. He was a prominent figure at the annual encampment of the Boy Scouts at the beach last summer."

It sounded good, but this new expedition never came together. Knowles must at least have visited the Bear River Mountains, however, because the Ilwaco Heritage Museum owns an excellent painting of his titled *Bear River* and dated 1917. It shows a shack by a river's edge, and is one of the only Knowles paintings to show the clear influence of Vincent van Gogh.

In the early 1920s, Knowles corresponded with a Portland, Oregon woman named Helen Gray Drollinger about the possible use of her property, known as Short Sand Beach—158 acres of ocean beach, woods, streams, and mountains on the Oregon coast near Tillamook Bay—for use as a nature school. Drollinger even suggested that he could take on "Nature Singer" Charles Kellogg, with whom she was in touch, as an instructor.

As late as 1931, Joe Knowles was still trying to renew his contract as the Nature Man. Chicago-based Harry Overman, an insurance agent, became Knowles's advocate and tried to put together a syndicate of papers, including the *Milwaukeee Journal, Detroit News,* and *Chicago Daily News,* to sponsor a new expedition, probably in the Michigan or Wisconsin woods (since, as Overman described it, "Illinois is too thickly populated to put it on"). But times were hard, and of the three the only paper willing to take part was the *Daily News,* which lacked the wherewithal on its own. That same year, Overman also queried the New York-based North American Newspaper Alliance, which replied, "I'm sorry, but we don't see our way clear to go into the Joe Knowles project."

Without work as a Nature Man, there was now the delicate question of how to make a living. Knowles never stopped trying to interest movie companies, newspapers, and book publishers in another nature jaunt, but he also recognized that after three well-publicized "experiments," his stunt may have played itself out.

In one early venture, Knowles was appointed as an unpaid deputy sheriff. According to a 1919 account in the *Ilwaco Tribune*, this unlikely post almost immediately landed him in trouble. Knowles was deputized to assist A. T. Samuels, described as "the sugar-coated songster of Ilwaco," in taking possession of a home occupied by "Portland author" M. E. Wells. It seems that Wells had sold his home to Samuels, but was reluctant to vacate the premises. Samuels and Knowles went to the house and occupied it, whereupon an enraged Wells appeared and ordered them to leave. When they declined, Wells "assaulted Mr. Knowles with a dangerous weapon, to wit, a hammer." Samuels and Knowles forcibly disarmed Wells, for which indignity Wells managed to have the pair arrested. Samuels then swore out a warrant for Wells's arrest, charging assault.

This sordid affair ended up before a justice of the peace in the summer of 1919. In a fit of honesty, Wells testified that if he had found a weapon at hand more effective than the hammer, he would not have hesitated to use it. He also admitted trying to push Knowles out of the house, leading the unknown reporter to comment that Wells's testimony "did not help his side of the controversy."

Knowles also testified, denying that he had beaten, bruised, choked, or otherwise manhandled Wells, as was alleged in the complaint, though he did subdue the man and hold him on the floor until he saw reason. Knowles and Samuels were eventually acquitted, as was Wells. It's interesting to note that Samuels retained the Astoria, Oregon, law firm of Norblad & Hesse. Albin Norblad later became governor of Oregon (1929–1931) and had his official portrait painted by Joe Knowles. This early connection may have helped Knowles get the commission.

But Knowles's career as a deputy sheriff was apparently short-lived, as was a brief stint later on as a wrestling promoter on the peninsula. He did spend a fair amount of time in court, but as either a litigant or a scofflaw.

A 1924 *Ilwaco Tribune* headline read: "Knowles Taken Under Traffic Laws." He was known as a wild driver. Neighbor Adele Beechey says her husband used to tell this story about Knowles: One time, when he was flush with cash, he bought a new car, a Rickenbacker, and took several "slightly intoxicated" cronies out for a test drive. Railroad tracks ran through Seaview then, and Knowles tried to outrun a train. Unfortunately, his Rickenbacker proved unequal to the task, so Knowles swerved it into a ditch at the last minute. The shaken passengers were reassured by Knowles, who said, "Don't worry, boys, it's fully insured!"

In another version of the story, Knowles actually managed to collide broadside with the train before his car was tossed into the ditch. He broke two ribs, but his two passengers, women in this version, escaped with only scratches and bruises.

In 1921, when Knowles was still finding his way as a resident of the peninsula, he was tracked down by Fred Lockley, a reporter for the *American Magazine.* The article Lockley wrote is fascinating, because it depicts Knowles as still very much the primitive nature man, living outside society, when in fact by that time he had largely put his bearskin away.

Lockley takes a walk along the peninsula coast, from Ilwaco to Long Beach, and there encounters a man hanging out salmon to dry on a line. It was Joe Knowles, and the salmon were a gift from local fishermen. He was, he said, still enjoying the simple life. "No," he said, "you wouldn't exactly say I have drifted into port, for I may feel the lure of the far horizon at any time." He once again attributed his restlessness to the Indian blood he had inherited from his father.

"I could never stay long away from the woods or the sea," he told Lockley. "In the city I always heard the call of the wild. . . . Time and again I have entered the woods both in Maine and here on the Pacific coast with the clothing I had when I was born. Naked and without a man-made thing, I depend on Nature who, if we will but realize it, is our friend and protector. . . . We have gone stale by living within brick walls and by depending on steam heat and push buttons."

Knowles was laying it on a bit thick for a willing listener. He sounded the familiar themes: the goodness of nature's bounty; the best ways to catch fish with homemade nets; making fire from sticks. He told Lockley that he was never lost in the woods. "I am at home, no matter where I am," he said. A photo of Knowles in his bearskin was captioned "He won't stay in civilization long. Soon he will be back again to the wilds."

In reality, this wild man was becoming increasingly domesticated. He'd decided that he had to find his place, if not in a city then at least in the company of other men. And once he found it, he rarely wandered far again. In a letter to his friend Ross Carpenter, gently declining an offer of a stay in California, Knowles said he'd love a change of scenery but would inevitably miss his "foggy coastline" and "the moaning of a distant sea."

Knowles had two serious options that he considered to be open to him: return to his work as an artist, or become a writer. While his heart seems to have been set on the latter, he had far more success at the former. But he pursued both at his own pace.

When it came to his art, Knowles was a persistent and often successful self-promoter. He sought and received many public commissions, and the results were usually pleasing to his patrons.

As a public artist and muralist, Joe Knowles bore almost no resemblance to Diego Garcia, the Marxist renegade whose master
work at Rockefeller Center was painted over in 1933 because it
depicted Soviet leader Lenin. As Knowles firmly declared in an
undated and unpublished essay, he was a proud traditionalist.

"Art," he wrote, "like every human developement [*sic*], has
gone through its periods of ups and downs, and has had to battle
against freakishness and vagaries of various kinds. But always
there has been a conservative, educated thinking majority that has
insisted on the great fundimentals [*sic*] which formed the foun-
dation of all Schools from the early Egyptain [*sic*] to the Modern
and which have always been at war [with] the revolutionary and
grotesque and looking to greater and greater expression of beauty
in line and color.

"Fifteen or more years ago," he continued in this impromptu
art history lesson, "a few medioccrities [*sic*] in Paris became discouraged over their lack of success in making a living and began to rail at Acedemicism [*sic*] and started out to found what has
become falsely styled Modernism. The real Moderns were [George
Van] Millett, Dias, Rouseau [*sic*], Degas, Renior [*sic*], Monet and
Manet in France; Turner, Constable and others in England; Rib-
era, Velasque [*sic*] and others in Spain; and El Greco (The Greek).
The little group composed of Picasso, Matisse, Gaugin [*sic*] and
others outdid all other attempts at producing the most hideous
and grotesque, meaningless trash the world has ever seen. No
wonder it attracted attention. Monstrosities, freaks, contorted
and distorted cripples have always been subjects of interest and
commiseration to the masses, and why not these like things
in art?"

Knowles was a modernist only in that his work was inspired by then-contemporary Western painters, such as Charles Marion Russell, George Catlin, and Frederic Remington. Perhaps because he was mostly self-taught, he respected the Academy and was outraged by attempts to storm its barricades. Happily for him, these elements combined to make his work eminently salable, particularly to patrons fond of declaring that while they didn't know much about art, they "knew what they liked."

Among his earliest lucrative ventures was a series of copper-plate etchings of storm-tossed sailing ships, feathered Indian chiefs, nostalgic farmhouses, rocky shores and more, all of it suitable for framing and display in the most genteel of living rooms.

In an essay on Knowles that was part of her *Observing Our Peninsula's Past, Volume 1: The Age of Legends Through 1931*, historian and artist Nancy Lloyd of Oysterville, Washington, writes that the artist's etchings "favored maritime scenes (ships under sail, fishing boats, men hauling in nets loaded with salmon) which sold well. . . . While it is fair, and even conservative, to define Knowles as an eccentric—his orbit did differ from most peoples'—there is no possible question about the excellence of his artwork."

Knowles addressed his etching technique in another unpublished writing fragment. "To make an etching in 'bitten line,' a polished copper plate is covered with a coating of 'etching ground' (a composition of wax, resin and asphaltum), then the ground is smoked on the surface of the plate, the design is drawn with a steel point, laying the copper bare wherever it passes. The plate is now ready for the acid which bites into the copper where the steel point has passed. The plate is now cleaned of the remaining

ground, the lines filled with ink, and the print made on a damp-
ened paper under extreme pressure."

Philippine Schmidt Rettenmayer, the San Francisco art dealer
who enjoyed Knowles's Indian heads, wrote to the artist in 1931
asking why he did not, as was common practice, number his etchings in a limited run, then destroy the plates. Knowles tended to
be cavalier about such things. Though his prints have a printed
and signed sticker identifying them as in either the first or second run, it's plain that some of his fuzzier prints were made from
badly worn and perhaps overworked plates.

He addressed this obliquely in his etching essay: "Since the
work is dormant in the copper plate and comes to life only in
the printed impression on paper," he wrote, "each print is really
original, placing us directly in relation with the artist." To Rettenmayer, he wrote back to say that the soft copper plates allowed
him to make only a few prints each, so this inherent limitation was
better than numbering.

According to Peggy Lucas, Knowles liked to work on his etchings at night, laboring straight through until dawn. "Knowles
often sang while he worked," Lucas wrote, "and the songs he min-
gled with the scratches of knife on copper were the chanties of
the sea and ballads he picked up from the backwoods guides
of Maine."

The artist's goal seems to have been volume, not artistic perfection. Ilwaco had already become a summer beach retreat,
and in the summer the many tourists became etching customers
at $3 each. Today, these same unchallenging but nonetheless
pleasing works (tinted a rich and nostalgic brown) are highly
sought after and enthusiastically bid for, on eBay and elsewhere. "It is a measure of the quality of his etchings and paint-

ings that 60 years after his death in the 1940s, Joe Knowles's work is still so valued by its owners that it rarely comes up for sale, regardless of price," wrote Nancy Lloyd in her *Age of Legends* essay.

Knowles's reputation as an artist grew on the peninsula and beyond. He took commissions large and small. One he accepted sometime in the early 1920s was for a large painting to be placed in Hellberg's Drugstore in the Astoria, Oregon, neighborhood of Uniontown. According to Bruce Berney, an ardent admirer of the work Knowles produced, Hellberg's had an ice cream fountain "where all the Finns chattered away."

The work was commissioned by Frostkist, a local creamery, to be placed prominently in the soda fountain. Knowles duly created a seven-foot-long, forty-inch-high oil painting on a wooden frame depicting two couples picnicking on an island beach with their canoes tied up in the background. In the lower left is a wicker picnic basket with a thermos and a box of Frostkist Ice Cream sticking out.

"The story is that Mr. Hellberg detested the picture," Berney wrote. "He thought the thermos was way too large, and that if those people had rowed all the way across the water on a hot summer day the ice cream would have melted." At the end of Prohibition in 1933, Hellberg decided he wanted to retail liquor instead of ice cream sodas and used that as an excuse to get rid of the Frostkist painting, which was donated to the city of Astoria. For more than thirty years, the painting hung in the publicly owned Shively Hall, where it sustained some damage from smoke and boys' basketballs.

Berney became the Astoria librarian in 1967 and soon afterward accepted the painting for display to the right of the library's main doors. Fortunately, it was completely restored by a young art instructor from the local community college. But after Berney retired in 1997 the painting was taken down and put in storage in the basement. "I am vexed that the present librarian won't put it back where it belongs," Berney says.

The story of the Frostkist picture has many echoes in Knowles's career. Some of his works thought lost have since turned up, and others languish in storage. For instance, the Columbia River Maritime Museum's fine art collection contains a splendid and atypical Knowles oil depicting a very turbulent sea with, in the far background, a three-masted ship under full sail and looking very fragile indeed. But the three-foot-wide work is in storage.

On the other hand, two very large and age-darkened Knowles landscape paintings have pride of place in the Ilwaco Heritage Museum. The evidence strongly suggests that these works were originally commissioned by Charles Strauhal (the Ilwaco Theater owner), in 1924. This silent film house showed the hits of the day for a mere thirty-five cents for adults, ten cents for children. Both Knowles and his wife Marion were regular patrons at the Ilwaco.

According to the *Astoria Evening Budget,* there had originally been six large paintings, measuring six feet by twelve feet, depicting, among other things, *Deadman's Hollow,* a cove into which the bodies of people drowned on the Columbia River were carried. Another was of a North Beach sunset. These were "mural decorations outstripping any of the northwest in point of beauty and value."

At some point, two of the paintings were sold to the Columbia Inn in Kalama, Washington, where they also had pride of place. If they hadn't fortunately been removed for cleaning at the time, they might have burned up in a spectacular fire that reduced the inn to a cinder in 1980. It's a guess whether these nearly-lost artworks are the same ones hanging in the museum, but it seems likely.

Unbeknownst to Knowles, soon after he arrived on the peninsula, events had been set in motion that would dramatically change his fortunes for the better. In 1918, Robert A. Long of Kansas City's Long-Bell Lumber Company was sixty-eight years old, with a fortune estimated at $20 million made from huge timber operations in Louisiana and Texas.

The future prospects for Long-Bell were excellent, except for one problem: The timber resources the company relied on were fast disappearing. Long could simply have retired and enjoyed his vast fortune, but instead he enlisted his company in a bold plan. Not only would they relocate logging operations to the Pacific Northwest, where the old-growth Douglas fir (some of it completely untouched by human civilization) stood 200 feet high, but they would build the world's biggest sawmill and a town to provide it with services.

Long's timber scouts located a 23,000-acre tract of fir, cedar, and hemlock belonging to the Weyerhauser Company and containing an astonishing 2.4 billion board feet of wood. To that they would add many other tracts, eventually totaling almost 70,000 acres. The trees were in Washington's Lewis and Cowlitz Counties, and the location of the sawmill was chosen carefully as offering both an excellent labor situation, a deep-water site on the Columbia where it converged with the Cowlitz River (offering easy access to Astoria and the major ports of the world), and excellent potential for developing a surrounding town. All the land necessary for the sawmill operation, some 2,600 acres, could be bought from just four landowners for $413,000.

The site was secured in February 1921, and the task of actually building the new town of Longview began. This considerable enterprise is detailed in John M. McClelland, Jr.'s book *R. A. Long's Planned City: The Story of Longview,* published in celebration of the town's seventy-fifth birthday in 1998.

Since Joe Knowles loved the untrammeled woods, he would presumably have deplored its sacrifice as toothpicks and two-by-fours for the building trade. By 1924, the new West Fir mill was churning out up to 800,000 board feet of lumber a day, much of it from magnificent heritage trees. The next year, East Fir was up and running with a similar, if not greater, volume. But while he may never have seen a poem as lovely as a tree, Knowles was also on the lookout for memorable art commissions.

The first settlement on the west bank of the Cowlitz River was named Monticello, and a visitor there in 1850 had prophetically announced that he envisioned the "greatest city to arise in the Northwest, with great buildings of stone and brick where now only log cabins or none at all stand." As it happened, the forward-looking planners of Longview paid little heed to the pioneer heritage there, declining to name any of the new streets after early settlers. But they did agree to the name for the Hotel Monticello, replacing a derelict but historic building of that name that had recently collapsed.

The new six-story hotel, a showplace in classic colonial style for the new town and necessary to house the many visitors arriving from Kansas City, had a steel-reinforced concrete structure. It was put up in a rush, with whole eighteen-car freight trains of furniture arriving express from Chicago. No expense was spared on the 160 rooms, each with its own bathroom, and mahogany paneling was applied to the lobby.

Such a richly appointed lobby deserved artistic enhancement. *R. A. Long's Planned City* relates that Hamilton Higday, one of Longview's real-estate salesmen, had been to the Long Beach Peninsula and there had encountered Joe Knowles, "an artist whose style and subjects had a remarkable resemblance to those of Montana's famous Charles Russell."

Higday was impressed when Knowles made fire for him with an Indian drill. "He is a man of poise, evident education and learning, and broad common sense," Higday said, although he was wrong about the education. He lobbied to give Knowles the commission to paint murals on the "winning of the west" in the lobby, but Long rejected this idea because the opening, scheduled for the summer of 1923, was on a tight schedule and it would take too much time.

The hotel's architect suggested that they should commission a fast and inexpensive frieze along the lobby ceiling line and then take their time finding appropriate paintings. But Knowles, ever resourceful when in search of a commission, went to Longview and argued forcefully that he worked quickly. Instead of murals that had to be painted in place, he would record the history of the founding of the Pacific Northwest in individual oils, which could be completed at his Seaview studio and transported to the hotel. He said he would complete the paintings for $500 to $600 each and would finish all forty-two in a record sixty days. Knowles painstakingly prepared a book of watercolor renditions of his proposed works and sent it to Long.

Knowles would form a lifelong friendship with Hughes Bryant, the manager of the R. A. Long Building in Kansas City and Longview's appointed building inspector. Bryant wrote to Knowles in December of 1923: "I shall be very glad indeed to look at this prospectus which you have presented to Mr. Long, as I know it will be quite interesting, and I sincerely hope that you may ultimately be favored with the order."

In January 1924, Bryant wrote again to say he had very much enjoyed the pictures and what he called "the narrative," so apparently Knowles had organized the disparate themes into a coherent story. "Mrs. Bryant and myself think the suggestions as you have presented them are splendid and the execution of the work quite wonderful," Bryant said.

It was obvious, however, that, beyond whatever aesthetic considerations he might have had, Bryant's principal concern was looking after the interests of timber magnate and civic visionary R. A. Long. "Perhaps you should have brought the narrative down to the Cowlitz River [bordering Longview] and not the Willamette," he wrote, "and that there should have been some pictures in the final narrative depicting the founding and the creation of Longview that is close to the heart of Mr. Long." He added: "By all means there should be some pictures portraying the vision and dream of Mr. R. A. Long in founding this wonderful new city. I merely offer this to you as a suggestion that may add more of an appeal to Mr. Long when he finally considers this matter."

Bryant and his wife loved the watercolor version of a painting tentatively called *The Wagon Train*, especially the "utter abandon" of its snorting horses, and asked Knowles if he could reproduce it for proud display above the Bryants' new fireplace in Kansas City. Knowles complied with this request, to the Bryants' complete satisfaction. The prospectus in which the early version of *The Wagon Train* appeared would later become a sore point, as in 1927 Knowles wrote Long-Bell seeking its return, and Bryant had to admit that he had searched the offices to no avail.

Bryant further suggested that his "good friend Mr. Knowles" might profit from contacting Washington Governor Louis F. Hart in Olympia, because similar pictures might be sold for display in the "magnificent new State House." Knowles later took up this idea, with great success.

Despite apparently ignoring Bryant's advice to add more work on the founding of Longview, Knowles got the Hotel Monticello job. But in fact he didn't work quite as fast as he'd said he would. By June 4, 1923, he had twenty canvases painted, eight of the portraits and twelve scenes of western pioneer days. The hotel opened on schedule with a grand banquet, attended by the governor, in the new Crystal Ballroom. It unfortunately opened without Knowles's completed panorama of paintings, though the gardens were enlivened with numerous rosebushes and 1,600 geraniums.

The full complement of paintings, now grown to forty-six with the addition of some decorative panels titled *Conquerors of the Trail*, was finally unveiled two years later. Knowles traveled to Longview to supervise the hanging of the works, and they were publicly revealed on August 5, 1925, in conjunction with the formation of the Cowlitz County Pioneer and Historical Society. According to a preview in the *Portland Oregonian*, both Knowles and R. A. Long would be on hand to give speeches. "Stereopticon [slide] views of the scenes will be thrown upon a screen outdoors," said the paper. "A few tableaux of historical events are included in the tentative program." The bill was lengthy, including vocalizing by the Kelso Ladies Quartette and songs by the Hotel Monticello Orchestra. There was even a picnic dinner.

The paintings were an immediate hit. It is impossible to gauge, in this television-sated age, the impact that an art exhibition could have had in an age with much less visual stimulation.

The lobby of Longview, Washington's Hotel Monticello, exhibits forty-six original Knowles paintings, including these portraits of (from left) John Jacob Astor, William Clark, Thomas Jefferson, and Meriwether Lewis. Jim Motavalli photo

According to the *Cowlitz Historical Quarterly,* "When [the paintings] were first displayed, they attracted attention throughout both Washington and Oregon and brought many guests to the Monticello. For example, it was quite the thing for Eastern Washingtonians on business trips to drive an extra 50 miles and spend the night at the Monticello in order 'to view the Knowles paintings, you know.'"

The Hotel Monticello is still there, and so is Joe Knowles's work, a permanent exhibition on display around the clock for more than eighty years. On a recent Friday afternoon, the virtually unchanged lobby of the recently renovated hotel was a bustling place, crisscrossed by guests and a multitude of workers. The framed paintings, newly cleaned by a curator, occupy nearly every free space along the paneled ceiling and are set off by a green carpet. Carved wooden details, gilded columns, and an ornate ceiling add to the period flavor.

The hotel's brochure misspells "Conquerors of the Trail," but it lists all forty-six works on display. Higday had apparently suggested to Knowles some of the subjects he might paint—Captain Gray discovering the Columbia River, the surrender of the Astorians to the British, Lewis and Clark in their canoes on the river, Hudson's Bay fur traders, immigrants on the Oregon Trail, and the coming of the railroad.

Knowles took some of these suggestions, but his Lewis and Clark are depicted on the arduous crossing of the Bitterroot Mountains, being led by a feathered Indian in the snow. He depicts numerous American Indian scenes, a variety of animals (wolves, buffalo, elk), and the emerging white man.

One of the finer works, situated over the front desk, is *The Wagon Train.* As much as seven feet wide, it shows a seemingly endless snaking loop of humanity moving relentlessly forward against a huge mountain landscape, with a sun-bleached cow skull in the foreground to remind the travelers of the dangers of the trail. It is indeed worthy of the best of Charles Russell. Like much of Knowles's work, it conveys its power with forceful composition and stylized movement rather than fine detail. Knowles admired the impressionists, if not some of their French contemporaries, and they had at least a minor influence on his work.

Another very dramatic painting is *The Wreck of the Ship Peacock,* which depicts a U.S. Navy ship coming to grief on the Columbia bar in 1841. Another strong maritime picture, *Gray's Ship The Columbia Rediviva,* with lots of wave action and flying seagulls, commemorates an eighteenth-century fur trader whose captain, Robert Gray, discovered and named the Columbia River in 1792. Knowles could always capture the romance of the ocean voyage in his work, a possible consequence of his own service.

Indian Cattle Rustlers will certainly catch the eye, because it is at least eight feet wide, with near-cinematic movement in the horses and cattle, set off by clouds of fine dust from the pounded sod. In *Attack on Fort Sheridan,* the horse-bound foray is enlivened by bold cloud formations.

The Vanishing Herd is one of the paintings that show the influence of Knowles's vigorous outdoors life. He had undoubtedly encountered its subjects in real life. Some of his white-rumped elk and reindeer gaze at the artist with apprehension, while others graze without fear. There is a great feeling of place in many of the paintings. A five-foot epic, *The Departing Red Man,* captures a moment of great poignancy as an Indian group, perhaps expelled from tribal lands, makes its way through a bleak landscape with Mount Hood in the background.

These paintings must have been very close to Knowles's heart, because taken together they firmly convey his lifelong love of animals, his affinity for nature, and his firm conviction that humans were ennobled by their exposure to it. As always, his American Indian subjects were sensitively portrayed.

In addition to their evocative scenes, the Hotel Monticello paintings include ten portraits that, amazingly enough, do not include R. A. Long. There are noble heads of William Clark and Meriwether Lewis, of course, plus many other historic figures in Pacific Northwest history: Vasco Nuñez de Balboa, the Spanish conquistador who discovered the Pacific Ocean in 1513 and claimed it for Spain; Sir Francis Drake, who reached the west coast of what is now the United States in 1579; Captain Robert Gray, the discoverer of the Columbia River; President Thomas Jefferson, who dispatched the Corps of Discovery; Sacagawea (the only woman in the group and an important guide for Lewis and Clark); John Jacob Astor, whose Pacific Fur Company established

Astoria as a trading post; and Chief Joseph, warrior chief of the Nez Perce tribe in northeastern Oregon. All these portraits are competent, though with some evidence of having been rushed. And some flatter their subjects rather more than others.

The Hotel Monticello lobby is a wonderful place to visit for a trip through the rich history of the region. And it's not bad for a look into the erratic but productive work ethic of Joseph Knowles, either.

According to several sources, Knowles's take for the Hotel Monticello paintings was $5,000, rather less than the $500 to $600 per painting he reportedly had sought but still an enormous sum at the time. Knowles was spectacularly imprudent with money, however, and he seems to have blown this fortune quickly. One major purchase, brought back from Portland, was the Rickenbacker touring car that he put in a ditch trying to outrace a train. The salesman was no less a personage than Eddie Rickenbacker himself. A hero approaching the luminosity of Charles Lindbergh (and just as conservative), Rickenbacker was a racing car driver turned pilot who had led the 94th Aero Pursuit Squadron in World War I and downed an amazing twenty-six enemy aircraft, winning the Medal of Honor in the process.

In 1921, faced with making a living, he started the Rickenbacker Motor Car Company and introduced a line of handsomely styled, mid-priced cars with the important engineering first of four-wheel brakes. This expensive innovation helped propel the company into insolvency by 1927, but not before the flush Joe Knowles bought one of its products.

By June 1928, Captain Rickenbacker was a hired hand at Cadillac, serving as sales manager of the LaSalle Division. In that capacity, he wrote to Knowles. "Your patronage and confidence in the writer and his product during the existence of the Ricken-backer Motor Car Company have not been taken lightly, as he is very grateful for same," he wrote in the third person, adding that he hoped to "again make possible the continuation of our old association."

It was a pretty good sales pitch, but there's no indication that Knowles bought a LaSalle. In 1923, he'd had no trouble paying $1,477 for a new Gardner complete with built-in radio, but by 1929, with the Rickenbacker possibly wrecked or out of com-mission, he was reduced to buying used, a 1926 four-cylinder Chrysler with payments of $37.08 per month.

Knowles's finances were always up and down, with windfalls fol-lowed by long periods of penury. "To him, money was so many pounds of copper," said Peggy Lucas. "Periodically he hit jack-pots, but the cash was stuffed back into ventures like fox farms and silver mines. And they didn't even pay out in bubble gum." It's even unclear if he was ever paid anything more than expenses for any of his nature expeditions. If he was, the details were kept quiet, and he likely spent the money quickly.

In 1924 and 1925, he borrowed money from banks in Ray-mond and Ilwaco in $300 and $400 increments. On June 24, 1925, his checking account had the grand total of 84 cents in it a perilous descent from the $3.51 he had on June 22. An exas-perated creditor with the prosaic name H. D. Thing wrote him many letters in 1929 and 1930 seeking payment of at least the $12 interest on a $100 loan he'd taken out. He was still begging for payments in 1932. "Now that the 'depression' is supposed to be about over, I would be pleased to have a payment on your note," Thing wrote.

Maxine Bown of Corvallis, Oregon, helped run her parents' store in Long Beach before World War II. She remembers Joe Knowles well as a man who would draw pictures of seagulls and ocean scenes on the store's eggs in lieu of repaying the money he owed. "My memory of him is that he was kind of slouchy, didn't care how he dressed," Bown said. "He wasn't too good about repaying debts, and would sometimes offer his pictures instead of money. I asked my dad, 'What's so great about this guy?' and my father said he was just really talented. It's too bad we didn't keep any of those eggs." But Bown does still have a Knowles etching, *The Lugger,* that her father took to fulfill a debt.

To make money, Knowles found himself increasingly looking beyond his small peninsula to the bright lights of Astoria, Oregon, across the river. In 1924, he was commissioned to produce six large paintings for The Lobby, a restaurant there. A bigger windfall while he was still working on the Hotel Monticello commission was for twelve thematically linked five-by-ten-foot trompe l'oeil works to grace the Liberty Theater in Astoria.

Astoria was then in the midst of rebuilding from a spectacular fire that had swept through the city on the night of December 8, 1922. A graphic description of this fire and its aftermath was given in a lecture by the novelist Matthew Stadler at the newly rebuilt Liberty Theater in February 2006.

The fire, Stadler said, "generated such intense heat that it jumped the 50-foot-wide [Commercial Street] and began feeding off itself up and down the block. A peculiarity of Astoria's downtown—the fact that everything was built on beams held on creosoted piling above a partial sand infill—created what one fire chief described as 'horizontal chimneys,' so that a fire that spread into a building's basement began to generate huge drafts throughout the downtown grid, drawing superheated air through the long tunnels of flammable creosote, which had predictably disastrous results."

Downtown Astoria was almost completely destroyed, and with it went the Liberty Theater. An epic rebuilding was necessary. Astonishingly, Astoria was then governed by the Ku Klux Klan, operating as a legitimate political party in that time and place, which had swept all of the major offices, including that of mayor, in the 1922 elections. The Klan was in power through 1926, but according to Stadler they were inept at actually governing, so much of the rebuilding effort followed the vision of professional city manager O. A. Kratz.

A temporary 600-seat Liberty Theater was completed by early 1923, but it was razed in 1925 to make way for a much grander vision, an Italianate thousand-seat entertainment palace incorporating stores and offices. A bid to decorate the Liberty with Oregon scenes by local artists was rejected. The plan for the Liberty, with what Stadler calls "a portal into the exotic," was echoed in other theaters built by the same owners in Portland.

The bold design of the new Liberty Theater needed suitable artwork, and, according to the *Astoria Evening Budget,* Knowles was selected to execute it in a sketch competition among twenty Northwestern artists. By February 1924 he was reported to be in Astoria studying the location and the interior of the building "with a view to taking advantage of all the characteristics of the theater and the lighting." The *Budget* story makes the rather outrageous claim that Knowles "has traveled through Italy and spent considerable time in Venice, so has thorough, first-hand knowledge of his subject."

Knowles certainly did travel widely during his days as a sailor on deepwater ships, and his itinerary did include Europe, but there's no indication that he spent much time in Italy. Certainly, he had no firsthand knowledge of the place and worked either from other paintings or photographs. Knowles could be a very convincing liar, and no doubt he told some very big ones to get this lucrative commission.

What the architects, John V. Bennes and Harry A. Herzog of Portland, wanted was no less than a fantastic visual effect. From this artist with the thorough knowledge of Venice, they wanted it to appear as if the theatergoer was in the Doge's Palace looking through its ornate, elliptical-top windows at the busy life on the Grand Canal. Intricate plaster detailing around the paintings heightened the illusion of windows, through which Knowles painted evocative gondoliers, the Bridge of Sighs, anchored sailing ships, and the classically beautiful buildings around the Plaza San Marcos. The dramatic clouds from the Monticello Hotel pictures reappear over Venice.

Bennes wrote to Knowles in February 1925, with the theater only a couple of months from opening. He suggested precise detailing in the paintings, which were being produced in the Seaview studio. "As a suggestion, please let us bear in mind that we should lend distance to the scenes as we look through the windows and not have any of the buildings to [sic] close to the foreground." Knowles had been given only six weeks to complete all twelve paintings, at a time when he was also still under pressure to deliver the Hotel Monticello work.

By February 27, he had completed the first of the paintings and took it to Astoria, the *Ilwaco Tribune* reported, to see how it looked "with the different lights thrown on it." The story added that Knowles was forced into some "rapid-fire work" to get the rest of the pictures done. The *Tribune* reported, and apparently

THE RESTORED TROMPE L'OEIL PAINTINGS OF VENICE IN THE BALCONY OF THE LIBERTY THEATER IN ASTORIA, OREGON. JIM MOTAVALLI PHOTO

believed, that Knowles painted his work entirely from memory. "When you consider that it has been more than 20 years since the artist visited the Mediterranean, you marvel at the remarkable memory displayed in handling a subject so unfamiliar," the paper said.

At the end of March, the Herculean labor completed, Knowles carried his finished canvases to Astoria, where they were warmly received. From the *Daily Astorian:* "The paintings . . . represent

Venetian scenes, so linked together that they give the effect of two continuous landscapes, each seen through six windows in the wall of the theater. The pictures carry out that sense of color values for which Mr. Knowles is widely known and bear in addition careful consideration of architectural detail." The theater, a proud symbol of Astoria's recovery, opened on April 4, 1925, with a Harold Lloyd silent film *Hot Water*. Elaine Hammerstein was still working regularly and made no fewer than six movies in 1925, but, alas, was not in the Lloyd film.

Knowles's paintings shone forth from the balcony of the Liberty for more than six decades, taking a bit of wear from the patrons in the process. The first two of the works on either side was accessible to loose feet or launched projectiles, and they got somewhat scuffed up. In the late 1990s, after the theaters had suffered from declining attendance for decades, the owner divided the property into a three-screen multiplex. In doing this (with two huge plywood boxes), he was fortunately guided by an historic preservationist and so the building suffered no lasting harm.

Today, the Liberty Theater is whole again, after $9 million in renovations with many projects still to be undertaken. No longer a movie palace, it now hosts concerts by country bands, plays from the Missoula Children's Theater, and lectures similar to the illuminating one delivered by Matthew Stadler.

The nonprofit Liberty Restorations has made the lovely old theater live again, and its rich Italianate period details are once more visible. One of the passionate figures behind the restoration is art collector, retired librarian, and history teacher Michael Foster, who lives in an art-filled eighteen-room Victorian in Astoria. Foster's grandfather, Charles Foster, was the highly competent fire chief when Astoria burned, but because he was Catholic he was fired by its Ku Klux Klan overseers, then rehired when they were ousted.

Michael Foster personally hand-gilded the columns in the theater's balcony, and he proudly leads a tour of the restored details. The ferns, scallop shells, urns, and winged lions sculpted into the plaster were all stylized symbols of Venice. Foster is a Knowles fan who owns more than thirty of the artist's original etchings. He points out that in Knowles's romantic paintings, all the important buildings that would have been on view from the Doge's windows are present and accounted for, but the landscape is somewhat simplified. Foster also believes that the eighteenth-century views of Venice painted by Giovanni Antonio Canal, known as Canaletto, were probably a source of inspiration for Knowles.

According to Foster, the Knowles paintings had to be cleaned in situ because they were nailed to the wall through the actual canvas. This presented problems for the expert art restorer, who agreed to do the work for $18,000 (later reduced to $12,000), because he was afraid of heights. "He turned visibly white when we told him," Foster said. An elaborate scaffolding was devised to ensure his safety.

Michael Foster sees something of an enduring mystery in the twelve canvases so quickly covered with paint by Joseph Knowles. Did he in fact produce them all himself? Foster doesn't think so. In fact, he can point to the six works he thinks were painted by Knowles, and the six that were the work of his alter ego and housemate, Edyth Henry.

The little driftwood home on the beach in Seaview turns out to have been rather crowded, raising eyebrows on the peninsula with the fact that not one but two additional women shared the abode with Knowles and his wife. "Neighbors were fascinated by the Knowles *ménage*," according to the *Cowlitz Historical Quarterly*. "'*La vie boheme* comes to the peninsula,' as one put it. Did illicit romance enter the picture? There were rumors, but apparently no one was sure. To fit three women into the Knowles's humble cottage must have been quite an accomplishment in itself."

Matthew Stadler tried to imagine the scene, with deadlines looming, as the Liberty Theater paintings were churned out. He conjures up "that amazing late winter, 1924–25, when Knowles and his wife and his friend [Edyth] hunkered down in their handmade house by the edge of the howling sea, burning the fires late into the night, painting Venice for the Liberty Theater, keeping their Longview patron at bay . . . and generally surviving the intractable problem of being an artist in a culture shaped by bureaucracy and business efficiencies."

The first to arrive at the handmade house was Nellie Carney, an old friend of Marion Louise from the east. She stayed at the cottage in Seaview as long as Joe and Marion both lived, and after that too, eventually working as a telephone operator in Ilwaco.

Edyth Henry (nicknamed "Sis"), a former teacher, apparently arrived later, in 1923. An accomplished artist, she came to Seaview to study with Knowles and stayed on. Carney and Henry shared the apartment over the cottage garage. Henry soon became an indispensable part of Knowles's etching operation, which perhaps explains his odd behavior when she finally departed the scene.

There's little question that Edyth Henry was the force that allowed Knowles to complete his Liberty Theater assignment. Stadler concurs with Foster. "The speed of the job, coupled with marked differences in the brushwork and brightness of some of the canvases[,] points to the possibility that Henry might have helped Knowles meet his deadline," he said in his lecture, adding that both artists somehow managed to make Venice's canals appear to be located on a tributary of the Columbia River. As he put it, "[F]ishing skiffs from Ilwaco have been stretched and then altered into gondolas."

Knowles was on a roll. One commission led to another, and it was a good thing he had the quiet, hard worker Edyth Henry by his side. In the spring of 1929, he went to Olympia as his friend Hughes Bryant had suggested and met with the Capitol Committee about painting the official portraits, in oil, of the last three governors of the state of Washington (Marion E. Hay, Louis F. Hart, and the then-current one, Roland H. Hartley). Hay had to be tracked down in Mexico. For this work, Knowles was to get $2,500, another big payday. It seems he prepared for this work in the Great Men of History series by painting the portrait of Raymond, Washington lumberman and school board member Charles L. Lewis, for display in the high school auditorium.

That trio captured on canvas, Knowles went on to a $600 commission to paint the portrait of an old acquaintance, Albin W. Norblad. By 1931, Norblad had risen far from the post of small-town lawyer, becoming city attorney, then president of the Oregon State Senate, and, finally, governor of Oregon. Knowles painted his official portrait shortly after he stepped down that year. Unfortunately, the painting was later destroyed in a statehouse fire.

Despite their lifelong camaraderie, there was a rather embarrassing misunderstanding between Knowles and Norblad about an earlier portrait. This one was not the governor's official portrait, paid for with state funds, but a private commission. Knowles thought he had Norblad's commitment for $50, but the august trappings of the official residence in Salem disguised a rather shocking truth: Norblad was flat broke. "I would be tickled to death to pay you fifty dollars if I had it but dam [sic] it frankly I am real broke," he wrote on executive stationery. "This office costs me a lot of money and I am way behind on the job. . . . The fact is that I have quite a number of debts that I owe that I can't take care of and my credit at the bank is exhausted. It's just hell." He definitely liked the "dandy" picture, though.

Norblad promised to try to get Knowles the official commission, and maybe his making good on that restored their friendship. Norblad was already a confirmed fan and patron of Knowles's art before the commission. In a 1930 letter, he commiserates with Knowles about a prominent client ("the notorious gentleman") who refused to pay him, and negotiates to buy an unnamed work by the artist (declining to take a picture by Edyth Henry instead). In 1931, ex-Governor Norblad made a speech at the local American Legion Hall for the official dedication of a stage curtain painted by Knowles. (Titled *The Spirit of Peace,* it depicted a bloody war scene with a beautiful woman calling the combatants to engage in commerce instead.) Norblad and Knowles could not have been from more disparate backgrounds, but they got along well and kept up a warm correspondence for the rest of Knowles's life.

As a free spirit, Knowles evidently made an impression on people of power, influence, and responsibilities who admired his independence. In 1923, at the instigation of the state bar association, he painted the chief justice of the Oregon Supreme Court, Thomas McBride, and they got along famously too. "I hear nothing but favorable comments on the portrait, and not a few of these are people who are more or less qualified to judge," McBride wrote Knowles, also announcing an impending visit to him in Seaview.

Knowles received a $1,000 check for the McBride commission, and took it to an out-of-town bank to cash. There was a problem because Knowles had no identification with him, but he got a spark of recognition when he said he'd been the Nature Man. The clerk had seen his vaudeville act. Knowles sealed the deal by making fire right there in the bank lobby. The clerk cashed the check.

Knowles had at least one more important commission. In 1933, he was chosen to represent the peninsula as part of Washington's exhibit at the Century of Progress Exposition in Chicago. He produced a huge canvas map designed to fit in the very limited exhibit space, twelve feet long and three feet wide. The *Ilwaco Tribune* described it as the view "one would get from an airplane flying along the ocean outside the surf." The full-color map showed "25 Miles of Silver Sand: A Beach Without a Pebble." It depicted lakes, pine woods, and cranberry bogs. In characteristic fashion, his own "artist's studio, home of Joe Knowles the Nature Man" was clearly marked. A white surf was seen beating against the rocky headlands of the North Head region "in a most realistic manner." Mount St. Helens and Mount Hood were visible in the background. Although it's a big dingy and frayed now, the map survives, and it was proudly on display when the Ilwaco Heritage Museum mounted a Knowles retrospective in 2007.

Each of the towns represented on the map kicked in a share to defray Knowles's fee. Unfortunately, when some representatives of the town of Long Beach came to see the undoubtedly impressive work, they were horrified to see that he had identified the re-

Knowles and wife Marion Louise with their much-loved dog Mukluks. courtesy of the ilwaco heritage museum

gion as "North Beach" instead of the alternative and preferred title, "Long Beach Peninsula." They demanded that this "error" be corrected or no cash would be forthcoming. Knowles, usually more conciliatory when money was involved, refused.

The standoff ended when the other communities came together and paid Long Beach's share. The North Beach name stayed on the map. Knowles couldn't resist writing a letter to the *North Beach Record*. "No hard feelings, Long Beach, for the criticism of your representatives," he wrote. "The map as it stands can do you no harm. And if it is any help, I'm pleased it didn't cost you anything, so don't kick."

To keep up with the volume of work, Knowles needed the active collaboration of master etcher Edyth Henry, an artist fully his equal. That may be one reason he was so distressed when Henry mysteriously disappeared in the fall of 1936, leaving a cryptic note saying she could be reached at her brother's home. "I can't bear to say goodbye even temporarily under the circumstances," she wrote. "I thank you for all the beautiful things you have taught me, all that you have done for me. . . . In sadness and tears, Sis."

The "circumstances" Edyth spoke of were singular. She had run off in the company of an elderly couple, Charles and Hattie Harmon. In a notice announcing a $25 reward for information leading to Edyth's discovery, Knowles describes Hattie Harmon as sixty-five years old, with piercing gray eyes and a large bandanna that she wore "gypsy fashion." She was a fortune teller, spiritualist, and "self-styled magnetic healer."

Mary Jane Walker remembers the arrival of the Harmons, who were offered a place to stay at a house the Walkers owned. They were later joined by a younger man, Charles Gattis, who may have become Edyth's lover. (Some go so far as to say Gattis and Edyth were married.)

Knowles never found Edyth, but he never stopped trying by writing letters and making inquiries. He believed that she had come under the sway of the couple, who had convinced her that if she followed their spiritual advice she would be "prosperous and happy." Further, he thought Hattie Harmon, "the old witch," had secretly poisoned Marion Knowles during a healing session, and would have poisoned him, too, if he had consented to her magnetic treatments when he came down with a gall bladder ailment.

"Seances were being regularly held and messages received from the spirit world," Knowles wrote in an unpublished account.

"I was supposed to die on the 22nd of October," after which, as detailed below, Edyth would have inherited the house and lucrative art business. Meanwhile, "Edyth was getting thin and looked worried. . . . She seemed to have lost all interest in everything but the Harmons. She was so completely under the control of the old witch that there was no advising her. . . . Poor Edyth is the unfortunate victim of the mangy outfit." He added, somewhat unnecessarily, "The whole thing reads like fiction."

The loss of Edyth's artistic hand was bad enough; but, in a protective legal strategy that backfired, she also was at least a part owner of his house. Knowles had long been embroiled in a court battle over his property boundaries (he was even hauled into court for damaging his neighbor's offending fence), and at some earlier point had deeded the house and grounds to her. But then to resolve the dispute, he needed Edyth's signature on a number of legal documents, only one of which she had provided before her abrupt departure. Knowles sent a quitclaim deed to Edyth's brother, Will Henry, in the hope that Edyth could be persuaded to sign it. It's unclear if she did so, but the Knowles couple held on to their house.

Will Henry wrote to Knowles in 1941, giving him a list of locations all over California from which Edyth had written letters, the last in 1938. "It does seem odd that we have not heard from her in something like two years," he said. Only months before he died, Knowles wrote the chief of police in Tulsa, Oklahoma, trying to find Gattis, who had apparently worked for oil companies there.

Knowles probably lost some of his focus after the unsettling Edyth Henry affair. His art career was winding down, though he found steady work from 1929 right through the end of his life in

1942 as a contract artist with a federal art project. This service was not without controversy, because Knowles became convinced that the Civil Works Administration on the peninsula was, in his words, "rotten to the core."

In 1934, Knowles wrote a series of letters to federal relief administrator Harry L. Hopkins and to President Franklin D. Roosevelt himself, complaining of cronyism in hiring, with jobs going to undeserving Republicans with political connections and private incomes. "It is being run by a political group almost to a man," he said to Hopkins. "[T]he many destitute families that need relief, and are entitled to it, cannot get a day's work at common labor." He was bitterly disappointed when his complaint was simply referred to the state-based agencies that he felt were responsible for the corruption.

According to Peggy Lucas, he was the project's only etcher, producing accurate images of ships that had come to grief in or near the Columbia River. One of his last jobs, boasted of in letters to old friends, was designing war propaganda posters. Sketches for these, some very clever, are in the Ilwaco Heritage Museum. The 13th Naval District commission to produce this work, four silk-screened posters per month, must have felt like vindication for an old Navy man who had left the service under ambiguous circumstances. "I'm in the Navy now!" he crowed to his friend Ross Carpenter in 1942. "I'm doing the old Navy as I know it for Uncle Samuel. The paintings are in watercolor of old ships in action, and the work is very interesting."

In 1940, when Knowles had only two years to live, the John Muir School in Seattle wrote asking if he'd care to produce a likeness of their namesake, the great naturalist. Knowles wrote back immediately, eager to comply and suggesting the modest price of $20 for the work. "He was a great lover of nature and a friend of man," Knowles wrote the school. Though he may not have been cut from the same noble bolt of cloth, the epitaph would apply to Knowles himself.

And so things might have stood, if Knowles had been content to go down in history as a successful artist who, at some time in the dim, dark past, had gone into the woods naked for reasons obscure. Knowles was a significant artist, whose work documenting the Washington coast is still highly regarded in the Pacific Northwest.

And Knowles left an artistic legacy that has sent out new roots in his Down East family. Though Knowles left Maine behind, the flame of his accomplishments still cast light there. The county highway passing their old family homestead is now known as "Knowles Road." Though he had no direct descendants, Joe's work is still influencing Knowles family members such as Susan Knowles Jordan of Ellsworth, Maine. Jordan says Joe Knowles was a great-uncle to her grandfather, which is a close enough connection to inspire her own wildlife painting. "Art runs in the family, I guess," she says. "My grandmother painted, and so did my dad, who is primarily a jazz bass player."

Jordan's wildlife paintings are beautifully rendered and painstakingly accurate. "It's really encouraging to think of the work Joe did in the woods, rendering colors from nature," she says. Jordan often goes out into the nearby marshes to see birds firsthand and render them accurately when photographs just won't do. "I spent a lot of time in the woods trying to see a yellow-throated warbler, and then one landed in a bush right outside my window," she said. "I was able to say, 'Oh, it's *that* shade of yellow.'"

Jordan says she has seen only a few Knowles works, in particular the drawings rather poorly reproduced in *Alone in the Wilderness*. There has been only one formal gallery show, a retrospective exhibit put on by the Lower Columbia Arts Association in Longview in 1951. It included an impressive 109 works of art, including sixty-six etchings provided by Nellie Carney. On view, among many other works (including portraits of both his dogs), was an etching of the steamship *Iowa* printed on paper salvaged from the ship itself. The well-regarded illustrator Elizabeth Lambert Wood provided seven works. She wrote the Association, "You are doing a very worthy bit of belated tribute to Joe Knowles. None of us appreciated him when he was our neighbor. As I look back I realize that he was kind to us all." Stewart Holbrook, who had profiled Knowles in the *American Mercury* many years before (and then included the profile in a book), offered some reminiscences. "I am very happy you are going to give him a memorial show," Holbrook wrote. He wouldn't get another until the summer of 2007, when the Ilwaco Heritage Museum mounted a major exhibition.

For the 1951 show, visitors could tour the gallery, then stroll over and see the paintings in the Hotel Monticello. The reviews were favorable, almost as much for the character of the "bighearted beach resident" as for the art. "Ask almost any longtime resident in the area about Joe and you touch off an anecdotal chain reaction," said the *Longview Daily News*.

But the Nature Man had a keen sense of his own place in history, and he wanted to be remembered as a man of ideas, as a bold thinker. He intended to do more with his pen than produce art on commission. He wanted to be a writer.

The archive at the Ilwaco Heritage Museum has file drawers full of Joe Knowles's short stories, some of them existing in a dozen drafts. They are all painstakingly typed on the same machine, and include novel spellings and a lot of crossouts and revisions.

Also in the files are poignant reminders that Joe Knowles's writing career was not to be. The *Saturday Evening Post* informed him in 1924 that it was declining to publish "Mat Moses of Canby, Maine," about a hunting guide who loved to fight and not one of his better efforts. "We are sorry to conclude that it is not a story that we can take for the *Saturday Evening Post*," it said. The *American Magazine* turned the piece down that same year, concluding that "it is well done but unfortunately not our type of yarn." The *American Mercury* got a similar submission in 1938, with the helpful thought that the editors were free to use the story "in whole or part at your regular rates," but it too was rejected.

Knowles worked hard to turn himself into the kind of writer these magazines accepted. He filled notebooks with elegant-sounding phrases, such as "he observed grimly," "every fiber of his being," and "hedged them in." He tried out a veritable feast of verbs, such as "He demanded . . . exclaimed . . . opined . . . bawled . . . directed . . . pointed." He wrote notes to himself— "Write pictures: real writing is the product of that and feeling"; "Write so your background may be read, and if you have a story, tell it"; "Always carry a notebook"; "Put the kick into your climax, and relieve your story with comedy." He ordered a correspondence course titled "The Blazed Trail to Successful Authorship," produced by the Palmer Photoplay Corporation. But neither his work nor his acceptance rate improved.

Knowles's best success as a writer was a column that appeared in the late 1920s in the *South Bend Journal.* It was a platform on which the Nature Man could perform, but for a man used to the national stage this must have seemed a minor role.

There are short stories, screenplays, and fragments of an aborted autobiography. Knowles must have told many friends he was working on the latter, because references to it appear in many letters. Attorney U. T. DeMartini asked him in 1935 about "the story of your life, which we are awaiting with so much interest." An interlocutor named "JBF" wrote that same year to let him know that the *Seattle Star* newspaper might be interested in writing a Knowles feature, and that its publication "could be used as a real plug for the book and for any yarns you might want to sell to magazines."

No book appeared, but the fragments in the files echo the material in *Alone in the Wilderness,* though without the efficient organization probably provided by Paul Waitt. Knowles often began on a topic with confidence and great vigor, but then lost the thread and trailed off into a favorite diversion, such as the social interaction of beavers on a pond. He revisited key incidents—such as his schoolboy confrontation with a bully—again and again.

Some of his stories have fascinating premises. "Girl of the Wilds" is about a young woman "born in the wild Sierra's [*sic*]," who learned the ways of the woods from her hunter-and-trapper father. "As a child, her favorite plaything was a bow and arrow, which she preferred to her wooden dolls, and so proficient did she become in their use that not an Indian boy in the Feather River Canyon could outshoot her." Perhaps he was reminded of besting Ishi with similar equipage. If the focus had stayed on Louise Geering, the girl of the wilds, it might have kept up interest, but she soon all but disappears and the piece devolves into a cinematic potboiler involving rivals for her affections.

Other stories have wonderful moments. "Spring Visitors," for instance, has a funny anecdote from Knowles's days as a trapper at King & Bartlett Camp in Maine. The camp cook, George Day, who "had never had no schooling," was somewhat less than skilled at making bread. "It was so hard a dog couldn't bite into it," wrote Knowles. He decided to take over the baking himself, but couldn't find the baking powder. Day pointed to a package. "It's right there in front of you. If it had been a dog it would have bit you." But the illiterate Day was pointing at a box of soap.

George Day was a real person. In 1903, Knowles decorated a trunk belonging to Day with a picture of a half-naked woman, and it survives today in Sean Minear's collection in Maine. If that bread story had been used to make a point, or been grouped with other attractive recollections, "Spring Visitors" might have found an eager buyer. But it's stuck rather aimlessly between a lengthy discussion of making the perfect pair of snowshoes and an account of a night of drunken revelry and sausage consumption.

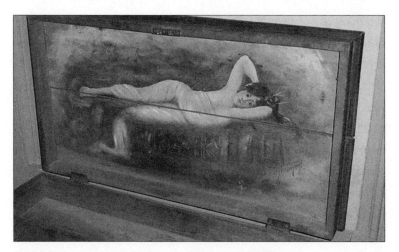

GEORGE DAY'S GAUDILY DECORATED TRUNK. COURTESY OF SEAN MINEAR

Some of Knowles's poetry has a rough power. Here's part of "No Man's Land," a possible response to a well-known World War I poem by James H. Knight-Adkin:

'Twas on the shore of "No Man's Land,"
At the closing of the day.
The golden sunset kissed the sand
Where a shipwrecked sailor lay.
And when the sign of life appeared
He crawled away to rest.
Beneath the shelter of the trees
And slept on Nature's breast.
With all the senses of the wild
He saw and felt and heard.
For he was part of Nature's wild:
The forest, beast and bird.

One of Knowles's best works is a lengthy essay on his beloved Siberian Husky, named Wolf in both the story and real life. It's impossible to say how much of the story is true, but it's a very good yarn anyway. The narrator first encounters the Alaska-bred Wolf tied to a log in Seattle. His old dog musher of an owner has just sold him to a bootlegger for a gallon of moonshine whiskey.

Wolf knows he's gotten a raw deal, so he immediately tries to follow the narrator—dragging the 200-pound log in the process. "'You poor devil,' I said to him. 'If you want to come with me as bad as all that then come on.' And I let him loose." Wolf becomes the best dog the narrator ever had, and page after page is devoted to closely observed comments on his singular and fiercely loyal behavior.

"Wolf was not a barking dog and had little respect for dogs that did bark," Knowles wrote. "He considered it a personal

insult whenever a dog barked at him or at his master, or at anything that belonged to them. And he was not slow at resenting the
insult." Wolf, who was pure white and immortalized in one of
Knowles's best etchings, did love to howl, however, and became
"a famous singing dog" whose favorite composition was "Roll on
Silvery Moon"—he could hit all the high notes. "Newsreel men
who filmed him said they had never heard a dog sing like Wolf,"
the story says.

The real Wolf died in 1935, and in a letter that year Knowles
said that "it was almost like losing one of the family. He was
loved by everybody that [sic] knew him. Neighboring children
continue to bring flowers to his grave in the garden where he
loved to lie. Pneumonia carried him away. He sank and melted
like a big white snowball and without a struggle died in my arms."
Knowles's Vermont friend, Katherine Baker, who received a version of this letter, wrote back to say that she found it so poetic
"that I could not bring myself to reply in my halting prose, utterly
inadequate to what I felt."

In a rather remarkable departure from standard obituary practice, the *Oregon Sunday Journal* published a long eulogy for Wolf,
complete with evocative photo, under the headline "Famous Husky
Dies." Alas, Wolf had gone to "the Happy Hunting Ground," a
victim of pneumonia. The obituary adds the song "When You and
I Were Young" to Wolf's singing repertoire, which it says was
filmed by Pathé News. His admirers, according to the paper, "included thousands of summer visitors to the peninsula and people
scattered all over the world."

Wolf was succeeded by Mukluks, a mixed-breed who eventually was as beloved as Wolf and died of distemper shortly before Knowles did. "In the afterlife, I want to be with my Mukluks,"
Knowles wrote. When Mary Jane Walker's appendix burst at age

seventeen, she was confined to bed rest and couldn't have human visitors. "But Joe would send in Mukluks carrying a big basket of food for me," she remembers.

As always, Knowles's mother—her kindness, her knowledge of Indian ways, her ability to keep the family going in the midst of dire poverty—was never far from his thoughts. Mary Knowles died in 1923, described in the local paper as "a most estimable woman, a lover of good books and a devoted Christian." There are many tributes to her among Knowles's papers.

Knowles must have visited his mother shortly before she died, because he writes movingly about a bedside encounter. Mary Knowles pulled her son to her and said, "Do you believe the dead ever come back to us? Your father comes back to me at night when everybody is in bed. He wakes me up and talks to me, turns me over and always tucks me in." Knowles says his sister Mary Jane (known as "Marme") could never understand how her mother had changed position in the night, as she lacked the strength on her own. Knowles sat with her for hours, supplied her with morphine tablets against the chronic pain, and massaged her stiffened arms until she could move them again. Among his personal effects is a lock of his mother's hair taken in 1916, when she was seventy-eight.

Knowles's writing is best taken in short doses, since he lacked the organizational talent for longer narratives. As a New England–born version of Will Rogers, he had his moments. "Religion is the world's greatest racket," he wrote in one short compendium of random thoughts. "Victims are usually hypnotized into their beliefs by professional racketeers. . . . Personally, I am a sun worshipper. The sun gives us light and life."

"If there is strength in unity, the wolves know it," he observed

KNOWLES AT HOME IN LATER
LIFE, AGAIN WITH MUKLUKS.
COURTESY OF THE ILWACO
HERITAGE MUSEUM

just before the U.S. entry into World War II. "While men fight single-handed with sticks and stones, the wolf pack unites against the common foe. Their instincts serve them better than reason serves the men of today."

On an envelope from the Imperial Hotel in Portland, he wrote, around the same time, "The politicians got us into this, and the boys at the front have to get us out of it. A lot of them will be dead before the job is finished. They say it is the people's war—I say it is the politicians' war."

Of his own experiences, Knowles could be amusingly philosophical. "From obscurity to fame in 60 days," he mused on a scrap of paper one day. "I made the grade and got a lot of fun out of it.

Nobody had paid much attention to me in the lean days but now that I had become famous everybody extended the glad hand."

Even the smallest Knowles observation could clearly convey his unique eccentricity. On one torn page he wrote only: "Height: 5'11", weight 190, eyes blue, a *nice* blue."

In the end, he grew philosophical and summed up his colorful life. In what was to have been chapter one of his autobiography, he admitted that impulse was often his driving force. "Chance has played her part in the ups and downs of my eventful life," he said. "Instinct has been my guiding star, and has led me swiftly over dangerous trails where reason dare not walk." He acknowledged more than a few disappointments. "I have sinned and suffered and repented," he said. "I have made mistakes and apologized for them." But though he admitted breaking most of the Ten Commandments, he seemed pleased with the way things had turned out. "It has all been very interesting," he wrote.

As Knowles sat at the window in his Seaview studio on a beautiful Indian summer morning, he looked out at the life around him—wild crabapple trees flaming with red, the faint sound of breakers at low tide, the call of the brown thrush mixing with the chirp of crickets—and he was satisfied. "I am thankful for my existence, and for all that Nature has done for me. . . . The school of experience has taught me more than I ever learned from books. Nature has been the best teacher I ever had. You may fool man and get away with it, but you cannot betray nature and escape."

He died facing the sea, on the other edge of America, but his native New England forests still had a powerful hold. "I have traveled over a good part of the world by land and by sea, always looking for someplace better than the woods, but I never found it," he told the *Raymond Herald* in 1921. "The earth belongs to nature, and we are her tenants."

———•◆•———

NINE

The Call
of Nature

IN THEIR BESTSELLING BOOK *THE CENTURY*, PETER JENNINGS AND Todd Brewster conclude that Joe Knowles's trip into the Maine wilderness "touched something deep in contemporary sensitivities. . . . Even as they marched eagerly into the exciting, industrial future, proud of their accomplishments, people simply couldn't resist looking back." As the authors note, Jack London's *Call of the Wild* was then the most popular novel in America, and the rapid progress of "civilization" was getting a critical reexamination.

But this yearning for a simpler life, almost a return to Eden, was hardly new. It fits into a long continuum of human activity, with precedents and antecedents. It would even be possible to follow the timeline back to the days of Knowles's most obvious inspiration—the cave man. Jim Mason, in his insightful *An Un-natural Order*, theorizes that our ancient ancestors of 40,000 years ago were more like "gatherer-hunters" than the "hunter-gatherers" often depicted in popular imagery going after big game. They knew the food and medicinal value of hundreds of plant species, felt a deep kinship with animals, and were, as he puts it, "intimate with the living world, not alienated and hostile to it."

Though our primary image is, perhaps, of a man in a Knowles-like bearskin with a club for big game in one hand and his woman's hair in the other, Mason says recent scholarship indicates that women and children were the main gatherers of the plants that constituted 80 to 90 percent of the diet in cave society. Mason traces most of our modern instinct to live apart from nature, and to subjugate it, to the pivotal period when humans began living a sedentary agricultural lifestyle and, approximately 11,000 years ago (in present-day Iraq), began domesticating animals.

Ancient England brought us the pagan "Green Man," whose image as a carved human-like head swathed in leaves dates back to the second century A.D. In medieval times, the Wild Men were thought to live in the forest wearing leaf garments. Nineteenth-century May Day revels brought us Jack-in-the-Green, who danced to wild music inside a wicker framework covered in greenery. They were perhaps symbols of what was already a rising discontent with modernism.

Fencing in animals, creating a garden, these were the first hesitant steps toward a modern civilization, and it immediately bred dissidents who preferred a freer life. Eighteenth-century lords and ladies found plenty of ready takers when they engaged "ornamental hermits" (i.e., "fake" hermits who live in an artificial hermitage and allow themselves to be seen by guests) for their country estates. As Dame Edith Sitwell describes the practice in her 1933 *English Eccentrics*, ". . . [C]ertain noblemen and country squires were advertising for Ornamental Hermits. Nothing, it was felt, could give such delight to the eye as the spectacle of an aged person with a long beard and a goatish rough robe, doddering about amongst the discomforts and pleasures of Nature. . . ." Hermits, exclusively male, signed five-year contracts.

The idea of the estate cave proved astonishingly durable. When the stately Shugborough Home in Staffordshire, central England, sought a "Professional Hermit for Cave-Dwelling Duty" in 2002, organizer Corinne Caddy told the *Daily Express* that she was "stunned" by the number of replies. Even though the gig lasted only a weekend, not five years, she commented that "It seems there are lots of people out there who just want to be a professional hermit."

But it would require another book to detail the "back to nature" movements that appear with astonishing regularity in human history. Instead, let's go back no farther than the eighteenth century, when industrial development began to take its toll on the natural world. The growth and rapid population of cities, with marginal sanitation (at best) and inadequate public health resources, soon led to a backlash and a yearning for a return to the bucolic ideal.

The ideas of the transcendental movement were laid down in a ninety-five-page book, *Nature,* written by Ralph Waldo Emerson in 1836. Like Knowles in his studio, gazing out at a Pacific beach, Emerson could find himself saturated by the beauty and order of everyday reality. "The lover of nature is he whose inward and outward senses are still truly adjusted to each other; who has retained the spirit of infancy even into the era of manhood. His intercourse with heaven and earth becomes part of his daily food. In the presence of nature, a wild delight runs through the man, in spite of real sorrows."

He expressed this "wild delight" personally, in full appreciation of the natural world around him: "In good health, the air is a cordial of incredible virtue. Crossing a bare common, in snow puddles, at twilight, under a clouded sky, without having in my thoughts any occurrence of special good fortune, I have enjoyed a perfect exhilaration. I am glad to the brink of fear. In the woods, too, a man casts off his years, and at any period whatsoever of life, is always a child."

Henry David Thoreau read *Nature* while a student at Harvard. He was a neighbor of Emerson in Concord, Massachusetts, and became his friend. The two-year period, beginning on Independence Day, 1845, that he spent at Walden Pond (on a woodlot offered for his use by Emerson) was a time of reflection and study. He conducted an accurate survey of the pond, gardened, wrote in his journals, and worked on his first book, *A Week on the Concord and Merrimack Rivers*.

Thoreau refused to be guided by the clock, saying famously that time "is but the stream I go a-fishing in." He wanted to get away from the manifold distractions of nineteenth-century life, to be awakened not by factory bells but by celestial music and aspirations from within. "Let us spend one day as deliberately as Nature, and not be thrown off the track by every nutshell and mosquito's wing that falls on the rails," he wrote. Like Emerson, he filled up his senses from everyday experience. He got up early and bathed in the pond, which he described as "a religious exercise, and one of the best things which I did."

The Transcendentalists were voracious readers, and in their search for enlightenment Emerson and Thoreau dipped into the major works of Hinduism and Buddhism. *Walden* quotes the Hindu *Vedas*, ancient sacred texts dating as far back as 1500 B.C. Their searching had reverberations and echoes in other parts of the world, particular Western societies experiencing industrialization and the alienation of labor. Around the same time that Thoreau was building his cabin at Walden Pond, the Scottish-born John Muir was experiencing the same kind of natural transcendence in rural Wisconsin. He writes in *The Story of My Boyhood and Youth* (first published in 1913) about discovering a bluebird's nest and beginning an acquaintance with the frogs and snakes and turtles in the local creeks. "This sudden plash into pure wildness—baptism in Nature's warm heart—how utterly happy it made us! Nature streaming into us, wooingly teaching her wonderful glowing lessons, so unlike the dismal grammar ashes and cinders so long thrashed into us."

The Transcendentalists loved nature, but they wanted its good offices to help them get in touch with the divine. A return to the primitive was not on their agenda. Although Thoreau writes in *Walden* that he "lived alone, in the woods, a mile from any neighbor," the truth is that he left often during his two years for paying work and to renew contacts with human society. His cabin may have been crude, but the cave man would not have recognized the life he lived there. He didn't become a vegetarian. He didn't turn his naked body to the sun. In the Europe of the time, they were doing both.

The father of the European back-to-nature movement was Jean-Jacques Rousseau (1712–1778). Rousseau's concept of the solitary "noble savage," who lived by his wits and good intentions in a pre-social natural world, was very influential in forging a more optimistic view of human nature. As Jim Mason does today, Rousseau set out the case that our ancient and benevolent ancestors were primarily vegetarians.

In his very thorough history of vegetarianism, *The Bloodless Revolution*, Tristram Stuart traces Rousseau's ideas as they filtered through European society. Rousseau had something of a breast fixation, and he argued that, in contrast to multi-nippled carnivores such as cats and dogs, "a woman's only having two teats and rarely giving birth to more than one child at a time is one more strong reason for doubting that the human species is naturally Carnivorous." These published observations, illustrated with pictures of bare-breasted women, helped launch a modest breast-feeding movement in France.

"In the 1780s the French court was overcome by a fad for rustic chic," Stuart writes. Fashionable women had their portraits painted wearing straw hats, or with one breast bared. Soon they were taking Rousseau's ideas even further in England, where John Frank Newton published his book *Return to Nature* in 1811, advocating a combination of vegetarianism and nudism. His friend, the poet Percy Bysshe Shelley, was an ardent convert to the former, and at least strongly sympathetic to the latter. He proclaimed Newton's five *au naturel* children "beautiful and healthy creatures." Shelley's wife, the former Mary Wollstonecraft, also gave up meat, and in 1817 she turned her Frankenstein's monster into an acorn- and berry-loving vegetarian.

There was a particularly strong back-to-nature movement in Germany, fueled by a longstanding fascination with the primitive. In 1874, a herd of reindeer was shown at the Hamburg Zoo—

and with them as part of the exhibit was a whole family of native Laplander Saami herders. A woman among them caused a furor by breastfeeding her child. It was a precursor of the grandly ambitious display of native peoples (including Ota Benga) at the 1904 World's Fair in St. Louis.

But the Germans wanted to do more than just look at primitives; they wanted to experience the primitive for themselves, and they did so in a spectacular fashion. All the elements that 1960s "flower children" may have thought they had invented—long hair, nudity, psychedelic art, vegetarianism, nature worship—were in place long before they were on the scene.

In the late nineteenth and early twentieth centuries, both before Knowles and after him, the German "Naturmenschen" and "Wandervogel" movements, which counted counterculture icon Hermann Hesse as an admirer, lived outdoors, went naked whenever possible, and practiced vegetarianism (an aspect of their culture that Knowles seems to have eschewed).

At the very end of his life in 1832, Johann Wolfgang von Goethe, one of Germany's literary giants, gave voice to a growing discontent with modernism. "Man in his misguidance has powerfully interfered with nature," he said. "He has devastated the forests, and thereby even changed the atmospheric conditions and the climate."

This sentiment was embraced by a growing movement. "By the early 20th century," according to *The Bloodless Revolution*, "the post-Rousseauist back-to-nature movement had sprouted into a thriving medley of naturopaths, nudists, mud-bathers, ecologists and vegetarians; this movement found its zenith in counter-culture nudist camps that promoted the idea that 'men could live a paradisiacal life in nature.'"

Few of the early practitioners are as renowned as Hesse, but they all created ripples on the placid German pond. As Gordon Kennedy notes in his book *Children of the Sun,* which follows the nature worshippers from Germany to California, one of the first of these "new men" was Louis Kuhne, who opened his "International Establishment for the Science of Healing Without Medicine and Operations" in Leipzig in 1883. His book *New Science of Healing,* praised by the Mahatma Gandhi, advocated a raw foods diet and sun baths.

Around the same time, Karl Wilhelm Diefenbach, an artist, healed himself from a debilitating illness with a nature cure that included going naked or barefoot, eating natural foods, and soaking up sunshine. He established a natural community called Humanitas that unfortunately suffered financial reversals. Diefenbach eventually established another community near Vienna (after an ill-considered trip to Egypt to build his own sphinx), but again fell victim to money problems.

Diefenbach is well remembered in Germany, where there are two museums devoted to his life and work. He inspired a young protégé, Hugo Hoppener, known as "Fidus." An artist of some ability, Fidus created relatively lurid and colorful paintings of naked men and women turning their shining faces toward a bountiful sun, work that looks decidedly psychedelic to our modern eyes. Any of his images could adorn a Deadhead's bus.

Adolf Just opened his own nature sanitarium in 1896, advocating the usual program of nudity and rigorous outdoor activities. Echoing the American pioneer Sylvester Graham (best remembered for the Graham cracker), he advocated consumption of raw foods and described water as "the only natural drink." He urged his fellow Germans to abandon the great cities, which he

An illustration by Fidus from 1904. from *CHIL-DREN OF THE SUN* (1998) by Gordon Kennedy

called "the hotbeds of everything unnatural," and move to the country.

This they did. Hermann Hesse's great teacher, a draft dodger named Gusto Graser, born in 1879, wore flowing robes (when he wore anything at all) and tied his long hair back with a headband. Wandering through Germany and Switzerland, he offered "forest meditations" when he wasn't railing against the confines of Christianity or translating the *Tao Te Ching* into German.

At the beginning of the twentieth century, many of the leading figures of Germany's new movement, including Graser, converged on Ascona, then a poor Lake Maggiore fishing village in Italian-speaking southern Switzerland. The twenty-year period—from 1900 to 1920—that an emerging counterculture flourished in Ascona is chronicled in Martin Green's book *Mountain of Truth*.

The book's title refers to Monte Verità, a vegetarian sanitarium established there, which attracted legions of nature-cure advocates. But Ascona was also a destination for early feminists, nudists, Dadaists, Theosophists, free-love advocates (especially Munich's

Franziska zu Reventlow), modern-dance devotees (who came to work with Rudolf Laban, a high priest of the form), vegetarians and, in 1904, the well-known anarchist Raphael Friedeberg.

Hermann Hesse, whose short book *Wandering* describes his own efforts to live unencumbered in the woods, visited Ascona for the sanitarium cure in 1907 and was taken not only with the place but with Graser (who sometimes lived in a cave near there).

Hesse couldn't commit himself totally to the lifestyle, but he sampled the fare readily enough. "Where am I going to sleep tonight? Who cares!" he wrote in an exuberant moment. While the human world was striving to get ahead, he contemplated a primrose blossoming, and a wind singing in the poplars. "I care about that," he wrote. "It is humming the song of happiness, humming the song of eternity."

But Hesse also recognized his limitations as he struggled toward enlightenment. "A thousand times, even in your poems and books, you have played the harmonious man, the wise man, the happy, the enlightened man," he wrote in *Wandering*. "My God, what a poor ape, what a fencer in the mirror, man is—particularly the artist—particularly the poet—particularly myself!"

Hesse dabbled, but Graser and Diefenbach were outstanding examples of what the Germans called "Naturmenschen," or natural men. It was a rather demanding discipline. Adherents gave away their possessions, adapted a strict vegetarian diet, and lived an itinerant life, preaching the gospel of the natural life. Their ideas took root and flowered as the well-organized "Wandervogel," the bands of young people who tramped the Alpine countryside in the early days of the new century. From the movement's beginnings in 1895, the group grew to 50,000 members in nineteen regional divisions by 1914. While in old photos they look wholesome

THIS IMAGE OF "HIPPIE" BILL PESTER IS FROM 1917. COURTESY OF THE PALM SPRINGS DESERT MUSEUM

in their lederhosen and Tyrolean hats, the program also included guitar music and mixed-sex nude swimming.

Since these Germans were wanderers, it was only a matter of time before their travels took them to the United States, where in California they found a welcoming attitude and a congenial climate.

Arriving in California around 1914 was fruitarian Arnold Ehret, the "Herr Professor" who ran Ascona's raw-foods sanitarium. His teachings found a ready audience in the United States, and he produced five books that have stayed in print and influenced the Los Angeles surf culture. Ehret and other German vegetarians also influenced Vera and John Richter, who started Eutropheon, the first raw-food restaurant in Los Angeles, in 1917. It stayed in business for twenty-five years.

Bill Pester, one of the first Naturmenschen transplants, arrived in the United States from Germany in 1906 after having fled compulsory military service. Pester practiced nudism and a raw-foods diet at his log cabin in Palm Canyon, California. "Man was intended to live in a state of nature," he said. Pester made his own sandals and farmed organically. A photo taken in 1917 shows the bearded, long-haired Pester playing slide guitar outside the cabin with only a towel for covering. It could have been taken in 1969.

Maximilian Sikinger, whose muscled body and flowing blond locks gave him the look of a young Adonis, came to the United States from Germany in 1935, when he was twenty-two. Sikinger, who frequented Palm Springs's Tahquitz Canyon area (now closed to the public because, according to one blogger, "large bands of hippies in the late 1960s held concerts there and trashed the place") in the winter and the high Sierras in the summer, emphasized fasting, deep breathing, nudity, naturopathic medicine, and body building. He lived long enough (to 2004) to influence a more contemporary and American breed of "Nature Boys."

Eden Ahbez (or, as he spelled it, eden ahbez) was born Jewish in Brooklyn in 1908. He hopped freight trains west and found his calling in California, where he befriended Pester and Sikinger. The by-now bearded, shirtless, and shoeless Ahbez preached Oriental forms of mysticism, played the flute, practiced vegetarianism, and sometimes camped out underneath the "L" in the Hollywood sign. By the late 1940s, there was an informal network of what were called "Nature Boys," living as clothes-free as they could possibly get away with in the southern California sun.

Although there were many others—Emile Zimmerman, Bob Wallace—Ahbez is the most famous "Nature Boy" because in 1947 he sold the haunting song of that name to Nat "King" Cole for a tidy sum. It became a huge hit and is now a treasured entry in the Great American Songbook. Ahbez's song, reportedly inspired by Pester and other German naturists, told of a "strange enchanted boy" who wandered far, only to discover that "the greatest gift" was "just to love and be loved in return."

An Ahbez contemporary, Gypsy Boots (born Robert Bootzin), also became a celebrity of sorts. He befriended Hollywood stars, ran the Health Hut in Hollywood, appeared at the Monterey Pop Festival, and made twenty-five appearances espousing the natural life on the *Tonight Show* with Steve Allen. He would swing onstage on a rope, then show Allen how to make organic juice. Many viewers certainly had a good laugh over the antics of Gypsy Boots, but others probably admired his free spirit and enjoyed what he had to teach about the natural life.

Boots died in 2004 and always maintained that his half-naked, food-foraging outdoor life with the "Nature Boys" had been inspired by the German example. He left a legacy, perhaps in the idyllic (at least initially so) communes that dotted the landscape in the 1960s and early '70s, many of them featuring farmers who tilled the land naked as had their German forebears. A more obvious descendant, the "nudist colony," embraces only the sun worship from the Nature Boys' canon: The family-oriented near-prudishness of these places would probably have turned them off.

Even today, the image of the human animal in his or her natural state has a powerful lost-Edenic appeal, reflected in the photographs of Justine Kurland, who, according to the *New York Times*, creates large-format works "populated by tribes of naked mature women, many of them pregnant or nursing, suggesting wandering fertility goddesses—who are playing with their children in paradisiacal settings of forest, meadow and sea." These tribes are viewed from a distance, with the camera's eye encompassing an entire unspoiled ecosystem, giving the photographs a resemblance to nineteenth-century American landscape paintings.

Scan the radio dial at random, and chances are you'll pick up a version of "Nature Boy"—there are dozens, from Frank Sinatra (his reached No. 18 on the *Billboard* charts in 1948) to *Star Trek* Vulcan Leonard Nimoy and even David Bowie. It has an enduring melody, sure, but it also has an alluring message. The Nature Boy wandered far, like the Naturmenschen, and carried with him some simple gifts that had great resonance in the booming postwar years, as Americans moved out of the urban "hotbeds of everything unnatural" and into suburbs that offered their own version of sanitized "country living."

It's hard to know what the Nature Boys and their German antecedents would have made of Joe Knowles. He hit many of the same notes in talking about the healing properties of Mother Nature, and espoused many aspects of their philosophy, but he almost completely lacked their obsession with natural food and health. He thought that living the primitive life fortified the character of modern man; the fact that, according to an eminent Harvard physician, he emerged from the woods with a physique more impressive than the legendary vaudeville strongmen of his day was incidental.

With songs on the radio and TV appearances, the message of the California Nature Boys probably traveled farther and had more lasting impact than Knowles's song of the woods. But Knowles did inspire a modest movement and some amusing copycats. There were the "Six Eves," who wanted to go into the woods under his supervision in 1916, and a leaf-clad fellow named

Bud Carson, who got his bare-chested picture taken alongside that of Knowles in *Physical Culture Pictorial.*

More serious were Carl and Margaret Sutter, who got themselves arrested by game wardens near Ashland, Maine, for imitating Knowles's stunt in May 1922. This "modern Adam and Eve" could at least go into the woods together, as they were united by the bonds of holy matrimony. The Sutters had the backing of the *Boston Advertiser,* but as with Knowles it was no protection against the unlawful taking of deer and partridge.

The Sutters were supposed to stay six weeks in the woods of Maine, but only made it through two. They did succeed in aping many of Knowles's best stunts: They went in naked and sent out regular reports on birch bark. Judging by the arrest reports, they seem to have been very good at catching game, both big and small. There were other obstacles beside the game wardens, however. Their timing was off: In late May and early June, not only are game wardens afoot, but Maine is really buggy. The *Portland Sunday Telegram* wrote in 1960, "[T]he back to nature stunt blew sky high when the pair surrendered to the summer insects which caused 'Eve' to become seriously ill."

The *Telegram* story also makes note of another attempt, sponsored by the paper itself. In the mid-thirties, the *Telegram* delegated reporter Bill Geagan and guide Charley Miller to watch over the Bangor-bred Bradley brothers, Arnold and Kenneth, as they plunged into the woods around Moosehead Lake. "And in the blue and gold of October's first morning, they disrobed, shook a few hands and while the cameras of national news services whirred, vanished into the perpetual twilight of the big woods that sprawls at the base of Big Squaw Mountain," Geagan wrote in 1960.

The Bradleys were to have stayed in the woods for a month, with a vaudeville contract awaiting their return. Charcoal reports on birch bark were dutifully prepared. The pair built a snug lean-to, created fire, and succeeded in gathering food. The lateness of the season kept the bugs off, but, as with Knowles in the Adirondacks, it also proved their undoing. After just thirteen days, a driving northeast snowstorm lashed the area and blanketed Big Squaw Mountain with seven inches of powder. "Another war with the woods of Maine was over," Geagan wrote. "Only Joe Knowles made a go of it."

Not all the nature men were out for publicity. Some were conventional hermits; some, like Hermann Hesse, seem to have become almost drunk with the intoxicating enticements of Mother Nature. Others were merely eccentric. Connecticut's "Leatherman," for instance, wandered a circuitous route for thirty years in the mid-to-late nineteenth century, wearing a crude suit of said material. He accepted gifts of food but rarely spoke more than a few words to anyone and slept in a network of rural caves.

Everett Ruess simply wanted to disappear. Ruess, born in 1914, was an accomplished landscape artist and, like Knowles, a printmaker. He was also a poet who pledged to follow "the sweeping way of the wind."

Ruess grew up out of place in Hollywood, California, with a gifted artist for a mother and a UCLA professor for a father. "How could a lofty, unconquerable soul like mine remain imprisoned in that academic backwater?" he asked. Ruess could be a bit precious in his youthful search for Beauty with a capital B. But he was so good at so many things (his artwork was praised by Ansel Adams, Edward Weston, and Dorothea Lange) and lived such a short time that he will remain always a fascinating enigma. "God, how the wild calls to me," he wrote. "There can be no other life for me but that of the lone wanderer."

In 1934, when he was just twenty, Ruess set off with two burros, Cockleburr and Chocolate, to explore the Southwest. He was last heard from among the canyons and mesas of Escalante, Utah, in what is now a national monument. He had given ample warning that he was looking to disappear forever: Three years earlier, he had predicted that he would go on one last wilderness trip and not return. Sounding like Hesse without the literary ambition, he wrote, "As to when I will revisit civilization, it will not be soon. I prefer the deep peace of the wilderness to the discontent bred by cities."

Ruess succeeded in disappearing; his donkeys were found, but little else. He left a final riddle: the word "Nemo," carved in a cave and in the doorstep of a home where he had lived for a short time with the Navajos. The fictional Captain Nemo had used a submarine to take his leave in *Twenty Thousand Leagues Under the Sea;* Ruess was an inner explorer, and he fulfilled his destiny.

Sylvan Ambrose ("Buckskin Bill") Hart lacked Ruess's romantic impulses, but he more than made up for it with practical ability. He is, perhaps, Knowles's true heir, because he lived alone in the wilderness not for two months but for more than forty-five years.

Hart, born in 1906, studied engineering at the University of Oklahoma. Finding jobs scarce in the depths of the Depression, he decided he'd be better off depending on his own wits than the sporadic employment offered by others. A natural loner, he headed for a remote spot that he thought had the resources to support a subsistence lifestyle: a stretch of Idaho's Salmon River 122 miles upstream from its confluence with the Snake.

Hart stayed there until he died in 1980, with a brief break to volunteer for the defense effort during World War II. He made his own three-room stucco house, his own clothes, tools, and cooking utensils—even a series of elaborately inlaid flintlock rifles and pistols used for hunting. Unlike Knowles, he made use of found materials, such as remnants of steel, lead, silver, and copper sourced from abandoned mines.

Buckskin Bill was no misanthropic hermit; he was friendly to the rafters who sometimes invaded his solitary homestead. But he was a kindred spirit to Daniel Boone in his love of the forest primeval. "If a man can look out his window and see another house, he's a poor man," he said.

Very close in spirit to Buckskin Bill was Dick Proenneke, a former diesel mechanic who waited until he retired in 1968 to turn his back on civilization. Proenneke lived on his own for more than thirty years in the remote Alaskan wilderness, accessible only by floatplane. Using only hand tools, he built a white spruce cabin that still stands today.

Like Buckskin Bill, Proenneke was friendly and liked company. On his rare visits to town, he was gregarious, marveling at such inventions as the VCR and the CD player. He was also a passionate environmentalist who recorded what he could of the natural world in his journals. When visitors to his home at Twin Lakes left their trash behind, it was Proenneke who cleaned up after them. He finally left his beloved wilderness in 1999, when he was eighty-two and increasingly infirm. He was comforted by the fact that Twin Lakes had a new guardian; it had become part of Lake Clark National Park and Preserve. The film about Proenneke's life echoes Joe Knowles; it's called *Alone in the Wilderness.*

There have been many others who answered the Call of the Wild, and it was often Alaska that called the loudest. Sometimes it ended in tragedy, as when twenty-two-year-old Christopher Mc-Candless, a recent graduate of Emory University, headed into the wilderness in 1992 and there slowly starved to death.

But others were hardier. Heimo Korth left Wisconsin in 1975 to find a sort of peace in a fourteen-by-nineteen-foot cabin 300 miles northeast of Fairbanks in the 19.5-million-acre Arctic National Wildlife Refuge (one of just seven people permitted to live there). The nearest town, Fort Yukon, is 110 miles away, and that means that Korth is probably living more remotely than anyone else in Alaska. But Korth is not the loner that Proenneke was; he found a wife, and they have two children. He's not going anywhere.

In *The Final Frontiersman,* a book about his cousin Heimo, James Campbell chronicles many stories of refugees from the Lower 48 who tried to make a go of it alone in frontier Alaska. A surprising number of them were able to make it as trappers and hunters, but it became only a temporary stopover before the monotony or the loneliness brought them out of the woods. Many are now married with children, living in Fairbanks or somewhere farther south, still dreaming of the wilderness but at best visiting it a few months a year. It probably helps that Korth married an Eskimo woman and his children were born into the life.

In 2004, thirty-year-old newspaper marketing man Guy Grieve left a well-paying job, along with his wife and two young sons, in Scotland for a year's stay in a tiny Alaskan cabin he built himself, sixty miles from the nearest settlement. Grieve was inspired by the story of British explorer Ernest Shackleton and the novels of Jack London. He burned his suit before he set out. And because he apprenticed himself to a local woodsman, he was able to successfully hunt grouse, trap beavers, and survive through a winter when the temperature fell to -74 degrees Fahrenheit. "You come to the wilderness to take your life right back to nature," he said. Grieve later wrote a book about his experiences, predictably enough titled *Call of the Wild*.

Many of our more modern Nature Boys have never even heard of Joe Knowles. Steve Gough, who in 2003 stripped off his clothes (except for hiking boots) and walked the length of Britain, from Land's End in the southwest of England to John o' Groats in the northeast of Scotland, says he was motivated not by wilderness survivalism but by a desire "to enlighten the public, as well as the authorities that govern us, that the freedom to go naked in public is a basic human right."

More in the spirit of Joe Knowles is Eustace Conway, who runs Turtle Island Preserve near Boone, North Carolina. Conway, who became something of a public figure for wilderness through his portrayal in Elizabeth Gilbert's 2002 book *The Last American Man,* has been living in the woods since moving into a teepee at age seventeen. When he was eighteen, he canoed 1,000 miles of the Mississippi River. Somewhat out of time in modern society, he set a record for crossing the United States in 103 days—by horse. A student of American Indian traditions, Conway wears buckskins, uses plant medicine, and stitches up his own wounds.

Conway was interviewed in a rare moment behind the wheel— of a horse trailer. Why was Joe Knowles so well received in 1913? Why were people not long off the land so amazed by his ability to make fire? Conway had an interesting answer. "He probably impressed the intellectual crowds in the Boston coffeehouses," he said, "but I bet people in the rural areas out West didn't find it so unusual." It's true that Knowles's awe may have been more of an urban phenomenon.

Conway asked if Knowles writes of the need to shape sharp stones, to make such tools as the knife, the ax, and the scraper. These in fact do get some attention in *Alone in the Wilderness*, but Knowles does not dwell on tool-making. He used stone tools to skin animals, but he was not specific about the process.

"The most important thing would be for him to have knowledge," Conway said. "He'd have to know how to make a shelter, to gather and use leaves. And it would be vital to know how to use the plant fibers he found to make rope, simple textiles, and clothing. He'd have to know a lot about tying knots."

The mention of knots set Conway off on a familiar diatribe against the American preference for instant gratification. "Outdoor survival schools are trying to make money," he said. "They need to sell something the public wants to buy, and that's the excitement of making fire by rubbing sticks together. Learning how to use fibers and tie knots is just as important, but they don't teach it because it's not exciting. It's all about marketing."

Conway added that knot-tying knowledge has disappeared as Americans have learned to depend on nuts, bolts, and plastic ties. There are two ways to tie shoelaces, he said, and most people nowadays do it the wrong way.

Joe Knowles did know how to tie shoelaces, and he certainly knew an immense amount about the proper use of plant fibers. Even in 1913, however, he found that interest in this craft learned from the Indians was fading. Would such patient craft have worked in his vaudeville show?

For a survivalist second opinion, there is Christopher Nyerges, who runs the School of Self-Reliance in California and is the

author of *Extreme Simplicity, Testing Your Outdoor Survival Skills,*
and *How to Survive Anywhere.* The latter is full of hardcore survivalist information. If you're trying to survive in a post-apocalyptic
city, for instance, it's nice to know that rats, squirrels, possums,
and pigeons can all be eaten—as long as you cook them well. Ter-
mite larvae can be collected from dead trees; and, as Knowles did,
you can also dine on salamanders and frogs' legs (though watch
out for the ones with toxic skin). Nets, blowguns, and arrows are
recommended. And Nyerges adds the helpful note that taking
these vermin out helps rid the city of possible sources of disease.
"In a genuine, large-scale emergency," he adds, "any domestic
animals will disappear somewhat quickly. If you love your cats
and dogs, hide them!"

In an interview, the California-based Nyerges said he had not
heard the strange saga of Joe Knowles:

> But I know of many people who have done similar feats. How hard
> would it be for me? I have gone into the woods for two weeks at a time
> without bringing any food and it was *easy* [emphasis in the original].
> I have gone into the woods with no gear—but wearing clothes—
> and I have made packs, carrying cases, shelters, nets, and fire (with
> a hand drill, with a bow and drill, even with a 'D' battery and a piece
> of steel wool). All of that is relatively easy as long as you have spent
> maybe three years mastering the basics, and as long as you are not
> afraid to get dirty. You also can't be too worried about occasional
> hunger, cold, and insect bites. Still, despite the fact that I know and
> understand the theory, it would still be very challenging for me—or
> anyone, really—to go and do this. Challenging, but not impossible.
> After all, it's what our ancestors did. It was the normal way of life that
> we've allowed to become dormant.

Nyerges says he's subsisted on snakes and grasshoppers, even eaten road-killed possum and deer when he's had to. He says that Knowles would have had a much easier time trapping deer than that bear that allegedly was caught in his deadfall trap. "Why? Well, the bear can kill you, and it runs very fast!"

Nyerges says that the journalists of 1913 who dismissed Knowles's bear trap as incapable of "holding a cat" were probably ill-informed. "Shallowness has nothing to do with it," he said. "In a deadfall, a large rock or logs are held up by some tentative trigger, and when an animal goes under it, the rocks or logs fall." Of course, Knowles's trap seems to have been a combination of a deadfall and a pit, since he plainly said that the bear survived the springing of the trap but was caught in place and needed to be dispatched with a club.

In the end, Nyerges concludes that he probably could duplicate Knowles's feat, but he just doesn't want to. "I don't feel any great desire to go out and kill animals just to prove I can do it," he said.

EPILOGUE

————— ·◆· —————

By disappearing into the wilderness when he was just twenty years old, Everett Ruess ensured his own continuing mystery. By contrast, Joseph Knowles lived to seventy-three, and he never stopped trying to explain himself—even when no one was listening. He wrote page after page about who he was and what he had done, though most of it never made it out of his little cottage on the Pacific.

Ironically, despite that torrent of words, we're closer to understanding the motivation of Ruess—a man who the evidence suggests died simply because he was tired of modern human life—than the voluble and publicity-loving Knowles. For though he talked and talked, he was like a magician bound by ancient codes never to reveal his secrets. He never admitted to being anything other than scrupulously honest, and he could summon great tempests of indignation when his veracity was questioned.

Knowles probably collaborated to defraud the readers of the *Boston Post* in 1913. The most likely scenario is that he wore store-bought clothes, received supplies, slept in a warm cabin, touched up his charcoal sketches with pencil, and let his story be scripted by the busy typewriter of Michael McKeogh.

But Knowles was a talented—and very complex—man. He *did* have many wilderness skills, in fact the unique skills necessary to survive such a feat. And that's why, in the scenario I can easily picture, he boasted of his ability to survive in the woods within earshot of a Boston newspaperman—Michael McKeogh. Together, as Richard Boyer wrote in the *New Yorker* in 1938, they hatched a credible plan.

If Knowles's narrative sounded plausible to newspaper readers, that's because it largely was. It combined the base of Knowles's wilderness skills and storytelling ability with McKeogh's ability to shape it into coherency, a story with arc and flow. Even better, it had Knowles's lively illustrations to bring it to life.

The timing of the wilderness experiment was also well-nigh perfect. Americans' flight from farm to factory was in full swing, and the city had become the unhealthy locus of pollution, crime, and exploited labor. Only the year before, the *Titanic* had sunk, making man's great works seem impermanent and tenuous. *The Call of the Wild* was a bestselling book, and *Tarzan of the Apes* was being serialized.

Knowles may well have been taken aback by his own success. The cycles of manic energy and lassitude that Boyer described may have been occasioned as Knowles contemplated living up to the image he had so vividly created for the reading public. Fortunately, however, when Knowles emerged from the woods, he discovered his own inner vaudevillian. He did indeed know how to make fire, and it was a spectacular stage trick that audiences would pay to see. He looked good in a bearskin, even if it was full of bullet holes. He evolved into, if not a raconteur, at least

KNOWLES OUT WEST: HIS TIMING WAS EXCELLENT. *BOSTON POST* PHOTO, FROM *ALONE IN THE WILDERNESS*

someone who could hold an audience with a well-honed story. He became an actor playing the part of the Nature Man, and he found that he enjoyed it—so much that when he lost that role, he kept trying to get it back.

It seems likely that the charges of fraud—even if true—struck Knowles to the quick. He was determined to prove that he really could survive in the wilderness and probably saw the trip into the

Siskiyous as a kind of redemption. He deliberately picked a destination so remote, so far from any friends or places he knew, that that deception would have been very difficult.

And survive he did. Though the second trip lacked the dramatic story scripted by McKeogh, its persistent and unremitting struggle has the ring of reality. The perpetually overconfident Knowles lost his cockiness in the face of the real thing. In the California border wilderness, he fought for everything: food, shelter, and scraps of clothing. Without his encompassing bearskin, he was something less than a majestic figure. He emerged from the woods half starved and half naked, but gloriously alive.

It is perhaps this image that sustained him during his long and somewhat anti-climactic aftermath. If he could have consoled himself with his artistic triumphs—"Conquerors of the Trail" at the Hotel Monticello, the Venetian panels in the Liberty Theater—then his fading image as the Nature Man might not have mattered as much. But it is apparent from Knowles's writing that for him the wilderness, and his own part in it, was paramount.

But to succeed as a nature writer, Knowles would probably have had to get a bit more of the poetry of the woods into his work. The naturalists whose work resonated with the public— Thoreau, John Muir, John Burroughs, Aldo Leopold, Rachel Carson later on—all wrote beautifully, and captured a bit of the transcendent in their work. Knowles was impatient with the majesty of the silent forest; he wanted to skip to the particulars. Rather than contemplate the grand designs in the animal kingdom, he chose to chronicle individual animal behavior. That's valuable, too, of course, but Knowles would get so caught up in his observations that he'd lose the thread of his story.

Knowles's attitude toward romantic writing is, in fact, amusingly summed up on a scrap of paper he left behind. In 1922, a friend sent Knowles an essay written by Phyllis Hocking, who lived on a houseboat in Sheepshead Bay, Brooklyn. She had taken out a canoe, and at midnight had had a near-mystical experience. "The sky was alight with many beautiful colors, which were reflected in the dark, roaring waves," Hocking wrote. "A slight breeze shook the trees on the shore, making their long branches move to and fro, causing a faint rustle almost ghostlike in its sound . . . . As I rode the waves in the face of the breeze, my hair was blown about. I must have looked terribly disorderly, but I did not care. I felt free and happy. My whole body quivered. I wanted to cry aloud out of sheer joy. Something seemed to call me with a pitiful yet beautiful voice, a voice filled with beauty, happiness, pathos—all together. Where was the voice? It seemed to come from those *fathomless waves* [emphasis in the original]."

Knowles sent back a grumpy reply. "I find it a letter of meaningless words rather than words inspired by the truth of the situation which she has so dramatically described. In the first place, she says, 'I was out in a canoe until midnight—the sky was alight with many beautiful colors, which were reflected in the dark roaring waves.' My criticism is that no reflections can be seen in 'dark roaring waves,' nor can a canoe live in them. Again, she is wrong when she describes the waves as 'fathomless.' I am inclined to think that your little friend has wild dreams and hallucinations."

Yes, Joe, but sometimes wild dreams and hallucinations add passion to the written word. Knowles, for all his eccentricities, was at heart a practical, can-do man who liked to proceed in a straight line to finish the task set before him.

What would Knowles have made of some of the passion-driven nature writers of today? My guess is he'd be dumbfounded by writers like Jay Griffiths, whose 2006 *Wild: An Elemental Journey* would seem to establish her as a kindred spirit.

Griffiths doesn't want to take a quiet walk on a well-marked nature trail; she wants the essence of wildness itself. In vehemently rejecting modern civilization and its temperature-controlled interiors, she wants to penetrate the deepest jungles and follow the bear into its lair, however ill-advised these adventures may be. "I felt that my blood could only truly flow if it coursed into red, red earth," she writes. "That I would only know my deepest glee if I could dive in an oceanful of trilling fish. I wanted to climb mountains till I cracked with the same ancient telluric vigor that flung the Himalayas up to applaud the sky. I was, in fact, homesick for wildness, and when I found it I knew how intimately—how resonantly—I belonged there. We are all charged with this. All of us. For the human spirit has a primal allegiance to wildness, to really live, to snatch the fruit and suck it, to spill the juice."

Though he'd sympathize with some of that—especially Griffiths's ringing denunciations of shrink-wrapped, antiseptic society— Knowles would probably have offered Griffiths something to calm her nerves. He would probably have judged her a tenderfoot, a person whose courage and passion for wilderness was matched only by her ignorance of its actual laws. She's the kind of person he'd expect to rescue when she failed to heed his voice of experience.

Knowles's writing in *Alone in the Wilderness* is not memorable for the visceral impact of its wild ideas, but it makes a quieter mark in another way. He wrote eloquently about the effects of loneliness on the human psyche. Humans are social animals, and none more so than Joe Knowles. He described the ache of separation from his fellows as more profound than hunger or cold. When he nearly gave up, he says, it was because he had no one to talk to, not because he was starving. Most people who try to make a go of it by themselves in the Alaskan wilderness eventually give up the life, and the loneliness of the life is a principal reason why.

The image of Tom Hanks in the film *Cast Away*, reasonably well fed but talking to "Spalding," his painted volleyball, comes to mind. In fact, the plot of *Cast Away* could be considered an update of Knowles's proposed script for *A Modern Robinson Cruso*, written in 1915.

Of course, *Alone in the Wilderness* could be as fictional as *A Modern Robinson Cruso*. If Knowles was actually holed up in a warm cabin with Mike McKeogh and Allie Deming, loneliness doesn't really enter into it. But in that case, the collaborators were prescient about forces that would act upon a man alone in the woods. It would also, of course, turn this nonfiction book into a novel, but a readable one with elements that ring true.

The concept of the marooned mariner or wilderness isolate has long been a popular one in legend and literature, from *Crusoe* onward. Jean Craighead George's 1959 *My Side of the Mountain* won enduring popularity with its story of Sam Gribley, a boy who spends a summer on his own in the Catskills. George, who won several major awards for *My Side*, was kind enough to respond to an e-mail query. No, she said, the book was not inspired by the story of Joseph Knowles, but "by the things I did in the woods with my family. But how interesting that someone lived off the land in 1913!" she wrote.

In 2007, we have the latest contribution to alone-in-the-wilderness literature. Georgina Harding's *The Solitude of Thomas Cave* is a novel about an English sailor who voluntarily agrees to be left for a year on a remote island off Greenland in 1616. As the wind howls outside during a long and dark winter, Cave has plenty of time to come to terms with himself and his troubled past. "The truth is that the hardest thing to bear through these frozen days has not been the dreams but the absence of them," Harding writes. "The loneliness."

Cave is changed forever by his experience, becoming a proto-environmentalist. For the first time, he sees clearly the ecological horrors wrought by his whaling compatriots. He remembered "how Adam had lived alongside the beasts in Eden, and made it his rule to kill no more than he needed." He looks around at herds of frolicking seals untouched by fear of humans and feels a kinship with no counterpart in his upbringing.

Knowles was not a religious man. He wrote in a note that he attended church a few times as a youth, "but I never did believe in the kind of God the minister preached about. The story of Christ walking on the water, being born without any earthly father, and Eve being made out of Adam's rib, I never could believe." But he did have a theology of sorts, a religion of the woods. "Modern civilization is a creation of man not of God," he wrote in *Alone in the Wilderness*. "Nature is God's creation." In his own way, he was a faithful congregant for the church of the woods, and because of his early lapses he became a penitent. It was probably deeply frustrating to him when the Adirondack trip descended into farce, and then was called off before the players ever strode onto the stage.

Elaine Hammerstein was not his soulmate, the names "Dawn Man" and "Dawn Woman" notwithstanding. To this product of an elementary school education in rural Maine, her New York sophistication would have been utterly alien. He wanted it to work, of course, and that's why he offered brave words about the blank slate on which he could inscribe his lessons in woodcraft.

Knowles felt that he had unfinished business, and that's why he did what he could to secure a new expedition. If he'd been left on a remote Mexican island (albeit with whirring cameras for company), he might have found his vindication. How could he have faked that? He never stopped talking about the next trip; when a reporter from the *American Magazine* tracked him down in 1921, he gave the impression that he was still taking off into the woods regularly.

"I could never stay long away from the woods or the sea," he told his interviewer. "In the city I always heard the call of the wild." He said he spent his "spare time" painting. Knowles wanted the world to see him as still awaiting the next adventure, but by the 1920s, nature anxiety was abating and modernity was taking firm hold. The evidence shows that the woods of Washington State never saw the bare Knowles posterior, but he still loved to talk about it. He wondered if the public had forgotten Joe Knowles, the nature man.

Unfortunately they probably had, human attention spans being what they are. There was a brief revival of interest when Knowles died on October 22, 1942, though there was a war on and attention was mostly elsewhere. The *South Bend Journal* said, "He never lost the interest in nature that won him national prominence." The *Chinook Observer* called him "one of the country's most colorful characters," and speculated he might actually have been born as late as 1879, which would have made him only sixty-three. "Joe had a trace of Indian blood on his mother's side [*sic*], and this influenced his entire life, giving him a love of the wild and a fearless nature," the paper said. At the time of his death, according to the obituary, he was working on a series of watercolor posters depicting sailing ships of the U.S. Navy that were to be displayed in factories and production centers. He had just completed the eighteenth installment, of the U.S.S. *Huron.*

Writer Peggy Lucas said in remembrance that "Joe's neighbors knew him as a jolly fellow who was more often than not smeared with ink or paint unless Louise Knowles or Nellie Carney got to him before he went in to town. But they also knew him as a fine artist who had done much to popularize the great Northwest he loved." She added that the brief outdoor ceremony was "the only kind he had wanted, on a spot that overlooks the Columbia River, a place where the birds gather to sing."

The *New York Times* obituary, published October 23, noted that he'd gone into the woods naked and without tools, weapons, or implements of any kind, "but when he came out he bore on his back a fire-making machine and other equipment he had fashioned to aid him in living the primitive life." The obit added that he had died in the house of driftwood near Cape Disappointment he had occupied for a quarter century. "He leaves a widow," it said.

Time magazine's obituary was unsporting enough to speculate that much of Knowles's time in the woods had been spent "hiding in a cabin with a Boston ex-publicity man . . . ," though it did acknowledge that he'd won "national acclaim and a 20-week vaudeville contract." Knowles's obit appeared alongside that of

his old car-selling friend Eddie Rickenbacker, who died somewhere over the Pacific on an Army inspection flight.

Marion Louise Knowles, with Nellie Carney at her side, remained there on the beach until she died at age sixty-one in 1947.
The *Chinook Observer* noted she had been married to the "well
known naturalist and author," but it seemed more interested in her
blue blood as a descendant of both a Declaration of Independence
signatory and a Revolutionary War soldier. An aunt was Dr. Elizabeth A. Follansbee, one of the first pediatricians in California.

Knowles and his wife are buried side by side in block twenty-
three, lot four of a picturesque cemetery, containing the remains
of many pioneer families in Ilwaco. The plain stone gives only
names and dates; if Knowles had been consulted, it's quite likely
that his status as the Nature Man would have been noted.

Standing on the Pacific shore in Seaview, watching the rough seas
that stretch to the horizon and the waves that wash detergent-
like foam on the beach, it's easy to feel Joe Knowles's presence.
The sand is scattered with driftwood and other debris, as if waiting to be picked up by him and applied to some constructive purpose. "Mother Ocean supplies all my wants," he said.

A thirty-eight-foot sub-adult gray whale washed up in nearby
Long Beach, and its skeleton stands sentry now, the display a re-
minder of the whale bones encountered near here by Lewis and
Clark in 1805. Ilwaco has gone into decline with the salmon fishing; these days, many of its former fishermen are telling stories
and hoisting beer in the Sea Hag bar (where the silent films once
flickered). But the rows of homes built by the Finns who would
have been Knowles's neighbors are still there, though weatherbeaten now.

Seaview and Long Beach have fared better than Ilwaco, because they adjusted to new realities and cater largely to the tourists
who crowd the place in the summers. But during the wet and
chilly winters, they too look forlorn. The tourist shops could perhaps enhance their trade by selling reproductions of Knowles's
etchings, which after all depict local scenes.

To follow the Knowles trail back in time, you go to the opposite
coast and start in Boston, where the Copley Plaza Hotel (now called
the Fairmont Copley) still features its 1912 decorative splendor.
The big dining room, with its intricately carved ceiling, looked down
on a splendid banquet for the Nature Man, with the floor strewn
with leaves to make him feel more at home. From Boston, head
straight north. In Maine, hop on Route 27 and journey into a rus-
ticity untouched by time. The narrow asphalt trail seems remote in
itself, but the journey gets even lonelier if you spot the tiny "King
& Bartlett" sign nailed to a tree and turn right onto dirt logging
roads. For Knowles this trip was harder, because he rode a buckboard over a rock-strewn track. The Civilian Conservation Corps built
new roads in the 1930s, though traces of the old trails are still there.

The ride in to King & Bartlett Fish and Game Club is a long,
bumpy one, passing active logging operations and covering more
than sixteen miles. But the camp, looking much as it did in
Knowles's time, is worth the drive. The main lodge and a row of
homey log cabins sit directly on big 538-acre King and Bartlett
Lake, presided over by a pack of friendly German shorthair bird
dogs. Meals are announced via a big dinner bell that was originally used on the local narrow-gauge railway.

From the shore of the lake, the view is a déjà vu. With no sign
of human habitation in the thick tree cover and bleached branch
litter lining the shore, it duplicates nearly perfectly a photograph

in *Alone in the Wilderness* that is captioned "A glimpse of the Spencer country in Northern Maine."

Danny Longley, the camp's resident historian, says that William King, Maine's first governor, built the camps in 1830 on land owned by his head lumberman, Bartlett. It's been a quiet 177 years, though Longley recalls the grim day during World War II when a deranged logger on a nearby Canadian woods crew killed himself and his wife, leaving their two kids to walk all the way to Stratton. Today, the operators lease 50,000 acres, catering to fishermen and hunters who go after moose, deer, wood ducks, grouse, and the bears descended from the one Knowles wore on his back. They fish in Spencer Lake and Lost Pond, his old haunts. For his part, Longley doesn't have too much to say about Joe Knowles. "He supposedly killed a bear with his bare hands, but he proved to be a fake, didn't he?" he said.

King & Bartlett Camp was the launch point for Knowles that rainy day in 1913, and from all appearances it could serve that same role again today. Set off on the same trail, and soon you'll be in the same thickets of dense underbrush that scratched and bruised the Nature Man's naked body.

For his 1997 book *The Sylvan Path,* Gary Ferguson walked Knowles's route from King & Bartlett to Spencer Lake and Lost Pond. It was not easy going. "When a moist northeastern woods is only 30 or 40 years from the saw like this one, there's enough sunlight reaching the ground to grow vegetation thick as fur on a beaver's butt, and full of tangles," he wrote. "By the time I've gone a hundred yards, my visibility has dropped to a lousy 15 feet. About every fourth or fifth step I trip over stumps or downed logs hidden by carpets of club moss and blueberry, several times actually falling, or else find myself mushing up to my ankles through sopping-wet cedar bottoms."

THE AUTHOR AND DAUGHTER MAYA AT KING & BARTLETT CAMP. GETTING THERE
IS STILL A ROUGH RIDE DOWN LOGGING ROADS. MARY ANN MASARECH PHOTO

He lurched and stumbled along a Bear Mountain trail "overgrown
with a loose weave of shoulder-high maples," swatting a growing
mist of flies and mosquitoes.

Ferguson finds Lost Pond largely overgrown too. He sees a loon
on its still surface, and the tracks of bears. It was on the banks of
Lost Pond, after the farcical bear-in-the-pit reenactment, that
Helon Taylor claimed to have seen a newly constructed cabin—
a structure Knowles said he'd somehow missed. Ferguson doesn't
find the cabin, but he does find a pile of cedar logs that had long

ago been worked with an ax and a saw. In the underbrush, he finds remnants of an encampment—including ancient bean and coffee cans. "Could this have been part of Knowles's trash pile?" he asks.

Who knows what Ferguson found. After ninety-four years, it's unlikely that the whole truth of that trip into the woods will ever be told. But Ferguson performed a valuable service no longer available to contemporary authors: He interviewed eighty-year-old Deb Sylvester, who was thirteen when his family bought King & Bartlett Camp.

Sylvester wasn't there in 1913, obviously, but in the late 1920s many of the oldtimers were still around King & Bartlett, including Allie Deming of Flagstaff (misidentified as "Demmins" in Ferguson's book) and another guide named Douglas, from Eustis. The latter may have been the father of Bana Douglas, possibly the mysterious woman who reportedly visited Knowles in 1913.

"What they told me," Sylvester said, "was that they had extra clothes waiting there, so after Knowles stripped down and headed off on the trail, he ran right over and got the spares. It was all planned ahead of time." He added that Knowles's groceries were kept at Deming's place, known as Twin Camps, "so Knowles could hike over and pick up his grub for the next couple of days—cans of stew and beans, even bottles of beer." Sylvester's conclusion: "There ain't no man in hell gonna go long without clothes with all those goddamned mosquitoes and black flies."

Ferguson decides that Knowles may indeed have been a fraud, but in the end it doesn't matter all that much. "More amazing than what Knowles did or didn't do," he wrote, "was the amazing effect the mere thought of such an adventure had on millions of Americans—husbands and housewives in Scranton and Cleveland and Des Moines eagerly reading headlines about the wild man, sipping dreams of the woods with their morning coffee."

Consider that Knowles had his impact in 1913, when Americans were only recently transplanted from farm and frontier. Contemporary youth, plugged in to iPods and virtual worlds, are far more alienated from nature than those ancestors of the new century. A new Adam with a reality show of his own would be a sure smash, wouldn't he?

But such programming is not merely theoretical; it's actually on the air. The Discovery Channel broadcasts the British Channel 4 production *Man vs. Wild,* starring the redoubtable Bear Grylls, a veteran of the elite Special Air Services (SAS) unit of the British Army. Grylls, dropped in various wilderness areas around the world, is shown eating the raw meat he captures on the hoof, straining elephant dung for water, and drinking his own urine. But is this Nature Man as tough as he looks? Not according to the British newspaper *Daily Mail,* which published an in-depth exposé in July 2007.

In an amazing reprise of the Knowles experience, the *Daily Mail* revealed that Grylls was actually spending many nights in fancy resort hotels. In an episode in California's Sierra Nevadas, viewers saw Grylls biting the head off a snake for breakfast, but the paper reported that "he was actually spending some nights in the Pines Resort hotel at Bass Lake, where the rooms have Internet access and is advertised as 'a cozy getaway for families' complete with blueberry pancakes for breakfast."

In an even closer parallel, Grylls filmed an episode describing himself as a "real-life Robinson Crusoe" marooned on a desert island, when, says the newspaper, ". . . he was actually on an outlying part of the Hawaiian archipelago and retired to a motel at nightfall." A Polynesian-style raft he supposedly hand-built (again following Knowles's script to the letter) had actually been assembled by the production crew, the paper said. There was more, including shots of Grylls lassoing "wild mustangs" that were actually tame and brought to the set in a trailer.

Channel 4 confirmed that Grylls occasionally stayed in hotels during expeditions, and added, rather weakly, "We take any allegations of misleading our audiences seriously. Bear does do all his own stunts and does put himself in perilous situations." The Discovery Channel also issued a carefully worded disclaimer: "The program explicitly does not claim that presenter Bear Grylls's experience is one of unaided solo survival. For example, he often directly addresses the production team, including the cameraman, making it clear he is receiving an element of back-up." But the Discovery Channel's own Web site claims that "Bear strands himself in popular wilderness destinations where tourists often find themselves lost or in danger," and it's unlikely that many viewers realize he's going to spend the night with a hot shower and room service.

Other TV nature shows have also fought charges that scenes were faked or misrepresented. So far unscathed is *Survivorman,* starring Les Stroud, who is dropped off in remote areas, from the Arctic to Central American jungles, with little but the camera equipment to film the program. Stroud, a Canadian, goes out for a week, not two months. This rugged survivalist started life as, of all things, a music video producer, but in 1987 he caught the wilderness bug that also bit many of the Alaska trekkers. He became a whitewater canoe guide and wilderness instructor. Eventually, he met a soulmate in Sue Jamison and, according to the Science Channel, "the two spent an entire year living in the remote boreal forest of northern Ontario. They lived as if it were 500 years ago—no matches, no metal, and no tent—just a stone axe and their knowledge of traditional bush survival." Take away their clothes, and they'd be modern iterations of Joe Knowles and Elaine Hammerstein.

Shows like *Survivorman* make it all look possible, even for former music video producers. A darker take on the same material comes from novelist T. Coraghessan Boyle. One of our foremost fiction writers, Boyle has always been, as he puts it, "obsessed with our animal nature versus our spiritual nature." His characters go wild in many different ways. In "Dogology," a story from his 2006 *Tooth and Claw* collection, a field biologist researching dog behavior "goes native," sheds her clothes, and becomes one of the pack. In his 1996 novel *The Tortilla Curtain,* a prim environmentalist and nature writer is outraged when a family of desperate illegal Mexican immigrants takes refuge in his pristine canyon.

It was inevitable that Boyle would have gotten around to Joe Knowles, and he does in his 2000 novel *A Friend of the Earth.* It is southern California circa 2025, and global warming is scorching the planet. Most animals are extinct, and Boyle's central character, Ty Tierwater, presides over a zoo holding the pitiful remnants. He is a former ecoterrorist, a friend of the earth.

Tierwater's wife, Andrea, turns out to be the great-granddaughter of Joseph Knowles. As Boyle describes it, Knowles was "one of the archetypal eco-nuts" who, one day in 1913, plunged into the woods to live off the land. "Two months later," he writes, "hard and brown and considerably thinner, not to mention chewed, sucked and drained by every biting insect in the county, he emerged at the same spot [*sic*] to an even larger crowd and proclaimed that his God was the wilderness and his church the church of the forest."

Ty and Andrea decide to spend their own month in the woods, the new Adam and Eve. They strip naked in front of a crowd of journalists and radical environmentalists and enter the forest primeval, headed for the Kern River in the Southern Sierras. Though Knowles's account of his experiences was strangely bug-free, Ty and Andrea are feasted upon by everything that crawls and bites. They struggle to make fire, and when they have it there's nothing for them to cook. They exhaust themselves trying to catch fish, their deadfalls trap nothing, and they play a losing cat-and-mouse game with a marmot. In place of Knowles's forest banquet, they are reduced to a warmed mash of beetles, salamanders, earthworms, and scorpions.

They don't saunter out wrapped in bearskins. "Tierwater lost 25 pounds, Andrea 19," Boyle wrote. "They were stick people, both of them, as hard and burnished as new leather, and they barely had the strength to drag themselves up and out of the canyon on the last day of their exile."

In an interview, Boyle said he was surprised by the huge reception Knowles received in 1913—mirrored in *A Friend of the Earth* as a cheering throng of one hundred is on hand to greet Ty and Andrea. "I really can't imagine it," he said, "because their pioneer forebears in that era lived much more primitively and much closer to the land than we do now. In 1913, I would think that half the population lived on farms. So it's surprising to me that they would have made a big deal about this guy going out and living rough."

When it was pointed out to him that frontier closures had provoked anxiety, Boyle agreed that was probably a factor. "Of course," he added, "the frontier continued in Alaska until 1970, when the Native Claims Settlement Act came in and you could no longer homestead. That's why I chose to set my novel *Drop City* in 1970, because I was wondering about the American character in response to that loss."

In the 2003 *Drop City*, which is about a clueless hippie commune relocated from sun-kissed California to the Alaskan wilderness, Boyle says he wanted to get at some fundamental questions. As he put it in an interview posted on his Web site, "Is nature nurturing? Can it support us? Will it, does it? Or is it purely harsh and will we be wiped out because of our own excesses?"

For Boyle, nature experiments tend to end badly. His animals are red in tooth and claw, not the gentle and friendly creatures created by the "nature fakers." Knowles was much more of an optimist who saw nature as nurturing, though the specter of global warming might have confounded and tested him.

Unlike Daniel Boone, Davy Crockett, and Teddy Roosevelt, Joe Knowles is not regularly trotted out for the kids as a role model of rugged individualism. His writings are not cited among the giants Thoreau, Carson, Muir, Leopold, and Burroughs. He is the forgotten Nature Man, and something of a punch line in Roderick Nash's *Wilderness and the American Mind*. But in his own way, Knowles has much to offer for our times. He may have been at least partly a fraud, but he was nonetheless successful in communicating a powerful and useful message to an anxiety-stricken age. As he entered the American home via its daily newspapers, he popularized the school of the woods as much as did any of his contemporaries. Who among us would not have been enthralled and inspired by one of his vaudeville turns? Who among us wouldn't want to see him in his bearskin even now?

PREPARING TO ENTER THE WILDERNESS

HE WAS ALWAYS READY TO DISROBE FOR ANOTHER ADVENTURE. *BOSTON POST* PHOTO, FROM *ALONE IN THE WILDERNESS*

NOTES

———— • ◆ • ————

1: A Modern Adam in Maine

It's hardly surprising that the Boston *Post* covered the Knowles saga exten-
sively. On Saturday, August 9, 1913, a few days after he'd entered the woods,
the paper ran a banner on the bottom of its front page: "Alone and Stripped of
Everything, Faces Existence in Maine Woods. Boston Artist's Exclusive Story
in Tomorrow's Post." The pattern of holding the big scoops until the Sunday
edition continued throughout the two-month saga. The last mention of Knowles
was on another Sunday, July 16, 1933, when a sixty-four-year-old Knowles was
discovered living in "healthy contentment," making a living from his art on the
Pacific Coast of the state of Washington.

The second major source for this chapter is Knowles's own book, *Alone in
the Wilderness* (Boston: Small, Maynard and Company, 1913). It is reputed to
have sold 300,000 copies. The book appeared within two months of Knowles's
emergence from the Maine woods. Since Knowles was busy with personal and
vaudeville appearances during that period, it is likely that the book was ghostwritten; if so, almost certainly by *Post* reporter Paul Waitt, who contributed
heavily to the paper's coverage.

The classic text *Wilderness and the American Mind,* by Roderick Frazier
Nash (New Haven: Yale University Press, 1967), is invaluable for placing
Knowles's first trip into the wilderness in context. "In fact, the Joe Knowles fad
was just a single and rather grotesque manifestation of popular interest in wildness," Nash wrote.

There are *many* short and colorful articles about Joe Knowles; some play
up the amusement factor and are fairly cavalier with the facts, but many are
well researched. Among the stories I found useful: "Joe Knowles, Seaview,
1869–1942," *Sou'wester,* Winter 1999, published by the Pacific County Historical Society and Museum (good data on Knowles in the West); "Where Are
They Now? The Nature Man," by Richard O. Boyer, *The New Yorker,* June 18,
1938 (Knowles exposed by Michael McKeogh); "Interesting People: A Modern Cave Man," by Fred Lockley, *American Magazine,* January 1921 (Knowles
at rest on the Long Beach Peninsula); "Tarzan of the Pines," by John Gould,
Christian Science Monitor, June 18, 1999 (factually questionable piece with a
wealth of information from a former *Post* insider); "Tarzan of the Maine Woods,"

by Lois Lowry, *Down East*, September 1979 (a pedestrian account with excellent photographs!); "The Saga of the Nature Man," by Herbert Adams, *Yankee Magazine*, October 1988 (a good, detail-filled account mostly of the first trip); "The Wild Man of Boston," by David Brown, *Washington Post*, October 8, 1997 (a nice overview); "The Original Nature Man," by Stewart H. Holbrook, *American Mercury #39*, 1936 (somewhat condescending, but informative); and "Yankee Tarzan," by Gerald Carson, *American Heritage Magazine*, April/May 1981 (Carson describes Knowles as "a man of shifting and uncertain moods," though his outlook brightened considerably after the mosquitoes stopped biting him).

And these sources were also consulted:

5 "As described in . . .": *American Humor: A Study of the National Character*, by Constance Rourke (New York: Harcourt, Brace and Company, 1931) provided insights into the Yankee character and its replacement in American tall tale and legend by the frontiersman.

5 "Harry Pierce's 34,000-acre King & Bartlett hunting camp . . .": The history of the camp was gathered in interviews at the camp itself and from K&B's website at www.kingandbartlett.com/tradition.html.

9 "The Jesuit Father Pierre Biard wrote in his book *Relation* . . .": An account of Father Biard's influence is set out in "The French Jesuits and the Idea of the Noble Savage," by George R. Healy, *The William and Mary Quarterly*, 3rd Series, Volume 15, Number 2 (April 1958), pp. 143–167. Another excellent source on early reactions to wilderness is *Reading the Roots: American Nature Writing Before Walden*, edited by Michael P. Branch (Athens: University of Georgia Press, 2004).

9 ". . . as dark as . . . Daniel Defoe's *Robinson Crusoe* . . .": There are, of course, many editions of Defoe's classic 1719 work. Paperback versions are available from both Modern Library and Penguin. A critical edition, *Robinson Crusoe* by Daniel Defoe (New York: W.W. Norton, 1994), offers modern interpretation of what can be a somewhat archaic writing style and the full, unabridged text.

12 "Even at a distance of one hundred years . . .": *The Chief: The Life of William Randolph Hearst*, by David Nasaw (New York: Houghton Mifflin, 2000).

2: The Makings of a Nature Man

26 "Edgar Rice Burroughs's *Tarzan of the Apes* was first serialized in 1912 . . .": The Yale-New Haven Teachers Institute offers "Would You Like to Swing on a Vine?: The Epic Tradition and Edgar Rice Burroughs," by Anthony F. Franco, posted at www.yale.edu/ynhti/curriculum/units/1987/2/87.02.05.x.html. Franco notes there were 24 Tarzan novels in all and "43 different film adaptations of the character to date since Elmo Lincoln starred in a silent version in 1918."

26 "According to an 1886 history . . .": The "History of Temple, Weld and Wilton, Maine" is taken from *A Gazetteer of the State of Maine*, by Geo. J. Varney (Boston: B. B. Russell, 1886). Varney on Wilton: "The chief occupation of the inhabitants is farming; and the well-cultivated appearance of the farms and the neatness and good repair of the buildings indicate thrift."

26 ". . . ice from the state's lakes and ponds was cut by horse-drawn teams
. . .": *The Edge of Maine,* by Geoffrey Wolff (Washington, D.C.: National Geographic, 2005). Wolff's short book is fascinating on many levels, but it's the description of Maine's huge ice industry that remains in the mind. Before refrigeration, ice packed in sawdust was shipped as far as Asia, where buyers complained that their expensive purchase melted.

28 "The 1890 census . . .": Research into the Knowles family census history was conducted by Sandra Tellvik of the Ilwaco Heritage Museum in Ilwaco, Washington, and Hazel M. Standeven of Scio, Oregon. Knowles (whose middle initial was "E" but whose middle name is unrecorded) had three siblings: George H., born in 1870; Leander W., born in 1871; and Mary J. (known as "Marme"), born in 1874. Mary Jane was later to marry Abbott Lathrop (known as "Bert") and have two daughters, Ethel Tyler and Lillian Lathrop. In a 1991 letter on file at the Ilwaco Heritage Museum, Douglas A. Lathrop, Sr., Mary Jane's grandson, describes spending many hours at her home in Wilton in the 1940s. "I kept her woodbox filled, cut her grass, ran errands and listened to her tell stories about Joe Knowles and the old family homestead," he said.

24 "Knowles gave a lengthy account of his younger days . . .": "From Woodsman to Artist: Child of the Forest, Guide and White-Waterman, Now a Successful Self-Taught Artist," by Fred Lockley, *Four L Bulletin,* August 1924. Lockley also wrote an important profile of Knowles for *The American Magazine* in 1921. In this story, Knowles describes his Navy service beginning at age nineteen. He says he was thrown into irons for insubordination, but picked the lock in the brig and went over the side. "I swam until the tide turned and was carried out to sea," he wrote. "At midnight an oyster boat picked me up and took me ashore. My muscles seemed to be have been paralyzed and for several days I couldn't walk or move my arms." He claims that the officer who put him in the brig was disciplined, and that he, Knowles, was eventually given an honorable discharge. But genealogist Hazel Standeven was unable to find records of Knowles's Navy service.

37 "A 1933 account . . .": "Original Back-to-Nature Man Now Happy on North Beach," by Edward M. Miller, *Portland Sunday Oregonian,* June 18, 1933. A photograph shows a somewhat portly Knowles, wearing a rare tie, with his much-beloved dog Wolf.

41 "Although he continued to design covers . . .": The covers of *National Sportsman* and *Baseball,* both from 1910, are in the Ilwaco Heritage Museum collection. The paintings are colorful and lively.

45 "One of its best ideas was the '*Boston Post* Cane'": There are several books about the canes, including: *The Bay State's Boston Post Canes: The History of a New England Tradition,* by Barbara Staples (Flemming Press, 1997).

46 "According to Mitchell Zuckoff's book . . .": *Ponzi's Scheme: The True Story of a Financial Legend,* by Mitchell Zuckoff (New York: Random House, 2006).

3: The Toast of Boston

I benefited from the archives of the Boston Public Library, which have both the *Boston Post* and *Boston American* on microfilm. The book *Desperate Journeys, Abandoned Souls,* by Edward Leslie (London: Macmillan, 1989), has a long and absorbing chapter on Joe Knowles, with much detail about the aftermath of the Maine trip.

An invaluable source for me about Knowles's reentry into Boston society was a long, unpublished paper written by Mark Neuzil, associate professor in the Department of Journalism and Mass Communication at the University of St. Thomas in St. Paul, Minnesota: "Applying Macro Media Theory to Journalism History: The Case of Nature Man and the Boston Newspaper Wars of 1913." It was delivered at the Kentucky Conference on Health Communication in Lexington, Kentucky in 1998 and will be excerpted by him for a forthcoming book.

Two avid Knowles collectors, Emery Neale and Charles Mulvey, put together large inventories of clippings and other material that are also in the Ilwaco Museum's collection and were drawn upon for this chapter. I am indebted to them for their diligence.

And these sources were also consulted:

50 "A *Boston Globe* story offers an intriguing addition": The *Globe* clippings, unfortunately undated, were sent to me by Brad Holden, operator of Attean Lake Lodge in Jackman, Maine. Brad's grandfather, Ruel Holden, provided Knowles with a banquet fit for a king after the Maine experiment.

51 "It compared in intensity to the 1850 concert tour . . .": "Mademoiselle Jenny Lind," *New York Herald,* September 16, 1850. Also, *P. T. Barnum Presents Jenny Lind: The American Tour of the Swedish Nightingale,* by W. Porter Ware and Thaddeus C. Lockard Jr., *American Music,* Volume 1, Number 1 (Spring, 1983), pp. 78–80. The authors say Lind gave ninety concerts on the tour, and she and Barnum parted as friends. Critics were rapturous in describing the Swedish Nightingale's voice, and tickets on her tour went for as much as $625. How great was Lind's voice? She was eventually recorded on a famous Edison cylinder, but it is now lost.

52 "One explanation for Knowles's nearly hysterical reception . . .": E-mail exchange, November 11, 2006, with Richard White, professor of American history at Stanford and author (with Patricia Nelson Limerick) of *The Frontier in American Culture* (Berkeley: University of California Press, 1994).

52 "Another specialist in this historical period . . .": E-mail exchange, December 1, 2006, with Louis S. Warren, professor of Western history at the University of California, Davis, and author of *Buffalo Bill's America: William Cody and the Wild West Show* (New York: Knopf, 2005).

56 "As described in Roderick Nash's book . . .": Nash, *Wilderness,* p. 142.

58 "(and sometimes fighting with) Beacon Hill philanthropist . . .": "The Philanthropist and the Physical Educator," by Betty Spears, *The New England Quarterly,* Volume 47, Number 4 (December 1974), pp. 594–602.

59 "Eugen Sandow, a vaudeville attraction . . .": An amusing collection of Sandow-related material is at the Online Physical Culture Museum, www.sandowplus.co.uk/sandowindex.htm.

63 "As *Sunday Post* editor Charles E. L. Wingate wrote . . .": *Sunday Post* editor Charles E. L. Wingate wrote to W. T. Stott of Portland, Oregon, about his involvement with the Knowles story on April 9, 1919. The letter is in the collection of the Ilwaco Heritage Museum. Wingate adds: "The Hearst people attacked the exploit and declared that Knowles had faked some of it. But the answer to that is simple enough: A few months later, the Hearst people in San Francisco and Los Angeles made arrangements with Knowles to do the same exploit in the California forests and he did so successfully."

63 ". . . the biggest fake of the century . . .": The editorial about Knowles appeared in the *Hartford Courant,* October 24, 1913.

64 "One contemporary vaudeville performer . . .": *Charles Kellogg: The Nature Singer (His Book)* (Morgan Hill, California: Pacific Science Press, 1929). Although probably hard to find, it's an enthralling read and might turn up on eBay or Amazon. Kellogg writes: "Through a strange whim of Nature, my throat, below the vocal chords, has the same physical structure as that of a bird, so that my songs are not imitations but genuinely my own, with the range and quality of the birds."

65 "A poster from that momentous occasion survives . . .": Interview with Sean Minear.

67 "Dr. Frederick A. Cook had claimed . . . ": The Frederick A. Cook Society has online resources at www.cookpolar.org. A collection of the man's works is maintained in Hurleyville, New York.

69　"According to the *Island Patriot* . . . ": "The Wild Man of the Woods Tells His Story," *Island Patriot,* December 6, 1913. Knowles was described as "clad in the garb of the wilds, his stalwart form draped with deer skin and bear skin," with "tattooed and bronzed muscular arms and shoulders."

69　"As a finale at the end of his Prince Edward Island lecture . . .": The December 9, 1913, *Charlottetown Guardian* account is colorfully summarized as the "Wild Man of Maine" chapter of Boyde Beck's book *Prince Edward Island: An (un)Authorized History* (Charlottetown, Prince Edward Island: Acorn Press, 1995). In an April 9, 2007, e-mail, he speculates that the bear probably originated in New Brunswick, ". . . since bears were becoming very scarce on PEI in 1913."

73 ". . . said one witness, fifteen-year-old Helon Taylor . . . ": The eyewitness interview with Helon Taylor, the fifteen-year-old who went into the woods with Knowles to see the second bear get clubbed, appears in the story "And Naked Into the Woods He Went," by Wendell Tremblay, *Maine Sunday Telegram,* August 12, 1973. This is an invaluable account, because, as the future superintendent of Baxter State Park, Taylor was an upstanding citizen and a very credible witness.

74 "In February 1914, *The Nation* proclaimed . . . ": The review appeared on February 19, 1914, in Volume 98, Number 2538 of *The Nation.* The reviewer noted that Knowles's "physical life, in brief, though not without tribulations, seemed to him of almost trifling importance in comparison with his mental life." London's *Chronicle* reviewed *Alone in the Wilderness* on March 7, 1914. It praised his "confidence as a former companion of Indian trackers. . . ."

75 "The Maine trail grew cold . . .": The *New Yorker* article, *The Nature Man*, by Richard O. Boyer appeared in the issue of June 18, 1938, under the heading "Where Are They Now?" The Nature Man's rebuttal, "Knowles Boos Story Charging Him Faker," appeared in the *Chinook Observer*'s front page on September 23, 1938. Boyer, who wrote for the *Daily Worker* as well as the *New Yorker*, was called before the Senate Internal Security Subcommittee in 1955 and refused to answer questions about his affiliation with the Communist Party. Knowles, who hated Boyer, would have had a field day with that information.

80 "Another curious footnote . . .": "Primitive Man in Maine Woods Sends President Birchbark Letter," *Washington Post*, September 15, 1913.

82 "Gould wrote his own account of Knowles's time in the woods . . .": "Tarzan of the Pines," by John Gould, *Christian Science Monitor*, June 18, 1999, p. 23. Gould says Knowles was "ready and willing to be [Roy Atkinson's] accomplice in the sensation that followed." But only Gould sees Atkinson's hand in the scheme. An appreciation of Gould's life and long-running column, "The Quintessential Downeast Storyteller," appeared in the *Monitor* on September 3, 2003.

4: Faking It in the Fading Frontier

For this chapter about frontier legends, I benefited from much recent scholarship that reveals the truth behind long-held myths. Books that I found useful for this reporting included: *Calamity Jane: The Woman and the Legend*, by James D. McLaird (Norman: University of Oklahoma Press, 2005); *Doc Holliday: The Life and Legend*, by Gary L. Roberts (Hoboken: John Wiley and Sons, 2006); and *Gunfighter Nation: The Myth of the Frontier in Twentieth-Century America*, by Richard Slotkin (New York: Atheneum, 1992). The solid reporting in these works contrasts sharply with the standard that existed at the turn of the century, as seen in entertaining but fanciful volumes like the 1903 *History of Our Wild West and Stories of Pioneer Life*, by D. M. Kelsey (Thompson & Thomas), which collects tall tales about Buffalo Bill, Wild Bill Hickok, Kit Carson, Davy Crockett, and others.

These sources were also consulted:

86 "Historian Frederick Jackson Turner cited this passage . . .": The complete text of Frederick Jackson Turner's influential paper, "The Significance of the Frontier in American History," is available online at http://xroads.virginia.edu/~Hyper/TURNER.

88 "Muir founded the Sierra Club in 1892 . . .": A newer biography is *John Muir: Family, Friends, and Adventures*, edited by Sally M. Miller and Daryl Morrison (Albuquerque: University of New Mexico Press, 2005). He was not the sole founder; according to the biography, he collaborated with "colleagues from the University of California, lawyers and others."

88 ". . . an 'interesting case history'": Interview with Jim Tantillo, a lecturer in environmental ethics at Cornell. A gallery of Knowles images is online as part of Tantillo's course curriculum for "People, Values and Natural Resources" at www.dnr.cornell.edu/courses/nr220/knowles/knowles1.htm.

88 ". . . a somewhat darker side . . .": Nash, *Wilderness*, p. 143. Nash's account of Knowles was first published in an essay entitled "The American Cult of the Primitive" (*American Quarterly*, Volume 18, Number 3, Autumn 1966), and then in the "Wilderness Cult" chapter of the book that appeared the following year. Dr. Nash was also kind enough to respond to my telephone calls and e-mails.

89 "There was also a distinct layer of anxiety . . .": *Idol Worship: A Shameless Celebration of Male Beauty in the Movies*, by Michael Ferguson (Herndon, Virginia: Starbooks, 2005). Masculinity was on the line, according to *This Mad Masquerade: Stardom and Masculinity in the Jazz Age*, by Gaylyn Studlar (New York: Columbia University Press, 1996). "Into the 1910s," he wrote, "the wilderness continued to be regarded as the site for a unique validation of masculinity mythically compatible with traditional values linked to America's frontier experience," he writes. And Studlar says that Knowles's "media-driven adventures" made this wilderness fascination explicit.

Nature and the Environment in Twentieth-Century American Life, by Brian Black (Westport, Connecticut: Greenwood Press, 2006), offers some insights. Black reports that "[Theodore] Roosevelt spurred a national interest in virility. He was concerned that young people growing up in a highly mechanized society would become soft. To keep this from happening, he worked with others to initiate various clubs and organizations, including the Boone and Crockett or Izaak Walton Clubs. Each group had an offspring for younger male members, with Sons of Daniel Boone proving the most popular."

Feminist writers also seized on this theme. In *Undomesticated Ground: Recasting Nature as Feminist Space*, by Stacy Alaimo (Ithaca: Cornell University Press, 2000), the author writes that Knowles "exemplifies the trend toward using the wilderness to rigidify rough-hewn ideals of masculinity." In *Reinventing Eden: The Fate of Nature in Western Culture* (New York: Routledge, 2003), Carolyn Merchant comments that Knowles's saga "epitomizes the male encounter with female nature to restore the frontier ruggedness lost to the soft, civilized, city life also gendered as female."

90 "The public was hungry for information . . .": *The Nature Fakers: Wildlife, Science & Sentiment*, by Ralph H. Lutts (Golden, Colorado: Fulcrum, 1990). A good short account of the controversy is in *American Heritage*, "T.R. and the 'Nature Fakers,'" by Gerald Carson (February 1971). Also of interest were some of the books of the period, including *The Kindred of the Wild: A Book of Animal Life*, by Charles G. D. Roberts (Boston: L.C. Page and Company, 1902).

92 "The wilderness craze . . .": A short stack of books offers insights into the early twentieth-century "nature cult," including *Reading the Trail*, by Corey Lee Lewis (Reno: University of Nevada Press, 2005). Lewis writes that as the western boundary was reached, "American attitudes toward the frontier began to shift from conquest to nostalgia. . . . It was during this period that Americans, especially easterners, began devouring the works of regional western writers like Mary Austin and [Sierra Club founder] John Muir."

95 "Eventually, even *Call of the Wild* . . .": Jack London's full essay on the nature fakers' controversy is online at http://london.sonoma.edu/Writings/Revolution/animals.html.

96 "The great showman Phineas Taylor Barnum . . .": *The Colossal P. T. Barnum Reader,* by P. T. Barnum, edited by James W. Cook (Champaign: University of Illinois Press, 2005). There are many wonderful books on the fabulous adventures of P. T. Barnum, and the old humbug's own writing is itself an excellent source.

98 "The quintessential exemplar . . .": *Daniel Boone: An American Life,* by Michael A. Lofaro (Lexington: University Press of Kentucky, 2003).

99 ". . . nineteenth-century legend Mike Fink . . .": Rourke, *American Humor.*

101 ". . . half a dozen different deaths were attributed to the boatman . . .": The 1847 article "Death of Mike Fink," by Joseph M. Field is online at http://xroads.virginia.edu/~hyper/detoc/sw/fink1.html.

101 "Crockett was a legend . . .": *The Frontiersman: The Real Life and the Many Legends of Davy Crockett,* by Mark Derr (New York: William Morrow, 1994).

102 "I . . . found my dogs . . .": From the *Narrative of the Life of David Crockett of the State of Tennessee.* The text is available free online, but there is also an annotated edition: *A narrative of the life of David Crockett of the State of Tennessee. A facsim. ed. with annotations and an introd. by James A. Shackford and Stanley J. Folmsbee* (Knoxville: University of Tennessee Press, 1973).

103 "One of the acknowledged masters of the genre . . .": *The Great Rascal: The Life and Adventures of Ned Buntline,* by Jay Monaghan (New York: Bonanza Books, 1951).

104 "But Louis S. Warren's 2005 . . .": *Buffalo Bill's America: William Cody and the Wild West Show,* by Louis S. Warren (New York: Alfred A. Knopf, 2005). Dr. Warren was also illuminating in an e-mail interview. This book is a model of modern scholarship on the old West.

105 "He staged this scene many times . . .": D. M. Kelsey, *History of Our Wild West.*

107 "Hickok also chronically exaggerated . . .": *Wild Bill Hickok: The Man and His Myth,* by Joseph G. Rosa (Lawrence: University Press of Kansas, 2007).

107 "Similarly given to tall tales . . .": The text of Calamity Jane's amusing but hardly factual autobiographical pamphlet is offered online by the valuable Project Gutenberg at www.gutenberg.org/dirs/etext96/cjane10.txt. McLaird, *Calamity Jane.*

109 "In the audience was an imaginative . . .": *Grey Owl: The Many Faces of Archie Belaney,* by Jane Billinghurst (New York: Kodansha International, 1999). A film titled *Grey Owl,* starring Pierce Brosnan in the title role, was directed by Richard Attenborough and released in 1999. The film focuses on the romantic relationship between Grey Owl and his Iroquois bride, Pony, and was generally well received (especially in Canada).

5: Knowles Makes Headlines out West

The primary source on Knowles's adventures in the Siskiyous is the *San Francisco Examiner,* which sponsored the trip and covered it in great detail. As in Boston, the grand adventure struck a chord with many. One of the latter was a seventy-five-year-old reader in San Francisco who sent Knowles a shirt made "while you were in the woods suffering with your sore feet. . . . It has been a great pleasure to me to read about you in the woods."

These sources were also consulted:

116 "According to a dubious 1976 column . . .": "Outdoors," by Bud Leavitt, *Bangor Daily News,* October 9–10, 1976. He tries to answer the question "Who in God's name is Joe Knowles?"

118 "The *Examiner* was close to Hearst's heart. . . .": David Nasaw, *The Chief* (New York: Houghlin Mifflin, 2000). This is the definitive book on one of America's most influential media moguls.

119 "He was at the time distracted by his foray into movies . . .": A great source on Hearst's involvement with motion pictures (including his dalliance with the Wharton Brothers in Ithaca) is *Hearst Over Hollywood: Power, Passion and Propaganda in the Movies* by Louis Pizzitola (New York: Columbia University Press, 2002). Another useful book is *Citizen Hearst,* by W. A. Swanberg (New York: Charles Scribner's Sons, 1961).

119 "In mid-June, Knowles was in Kansas City . . .": "As Adam Lived in Eden: Joseph Knowles, in Kansas City Today, Tells of New Plan," *Kansas City Star,* June 20, 1914. Charles Mulvey's Knowles collection was kept in a big leatherbound scrapbook, and this piece was in it. Knowles gives a novel account of how he went into the woods: A friend told him nobody could live in the woods without a gun, rod, fire, and clothes. "Don't believe it," Knowles replied. He sat down with a long list of supposed "necessities," and gradually struck off everything he knew he could do without. "And you know what?" he asked. "There wasn't a necessity left. Then I decided to make the experiment."

120 "A 1991 story in . . .": "Joseph Knowles: The Story of the Hotel Monticello Murals," by Virgil Elizabeth Hopkins, *Cowlitz Historical Quarterly,* Volume XXXIII, Number 4, 1991. The lengthy piece was helpful both at this juncture and later on, when Knowles had moved to Seaview, Washington. The periodical is published by the Cowlitz County Historical Museum, 405 Allen Street, Kelso, WA 98626.

125 "Christofferson is best remembered for setting a world altitude record . . .": "Rose Festival Takes Off," *The Oregonian,* January 8, 2007. Christofferson was also quoted in *The Oregonian* of June 10, 1912: "This is an age of do it first. Be original; don't copy. When a feat has once been performed, the people tire of it and expect the next performer to give something entirely new. That is the only reason I have decided to make a flight from the top of the Multnomah Hotel building on Tuesday afternoon. It will be the first exhibition of the kind in the history of aviation."

126 "Biographer Alex Kershaw . . .": Telephone interview with Alex Kershaw, December 29, 2006.

135 "On July 28, Austria-Hungary declared war on Serbia . . .": *A Short History of World War I*, by James L. Stokesbury (New York: Harper Paperbacks, 1981).

137 "F. L. Brown of Hartford, Connecticut . . .": "Joseph Knowles, Who Gets Back to Nature," *Hartford Courant*, September 13, 1914.

143 "Joe Knowles was a big hit in Oregon.": "Joe Knowles Seen in Primitive Garb," *Morning Oregonian*, September 5, 1914.

6: Ishi and the Native Tradition

149 "He expounded at some length . . .": We know that Knowles visited the Penobscot Indians in Old Town because Charles Mulvey collected an undated clip on the subject from the *Bangor Daily News* entitled "Joe Knowles Visits Penobscot Indians." The story said he was "warmly greeted by the governor and all the island residents." Among the Penobscots, he said, "for the first time since my return to the civilized world I met the people whose forefathers (and they themselves) have lived closer to nature than any others to whom I have been telling the story of my past two months' existence."

149 "Knowles's interest in Indian subjects . . .": Letter to Joe Knowles from Philippine Schmidt Rettenmayer of San Francisco, August 22, 1931.

150 "The midwife of that transformation . . .": *Black Wolf: The Life of Ernest Thompson Seton*, by Betty Keller (New York: HarperCollins, 1986). A well-annotated discussion of Seton's conflict with Baden-Powell is available at www.infed.org/thinkers/seton.htm. Ernest Thompson Seton's *Wild Animals I Have Known*, which features 200 illustrations, is available in a 2006 edition from Hard Press.

152 ". . . both Ishi and Pope enjoyed this carnival of cowboys . . .": *Ishi's Brain*, by Orin Starn (New York: W.W. Norton, 2004), shows great energy in pursuit of its quarry, which is considerably more than the man's gray matter. Starn also granted me an interview and we exchanged several e-mails. *Ishi in Two Worlds*, by Theodora Kroeber (Berkeley: University of California Press, 2004), is the most recent edition of the 1967 standard text on Ishi. Another book for younger readers is *Ishi: The Last of His People*, by David R. Collins and Kristen Bergren (Greensboro, North Carolina: Morgan Reynolds Publishing, 2000). Alfred Kroeber's involvement in the farce at the American Museum of Natural History involving the corpse of the shaman Qisuk is described in *Give Me My Father's Body*, by Kenn Harper (London: Profile Books Ltd., 2001).

152 ". . . the information Kroeber gathered from Ishi . . .": *Handbook of the Indians of California* (Smithsonian Institution, Bureau of American Ethnology), by A. L. Kroeber (Mineola, New York: Dover, 1976).

154 ". . . discovered the singer Leadbelly in 1933 . . .": *The Life and Legend of Leadbelly*, by Charles K. Wolfe and Kip Lornell (Cambridge, Massachusetts: Da Capo, 2006). Leadbelly was serving a term in prison and made a plea in song for his release to Louisiana governor O. K. Allen. He was released in 1934 into the personal recognizance of Lomax, who employed him as his personal chauffeur. Leadbelly's marriage certificate is on file in the Wilton, Connecticut town hall.

154 "And Ishi was certainly treated much better than Ota Benga . . .": *Ota Benga: The Pygmy in the Zoo*, by Phillips Verner Bradford (New York, St. Martin's Press, 1992), tells that whole story. The missionary who brought Ota Benga and eight other Congolese pygmies to the United States in 1904 for exhibit at the St. Louis World's Fair was the author's grandfather, Samuel Phillips Verner. Ota Benga later committed suicide.

157 "According to Steven Shackley . . .": The 1996 press release about University of California at Berkeley researcher Steven Shackley and his conclusions about Ishi's arrowpoints is at www.berkeley.edu/news/media/releases.

7: Dawn Man Meets Dawn Woman

161 "Public records in Pierce County, Washington . . .": Genealogical information on Joseph Knowles was gathered by Hazel M. Standeven of Scio, Oregon and was submitted for publication in the journal of the York County (Maine) Genealogical Society in 2006. Census records for Eustis, Maine, in 1900 record Knowles's marriage to Sadie O. Knowles (formerly Sadie Andrews) as having taken place in 1892. But the Boston census of 1910 dates the marriage to 1895. Sandra Tellvik of the Ilwaco Heritage Museum complemented Standeven's research with additional work on the genealogical record in early 2007. She reveals that Sadie Knowles was divorced by 1910, living with her sister and working as a hotel chambermaid.

161 "According to her obituary in 1947 . . . ": The obituary as found in the records of the Ilwaco Heritage Museum is undated and unidentified, though it is probably from the *Chinook Observer*. The obituary notes that the services were "arranged by her lifelong friend and home companion Nellie Carney."

163 ". . . he had many female admirers . . .": These letters are part of the collection at the Long Beach Peninsula Trading Post in Ocean Park.

163 "Knowles had a very good experience . . .": It proved impossible to confirm that either of Knowles's nature films, *Alone in the Wilderness* and *The Nature Man*, still exists, though rumors indicated that at least one of them is still extant. The Internet Movie Database (www.IMDb.com) is a very valuable research tool, but its information on Joe Knowles's films is neither comprehensive nor accurate.

166 ". . . the *Atlanta Constitution* advertised local showings . . .": The ad appears Sunday, January 9, 1916. In a bit of hyperbole, it was described as "the mightiest, most fascinating, most remarkable of all nature pictures."

166 "One of Knowles's many side trips . . .": "Joe Knowles Talks to Students, Makes 'Nature Fire' for Them," *Los Angeles Daily News*, September 22, 1914. Knowles appeared in "the conventional garb of 1914," rather than the much-traveled bearskin.

169 "With no intention of leaving . . .": What is probably the only copy of Knowles's original screenplay *A Modern Robinson Cruso* [*sic*] and correspondence relating to it are preserved in the personal collection of Brenda Hill, who runs the Long Beach Peninsula Trading Post on the peninsula in Ocean Park.

172 "Knowles wrote to the newly elected mayor . . .": This undated letter to William Hale "Big Bill" Thompson is also at the Long Beach Peninsula Trading Post. Thompson's reply was sent on May 31, 1916.

173 "The news came in July 1916 . . .": The *New York American* and its sister paper, the *Evening Journal,* are on microfilm in the main 42nd Street branch of the New York Public Library. Unfortunately, the work was not done well, and some of the relevant stories are only partly readable.

174 "In 1887, *Treasure Island* author Robert Louis Stevenson . . .": The Stevenson Society of America owns Robert Louis Stevenson's memorial cottage and museum in Lake Saranac, New York. There are dozens of Stevenson biographies, but if you simply want to read about the Scottish author playing the pennywhistle in Lake Saranac, go to http://pennypiper.org/ssindex.HTM.

175 "It was also to the neighboring Adirondacks . . .": "Following a Hermit's Footsteps," by John Motyka, *New York Times,* "Escapes" section, October 7, 2005.

176 ". . . in a bemused account that July . . .": "Six Eves to One Adam," *Washington Post,* July 16, 1916. The article describes them as a "sextet of wood nymphs."

177 "Elaine Hammerstein had an impeccable theatrical pedigree.": There is, unfortunately, no biography, auto or otherwise, of Elaine Hammerstein. In fact, the longest treatise I found relating to her is a six-page sketch in a long-out-of-print book, *Ladies in Distress,* by Kalton C. Lahue (New York: A.S. Barnes, 1971). "Among the several stars who carried the banner of [Lewis J.] Selznick Pictures to the screen was the young and attractive daughter of Arthur Hammerstein, the well-known theatrical producer," Lahue writes. "Born in Philadelphia in 1897, Elaine Hammerstein's close connection with the theatre almost guaranteed her success in show business, with or without talent." But talent she had. Lahue notes that after Selznick left World Pictures to found his own company, he approached Hammerstein, contract in hand, because she had "a name that could be easily exploited."

   Elaine is barely mentioned in the books on the Hammerstein family and on Rodgers and Hammerstein. These include *The Sound of Their Music: The Story of Rodgers and Hammerstein,* by Frederick Nolan (New York: Walker, 1978), and *They're Playing Our Song,* by Max Wilk (New York: New York Zeotrope, 1973, expanded 1986), though both of these were helpful in getting to know Elaine's cousin, Oscar Hammerstein II. Keeping the flame alive is the Rodgers and Hammerstein Organization, 1065 Avenue of the Americas, Suite 2400, New York, NY 10001.

178 "In his amusing book on vaudeville . . .": I had several conversations with Travis Stewart, a/k/a Trav S.D., author of *No Applause—Just Throw Money: The Book That Made Vaudeville Famous* (New York: Faber and Faber, 2005). This is a very funny and readable history of the almost-forgotten vaudeville stage,

with priceless information on Oscar Hammerstein I, Willie Hammerstein, and Elaine's father Arthur Hammerstein. Playwright, actor, and historian Stewart founded the American Vaudeville Theatre in 1996, and its productions (which include radio plays) should be sought out.

181 "Terry Harbin, whose day job . . .": The records of the Wharton Releasing Corporation are held by the Division of Rare and Manuscript Collections at the Cornell University Carl A. Kroch Library in Ithaca, New York. Terry Harbin, who works at the Tomkins County Public Library, is the best source for filmmaking in Ithaca. He was kind enough to talk to me at length and e-mail me followup information. For a great archive of "Ithaca-Made Movies," go to http://home.twcny.rr.com/imm. For some reason, this corner of William Randolph Hearst scholarship is little visited.

184 ". . . help explain the world . . .": I interviewed Oscar Hammerstein III, better known as Andy, at the Ridgefield, Connecticut Starbucks on January 26, 2007. The family historian and a significant visual artist, he was helpful and very funny. What he couldn't remember, he looked up on his laptop.

187 "But Arthur was named as a co-respondent in a divorce case . . .": "I Couldn't Promise to Stay Married," *Indianapolis Sunday Star Magazine*, September 10, 1922. This lurid article certainly succeeds in painting Arthur Hammerstein's picture as a proud serial philanderer.

187 "He always referred to it as . . .": The quote from William Hammerstein about *The Light That Failed* is from Max Wilk's book *They're Playing Our Song*.

188 "According to the biography that appeared . . .": The 1923 *Blue Book of the Screen* is online at http://silentgents.com/indexBlueBook.html.

190 "This angle takes center stage . . .": Peter Bogdanovich's film of *The Cat's Meow* (2001), based on a play, makes good viewing, though its content is highly speculative.

196 "He was a committed eugenicist . . .": Twelve linear feet of records pertaining to the American Eugenics Society, 1916–1973, is held by the American Philosophical Society, 105 South Fifth Street, Philadelphia, PA 19106–3386. To read some actual (and chilling) original eugenics documents, visit the American Eugenics Movement Image Archive at www.eugenicsarchive.org.

196 "The Whartons made the infamous film *The Black Stork* . . .": The unbelievable story of the Wharton brothers' eugenics film is told in *The Black Stork: Eugenics and the Death of "Defective" Babies in American Medicine and Motion Pictures since 1915* (New York: Oxford University Press). Author Martin S. Pernick, a professor of history at the University of Michigan at Ann Arbor, shared insights with me. "Hearst himself was at the Wharton Studio in Ithaca during the final editing of *The Black Stork* in mid-September 1916," he told me. "But by mid-1917, Hearst enterprises appear to have backed off their support. I discuss several likely reasons on pp. 152–53 of my book, including the coincidence that Hearst and Wharton became embroiled in a lawsuit over credits."

203 "Elsie Frick of 148th Street in New York City . . .": This letter, dated September 28, 1916, is in the collection of the Ilwaco Heritage Museum.

203 "Knowles never saw Elaine Hammerstein again . . .": It would have been interesting to know what Knowles made of Hammerstein's ascendant career. His moment in the national spotlight was over after 1916, but hers was just beginning. An inability to kill her own game proved no hindrance to a successful film career.

According to statistics published by theater owner William Brandt, she was popular enough to earn an estimated $2,500 per week in 1923 (more than the "man of a thousand faces," Lon Chaney, and on a par with major star Wallace Beery). But Hammerstein's films—she made more than forty, mostly melodramas and comedies—are not easy to find these days. At least eighteen of them survive in various film libraries, ranging from the George Eastman House in Rochester, New York, to the British Film Institute in London. But by far the biggest cache is at the Library of Congress's Motion Picture, Broadcasting and Recorded Sound Division, located just across the Mall from the Capitol Building in Washington, D.C.

Patrons do not see these films in a darkened theater, seated on velvet cushions and clutching a bag of popcorn. Instead, they seat themselves at old Steenbeck editing tables and thread big rolls of 35- or 16-millimeter film, which they view on a flickering screen. They must wear white gloves when handling the film, and no food or drink is permitted.

Some of Hammerstein's films are pristine, but others were badly damaged by improper storage. Fortunately, there's enough left to see that Elaine Hammerstein was, if not a groundbreaking, risk-taking actor, certainly a competent and immensely appealing one. She had a dark beauty in a heart-shaped face, a wide, hearty smile, and a range of emotional resources that ran from juvenile exuberance to tear-stained heartbreak. She looked a bit like Pola Negri or Louise Brooks, but was much more wholesome; she had none of Negri's vampish intensity or Brooks's exoticism.

Hammerstein almost always played a good American girl beset by circumstances. In William P. S. Earle's *The Way of a Maid,* a brisk comedy produced for Selznick in 1921, she is genuinely funny as a merry Jazz Age party girl heiress who is mistaken for a maid by a drunken playboy (Niles Welch), then must actually take the job when her wealth evaporates. Welch and Hammerstein were paired in several pictures and had a definite chemistry.

Paint and Powder is also noteworthy, not only for Hammerstein's lively performance as Mary Dolan, a rags-to-riches dancer who hits the big time on Broadway, but for its rich, atmospheric photography. Unusually for an Elaine Hammerstein picture, it has a tragic ending when the male lead (Theodore Van Eltz) waits too long to claim her hand.

One gets the impression that Hammerstein didn't take herself or her film career too seriously. It's all a lark, and a little girl is playing dress-up. (Hammerstein was a fashionable dresser, on and off screen. She made the tabloids in 1920 by claiming that women were paying too much for fancy clothes with designer labels.) In his book *Ladies in Distress,* author Kalton C. Lahue asks

"What made Elaine Hammerstein's films so enjoyable? This same lightheartedness with which she regarded her career came across boldly on screen. Here was an actress who bore her distinguished name without pretensions, and even in the deepest of melodramatic moments seemed to be saying, 'It's only a great big make-believe world.'"

She exuded a Jean Arthur-like breeziness that worked particularly well in movies of the 1920s, especially comedies. She should have made more of those. It's quite possible that, had she stayed with film, she would have transitioned relatively easily to sound a few years later.

And Hammerstein had a ready path to sound: She married Alan Crosland, director of both the first film with synchronized music and sound effects, *Don Juan* (1926), and *The Jazz Singer* (1927), the first picture with synched dialogue. The path to the marriage followed a familiar scenario, since Crosland directed her in the 1920 drama *Greater Than Fame* and the 1922 *Why Announce Your Marriage?* (with Niles Welch).

The marriage, his second and her first, did not last long, from 1925 to 1926. Crosland, like Elaine's uncle Arthur, was a man about town in that period, driving fast cars around Hollywood with one starlet after another on his arm. The brief marriage produced no children, and Crosland would be married again in 1930. *The Jazz Singer* would prove to be Crosland's career high point; by the time of his death in 1936 he was directing B pictures. His death prefigured Hammerstein's more than twenty years later. Crosland was driving on Sunset Boulevard and hit some road debris from a construction site, flipping his car twice. He died several days later, aged just forty-one.

Hammerstein bounced back quickly from her dalliance with Crosland. In 1926, having relocated with her former husband to California, she got married once again, this time to Los Angeles fire commissioner James Walter Kays. She was 28; he was 42, and they'd been engaged for six months. The announcement of the marriage in the *Oakland Tribune* on June 10, 1926, appeared on the front page, with a large picture of Elaine dressed as a flapper. But it contained two serious errors of fact, claiming that the marriage was her first and that she was the daughter of Oscar Hammerstein. *Time* magazine noted the nuptials also, getting more of the facts right but describing Elaine as a "fluffy cinema actress." The Kays/Hammerstein wedding was apparently a very quiet affair, with only Elaine's mother and "several immediate friends" in attendance.

Hammerstein was evidently looking for stability, and she found it with Kays. Despite the poor example of her much-married father (who never made it to his daughter's wedding), and her own earlier history, she lived quietly with her new man for more than twenty years. She also quit the movies cold, never making another after *Ladies of Leisure* that same year of 1926.

Kays became an insurance broker and stayed active politically.In 1940, he againhelped raise money for the Democrats, serving as financial chairman for the Franklin D. Roosevelt reelection campaign. The couple might have been expected to enjoy a comfortable late middle age, but fate intervened with a horrendous 1948 car crash in Mexico.

Hammerstein, then fifty, and Kays, sixty-six, were passengers on August 13

in a car driven by Richard Garvey, scion of a well-known Los Angeles landown-
ing family. The party of five was traveling near La Gloria, twelve miles south
of Tijuana, when they collided head-on with what the *Los Angeles Times* described as "a machine driven by a Mexican."

According to the *New York Times,* the driver of the Mexican car reported that
the other vehicle (registered to Kays) approached on the wrong side of the road
at a high rate of speed, collided with him, and then caromed off the road into
a hillside. All the passengers in Hammerstein's car died instantly, except for
Garvey who died later in a Tijuana hospital. The passengers in the Mexican
car escaped serious injury.

Elaine Hammerstein is buried in Los Angeles's Calvary Cemetery, which is
Catholic-affiliated. It seems likely that Hammerstein converted to her husband's faith, thus putting some distance from her origins among the wildly colorful Hammersteins of Broadway.

8: The Artist out of the Woods

For much of the material in chapter eight, I am indebted to the voluminous
Joseph Knowles files in the collection of the Ilwaco Heritage Museum in Ilwaco,
Washington (www.ilwacoheritagemuseum.org). The museum owns not only a
large collection of Knowles paintings, drawings, and etchings, but also some
of the copper plates used to make the latter. In a file cabinet are Knowles's original stories, his bank accounts, correspondence, and many fragments written
on whatever was handy.

These sources were also consulted:

209 "When Lewis and Clark's 'Corps of Discovery' . . .": Lewis and Clark's
diaries for 1804–1806 are online at the Internet site of the Lewis and Clark
Trail, http://lewisandclarktrail.com/diary.htm. Bernard DeVoto edited a version
titled *The Journals of Lewis and Clark* (New York: Mariner, 1997), with a fore-
word by historian Stephen Ambrose.

211 "In 1917, the year Knowles arrived . . .": "Graveyard of the Pacific: Shipwrecks on the Washington Coast," essay posted at www.historylink.org/
essays/output.cfm?file_id=7936.

211 "The water was always rough . . .": Author interview with Adele
Beechey, December 12, 2006.

211 ". . . a pudgy 'W. C. Fields type of character' . . .": Author interview with
Theresa Potter, January 9, 2007.

212 "Rodney Williams, who still lives in Long Beach . . .": Rodney
Williams's letter was dated January 15, 2007. He recalls meeting Knowles
around 1937, when Williams was ten years old. The location was Warner Smith's
grocery store in Seaview. Knowles told the young man that the Williams family had ended up in Ilwaco because the devil had decided to pick up all the
"imps" in the country and drop them in the ocean, but miscalculated and
dropped them in Ilwaco instead. He added, "I remember during the late 1930s
or early 1940s of [*sic*] going to the Knowles house with my parents and being

shown, I believe by Mrs. Knowles, various copper plates of his making including one of the 'Flying Dutchman.' We were told that the plates were only good for a certain number of reproductions and then became unusable. My parents purchased an etching by Miss [Edyth] Henry titled 'Windswept' which is still in our beach house living room."

214 "Ross Carpenter, an artist friend . . .": The letter is dated January 7, 1931. Carpenter, who admires Knowles's carefree approach to work, asks, "How would you like to primp yourself up in a stiff collar, highly polished shoes (and a few other glad rags) and make the rounds of the skyscraper offices trying to get an interview with some self-important, hard-boiled, half-baked moron, called in the vernacular 'an executive,' in order to plead with him to put you on the payroll?"

215 "Mary Jane 'Fuzzy' Walker . . .": Walker of Ilwaco invited me into her home in Ilwaco and showed me her scrapbook full of photographs. She was interviewed on December 21, 2006, by telephone and on January 6, 2007, in person. Asked about Joe Knowles, she said, "We lived side by side practically." Walker had several husbands. One was a commercial fisherman whose ship, *The Harvest Queen,* was lost at sea.

219 "Avast there, Sailor Knowles! . . .": The letter is dated September 15, 1935.

221 "Knowles was appointed as an unpaid deputy sheriff . . .": "Seaview Notables in a Lovely Tangle," *Ilwaco Tribune,* June 13, 1919. Also, "Knowles and Samuels are Acquitted," *Ilwaco Tribune,* June 20, 1919. Historian and artist Nancy Lloyd of Oysterville, author of *Observing Our Peninsula's Past,* provided the clippings about Knowles's brief career as a deputy sheriff. She writes in *Observing Our Peninsula's Past,* "And so Joe Knowles arrived in Seaview, liked what he saw and, on the rocks off of Holman Road, cobbled together a three-room cabin from beach flotsam."

222 "In 1921, when Knowles was still finding his way . . .": Lockley, *American Magazine.*

227 "According to Bruce Berney . . .": E-mail message from Bruce Berney to Sandra Tellvik of the Ilwaco Heritage Museum, November 19, 2005.

228 "According to the *Astoria Evening Budget* . . .": "Joe Knowles Paints Mural Decorations for Ilwaco Theater," *Astoria Evening Budget,* December 29, 1924.

229 "Unbeknownst to Knowles . . .": A detailed account of the Hotel Monticello commission is in *R. A. Long's Planned City: The Story of Longview,* by John M. McClelland, Jr. (Longview: Westmedia, 1998). Other sources are the aforementioned "Joseph Knowles: The Story of the Hotel Monticello Murals" in the *Cowlitz Historical Quarterly;* a personal visit to Longview with two hours spent in the company of the pictures; and contemporary documents in the Ilwaco Heritage and Brenda Hill collections.

It is, in fact, impossible to overestimate the value of the latter trove, part of which is on public view at the Long Beach Peninsula Trading Post in Ocean Park. Thanks to Brenda Hill, many important documents that fill in holes in the Ilwaco Heritage collection were preserved. Hill has several letters pertaining to the

Hotel Monticello paintings, as well as extensive correspondence with members of Knowles's family (especially his sister, Marme, who seems to have been the force holding the family together). Included is what is probably one of the only letters his brother George, a night watchman at the T. A. Huston baking company in Auburn, Maine, ever wrote. "i dont rite verry much," he said.

232 "In January 1924 . . .": Hughes Bryant wrote from Kansas City on January 28, 1924. It was three years later, on November 2, 1927, that he wrote Knowles to say the watercolor "Conquerors of the Trail" book was missing.

237 "By June 1928 . . .": Eddie Rickenbacker wrote on Cadillac stationery on June 23, 1928. He wanted Knowles to join the "large and happy family of LaSalle and Cadillac owners."

238 "In 1924 and 1925 he borrowed money . . .": These records are in the Ilwaco Heritage Museum collection.

239 "Maxine Bown of Corvallis. . . .": Maxine Bown of Corvallis, Oregon was interviewed by telephone on March 8, 2006. She was located with the help of a relative, Allen Dickinson, who had bid on a Knowles etching on eBay.

239 "Astoria was then in the midst of rebuilding . . .": For information and insight into Knowles's (and Edyth Henry's) paintings at the Liberty Theater in Astoria, Oregon, I relied on a personal visit and an encounter with historian and restoration specialist Michael Foster.

239 "A graphic description of this fire . . .": Matthew Stadler's lecture at the Liberty Theater was delivered on the night of February 24, 2006, and was sponsored by the Oregon Humanities Council, which also published it as a booklet. Although Stadler isn't strictly accurate when it comes to Joseph Knowles, he compensates with considerable color (including a detailed description of Edyth's disappearance with the Harmons). Stadler believed that the "marked differences in the brushwork and brightness of some of the canvases points to the possibility that Henry might have helped Knowles meet his deadline."

241 "By February 27, he had completed . . .": "First Big Picture is Ready for Hanging," *Ilwaco Tribune*, February 27, 1925. Also, "Delivery Made of Knowles's First Set of Paintings," *Ilwaco Tribune*, March 27, 1925.

247 "Norblad was already a confirmed fan . . .": Letter from Albin Norblad, October 20, 1930.

247 ". . . he painted the chief justice of the Oregon Supreme Court . . .": Letter from Thomas McBride, March 20, 1928.

248 ". . . he had at least one more important commission . . .": "Beautiful Painting of the Peninsula Made by Knowles," *Ilwaco Tribune*, June 2, 1933.

250 "The 'circumstances' Edyth spoke of were singular . . .": Knowles's records of this affair and related correspondence are in the Ilwaco Heritage Museum collection.

252 "In 1940, when Knowles . . .": Letter from Kenneth E. Selby, dated April 24, 1940.

253 "Knowles family members . . .": Author interview with Susan Knowles Jordan, March 15, 2007. Her father, jazz bassist Donald Knowles, was also interviewed on March 8, 2006 and March 14, 2007.

254 "There has been only one . . .": "Art Showing is Featuring Local Work," *Astoria Evening Budget,* September 19, 1951. Also, "Joe Knowles Exhibit Brings Tributes From Many Sources," *Ilwaco Tribune,* September 21, 1951.

255 ". . . file drawers full of Joe Knowles's short stories . . .": Knowles's short stories exist in many drafts, now yellowed with age. He rarely managed to improve them in subsequent versions. Sometimes writer's block is evident. An aborted stab at "Mat Moses of Canby, Maine" ends in repeated lines (a la *The Shining*) of "Now is the time for all good men to come to the aid of their country. . . ." He had trouble getting to a point, or sticking to it when he found it. A piece headed "Memoirs: Psycology [*sic*] of Life" never actually gets to any psychology—it's mostly about his friend, the trapper Andy, who could talk to beavers and imitate the call of the whippoorwill. It's unclear why Knowles kept his rejection notices; perhaps he thought they'd be a spur to more inspired composition.

9: The Call of Nature

263 "In their bestselling book . . .": *The Century,* by Peter Jennings and Todd Brewster (New York: Doubleday, 1998), repeats the impressive but unfortunately mistaken notion that Knowles's book sold 300,000 copies, but is otherwise accurate in two long paragraphs. They point out that Knowles kept readers up to date, "even taking time to philosophize along the way, extolling the virtues of the natural life and scolding readers for being too 'civilized.'"

264 "Jim Mason, in his insightful . . .": *An Unnatural Order: Uncovering the Roots of Our Domination of Nature and Each Other,* by Jim Mason (New York: Simon and Schuster, 1993), might be hard to find, but it's worth the effort. For Mason, "the agrarian worldview sees the natural order of things as sometimes disordered, sometimes hierarchical, sometimes dualistic, but ever in need of human intervention to bring about proper order." Mason coined the term "misothery," meaning hatred of animals, which he sees as a necessary adjunct to human dominion over the rest of the planet. "And since animals are so representative of nature in general it can mean hatred and contempt for nature," he writes.

265 "As Dame Edith Sitwell describes . . .": *The English Eccentrics,* by Edith Sitwell (Boston: Houghton Mifflin, 1933), is an amusing romp through peerless eccentricity, or the eccentricity of the peers—including one who set fire to his own nightshirt to cure the hiccups.

265 "The ideas of the transcendental movement . . .": *Nature and Other Essays,* by Ralph Waldo Emerson (New York: Penguin Classics, 2003), contains the influential short book of 1836 and other useful works. Among the books it influenced was Henry David Thoreau's *Walden,* which needs no elaboration here. Because of its enduring popularity and expired copyright, there are dozens of editions, some illustrated and some annotated. The book celebrated its 150th anniversary in 2004.

267 ". . . the Scottish-born John Muir was experiencing . . .": *The Story of My Boyhood and Youth,* by John Muir (Edinburgh: Birlinn, 2006).

268 "In his very thorough history . . .": Because vegetarianism, nudity, and sun worship often went together in human history, *The Bloodless Revolution: A*

Cultural History of Vegetarianism From 1600 to Modern Times, by Tristram Stuart (New York: W.W. Norton, 2007), turned out to be quite useful.

269 "In the late nineteenth and early twentieth centuries . . .": The only book I found that focuses solely on the "Naturmenschen" and their descendants is *Children of the Sun: A Pictorial Anthology from Germany to California, 1883 to 1949,* by Gordon Kennedy (Ojai, California: Nivaria Press), 1998. Fidus's turn-of-the-century "psychedelic" art is particularly eye-opening.

277 "The *Portland Sunday Telegram* wrote in 1960 . . .": "Did Joe Knowles Roam State Woods in a Bear Skin?" by Bill Geagan, *Portland Sunday Telegram,* February 28, 1960.

278 "Not all the nature men were out for publicity . . .": The Leatherman deserves a book of his own, but doesn't seem to have gotten one. Books with "leatherman" in the title are usually about something entirely different. I relied on a comprehensive feature, "Mystery Still Conceals the Identity of Meriden's Legendary Leatherman," by Eric P. Sandahl, which appeared in the *Meriden Record,* July 22, 1948.

278 "Everett Ruess simply wanted to disappear . . .": There are several short biographies of Everett Ruess on the Web, including at www.everettruess.net and www.angelfire.com/sk/syukhtun/everett.html. There is also a book, *Everett Ruess: A Vagabond for Beauty,* by W. L. Rusho with Edward Abbey and John Nichols (Layton, Utah: Gibbs Smith, 1983).

279 "Hart, born in 1906 . . .": *The Last of the Mountain Men,* by Harold Peterson (Cambridge, Idaho: Backeddy, 1983), tells the story of Sylvan "Buckskin Bill" Hart. There's also an informative article about him by one "Grits" Gresham from *Hunting* magazine at www.huntingmag.com/big_game/mountain_men. Considering the source, it's not surprising that it focuses on the pistols and rifles Hart built from scratch.

280 "Very close in spirit . . .": *One Man's Wilderness: An Alaskan Odyssey,* by Sam Keith and Richard Proenneke (Portland, Oregon: Alaska Northwest Books, 1973), tells the late Proenneke's story. The video about him is titled *Alone in the Wilderness,* available online at www.dickproenneke.com.

281 "But others were hardier.": *The Final Frontiersman: Heimo Korth and His Family, Alone in Alaska's Arctic Wilderness,* by James Campbell (New York: Atria, 2004), is a very sympathetic portrait by his cousin. It's amusing to note how many of these books use words like "last" or "final" to describe their protagonists. It really doesn't seem likely we'll run out of mountain men or frontiersmen any time soon.

281 "Grieve was inspired by . . .": *The Call of the Wild: My Escape to Alaska,* by Guy Grieve (London: Hodder and Stoughton, 2006), is another finding-refuge-in-the-wilderness tale.

282 "More in the spirit of Joe Knowles . . .": Eustace Conway telephone interview, March 18, 2007. *The Last American Man,* by Elizabeth Gilbert (New York: Penguin, 2003).

283 "For a survivalist second opinion . . .": *How to Survive Anywhere: A Guide for Urban, Suburban, Rural, and Wilderness Environments,* by Christopher

Nyerges (Mechanicsburg, Pennsylvania: Stackpole, 2006), is just the latest guide by the prolific author and survivalist. He's written several others, including *Extreme Simplicity, Guide to Wild Foods and Useful Plants,* and *Enter the Forest.* Nyerges's School of Self-Reliance can be contacted at P.O. Box 41834, Eagle Rock, CA 90041, or through www.christophernyerges.com.

Epilogue

The archives of the Ilwaco Heritage Museum and Brenda Hill's collection at the Long Beach Peninsula Trading Post once again delivered the goods for many references in this chapter.

These sources were also consulted:

292 "What would Knowles have made . . .": *Wild: An Elemental Journey,* by Jay Griffiths (New York: Jeremy A. Tarcher, 2006).

293 "The concept of the marooned mariner . . .": Jean Craighead George was kind enough to respond to e-mail queries about her 1959 book *My Side of the Mountain,* which won the Newbery Honor and had two sequels. The trilogy is available as the *My Side of the Mountain Trilogy* (New York: Dutton Junior, 2000).

294 "In 2007, we have the latest contribution . . . ": *The Solitude of Thomas Cave,* by Georgina Harding (New York: Bloomsbury, 2007). In the end of the book, Cave has become a hermit again. He becomes convinced that whaling is a violation of nature.

296 "The *New York Times* obituary . . .": "Joe Knowles, Lived in Wilds Unarmed," *New York Times,* October 23, 1942. Also, "Last Rites Held for Seaview Artist," *South Bend Journal,* October 30, 1942. And "Joe Knowles Dead," *Chinook Observer,* October 23, 1942.

299 "For his 1997 book . . .": *The Sylvan Path: A Journey Through America's Forests,* by Gary Ferguson (New York: St. Martin's Press, 1997). This is not a book about Joe Knowles, but instead a beautifully written travelogue that uses Knowles's 1913 Maine trip as a guiding metaphor. Ferguson says "the lion's share of my childhood memories is shot full of leaves. Which is why it was such a sad surprise when in my mid–30s I looked over my shoulder to find that the trees had shrunk from my life. . . ." Hence the book. Ferguson writes, "As unlikely an inspiration as Joe Knowles might be, he's the one who left me hungry to go back out and roam the last wild places, places like Maine and Appalachia and the North Woods, looking for the people who still had pieces of the old American imagination in their pockets, people who never forgot how to warm their lives with the woods."

303 "Other TV nature shows . . .": Read all about Les Stroud, the Survivorman, at www.survivorman.ca or www.lesstroudonline.com. On The Science Channel's Web site, he is asked which books he considers indispensable for roughing it in the bush, and he recommends: *The Psychology of Wilderness Survival,* by Gino F. Ferri (Skyway Printing, 2000); *Wilderness Living and Primitive Skills: Naked into the Wilderness,* by John and Geri McPherson (self-published by Prairie Wolf, P.O. Box 96, Randolph, KS 66554); *Bushcraft: Outdoor Skills and Wilderness Survival,* by Mors Kochanski (Lone Pine Publishing, 1998); *Outdoor Survival Skills,* by Larry Dean Olsen (Chicago: Chicago Review Press, 1997); and any of the *Peterson Field Guides.*

304 "It was inevitable that Boyle . . .": *A Friend of the Earth,* by T. Coraghessan Boyle (New York: Viking, 2000), is just one of this prolific author's books to take a deep dive into the human/animal divide. Also essential are *Drop City* (2003), *The Tortilla Curtain* (1996), and the short-story collection *Tooth and Claw* (2006). His Web site at www.tcboyle.com contains book reviews, excerpts, links to interviews, a message board, and even contests.

BIBLIOGRAPHY

———•◆•———

Billinghurst, Jane. *Grey Owl: The Many Faces of Archie Belaney*. (New York: Kodansha International, 1999.)

Black, Brian. *Nature and the Environment in Twentieth-Century American Life*. (Westport, Connecticut: Greenwood Press, 2006.)

Boyle, T. Coraghessan. *A Friend of the Earth*. (New York: Viking, 2000.)

Bradford, Phillips Verner. *Ota Benga: The Pygmy in the Zoo*. (New York, St. Martin's Press, 1992.)

Branch, Michael P. (ed.). *Reading the Roots: American Nature Writing Before Walden*. (Athens: University of Georgia Press, 2004.)

Campbell, James. *The Final Frontiersman: Heimo Korth and His Family, Alone in Alaska's Arctic Wilderness*. (New York: Atria, 2004.)

Defoe, Daniel. *Robinson Crusoe*. (New York: W.W. Norton, 1994.)

DeVoto, Bernard (ed.). *The Journals of Lewis and Clark*. (New York: Mariner, 1997.)

Emerson, Ralph Waldo. *Nature and Other Essays*. (New York: Penguin Classics, 2003.)

Gilbert, Elizabeth. *The Last American Man*. (New York: Penguin, 2003.)

Grieve, Guy. *The Call of the Wild: My Escape to Alaska*. (London: Hodder and Stoughton, 2006.)

Harper, Kenn. *Give Me My Father's Body*. (London: Profile, 2001.)

Jennings, Peter, and Todd Brewster. *The Century*. (New York: Doubleday, 1998.)

Keith, Sam, and Richard Proenneke. *One Man's Wilderness: An Alaskan Odyssey*. (Portland, Oregon: Alaska Northwest Books, 1973.)

Keller, Betty. *Black Wolf: The Life of Ernest Thompson Seton.* (New York: HarperCollins, 1986.)

Kellogg, Charles. *Charles Kellogg: The Nature Singer (His Book).* (Morgan Hill, California: Pacific Science Press, 1929.)

Kelsey, D. M. *History of Our Wild West and Stories of Pioneer Life.* (Whitefish, Montana: Kessinger Publishing, 2004.)

Kennedy, Gordon. *Children of the Sun: A Pictorial Anthology from Germany to California, 1883 to 1949.* (Ojai, California: Nivaria Press, 1998.)

Knowles, Joseph. *Alone in the Wilderness.* (Boston: Small, Maynard and Company, 1913.)

Kroeber, A. L. *Handbook of the Indians of California.* (Mineola, New York: Dover, 1976.)

Kroeber, Theodora. *Ishi in Two Worlds.* (Berkeley: University of California Press, 2004.)

Lahue, Kalton C. *Ladies in Distress.* (New York: A.S. Barnes, 1971.)

Lloyd, Nancy. *Observing Our Peninsula's Past, Volume 1: The Age of Legends Through 1931.* (Oysterville, Washington: The Chinook Observer, 2003.)

London, Jack. *The Call of the Wild.* (New York: Scholastic, 2001.)

Lutts, Ralph H. *The Nature Fakers: Wildlife, Science & Sentiment.* (Golden, Colorado: Fulcrum, 1990.)

McClelland, John M., Jr. *R. A. Long's Planned City: The Story of Longview.* (Longview, Washington: Westmedia, 1998.)

Mason, Jim. *An Unnatural Order: Uncovering the Roots of Our Domination of Nature and Each Other.* (New York: Simon and Schuster, 1993.)

McLaird, James D. *Calamity Jane: The Woman and the Legend.* (Norman: University of Oklahoma Press, 2005.)

Merchant, Carolyn. *Reinventing Eden: The Fate of Nature in Western Culture* (New York: Routledge, 2003.)

Miller, Sally M., and Daryl Morrison (eds.). *John Muir: Family, Friends, and Adventures.* (Albuquerque: University of New Mexico Press, 2005.)

Muir, John. *The Story of My Boyhood and Youth.* (Edinburgh: Birlinn, 2006.)

Nasaw, David. *The Chief: The Life of William Randolph Hearst.* (New York: Houghton Mifflin, 2000.)

Nash, Roderick Frazier. *Wilderness and the American Mind.* (New Haven: Yale University Press, 1967.)

Nyerges, Christopher. *How to Survive Anywhere: A Guide for Urban, Suburban, Rural, and Wilderness Environments.* (Mechanicsburg, Pennsylvania: Stackpole, 2006.)

Pernick, Martin S. *The Black Stork: Eugenics and the Death of "Defective" Babies in American Medicine and Motion Pictures since 1915.* (New York: Oxford University Press, 1996.)

Peterson, Harold. *The Last of the Mountain Men.* (Cambridge, Idaho: Backeddy, 1983.)

Roberts, Gary L. *Doc Holliday: The Life and Legend.* (Hoboken, New Jersey: John Wiley and Sons, 2006.)

Rourke, Constance. *American Humor: A Study of the National Character.* (New York: Harcourt, Brace, 1931.)

Slotkin, Richard. *Gunfighter Nation: The Myth of the Frontier in Twentieth-Century America.* (New York: Atheneum, 1992.)

Starn, Orin. *Ishi's Brain.* (New York: W. W. Norton, 2004.)

Stewart, Travis. *No Applause—Just Throw Money: The Book That Made Vaudeville Famous.* (New York: Faber and Faber, 2005.)

Stuart, Tristram. *The Bloodless Revolution: A Cultural History of Vegetarianism from 1600 to Modern Times.* (New York: W. W. Norton, 2007.)

Warren, Louis S. *Buffalo Bill's America: William Cody and the Wild West Show.* (New York: Knopf, 2005.)

White, Richard, and Patricia Nelson Limerick. *The Frontier in American Culture.* (Berkeley: University of California Press, 1994.)

Wilk, Max. *They're Playing Our Song.* (New York: New York Zeotrope, 1973.)

Wolff, Geoffrey. *The Edge of Maine.* (Washington, D.C.: National Geographic, 2005.)

Zuckoff, Mitchell. *Ponzi's Scheme: The True Story of a Financial Legend.* (New York: Random House, 2006.)

ACKNOWLEDGMENTS

———·◆·———

I owe a great debt of gratitude to two establishments on Long Beach Peninsula: The Ilwaco Heritage Museum in Ilwaco, and the Long Beach Peninsula Trading Post in Klipsan Beach. At the former, research librarian Joan Mann, collections manager Barbara Minard, and executive director Nancey Olson went well beyond their job descriptions in accommodating a demanding patron (and new Museum member!). At the latter, Brenda Hill was kind enough to open her considerable Knowles archives to my day-long perusal, even if my research blocked the aisles of her busy store. The co-workers who assisted me during my visit there were Bessie Poe and Stacy Barrett.

Also on the Peninsula, Mary Jane "Fuzzy" Walker, Adele Beechey, and Theresa Potter offered precious first-hand accounts of meeting the Nature Man. Kaye Mulvey-Cowan and Les Cowan allowed me access to their invaluable collection of Knowles correspondence, artwork, and photographs. Mary Alice Neal led me to her late husband's collection of Knowles memorabilia. Rodney Williams of Long Beach, who met Knowles when he was ten, sent an illuminating letter. Maxine Bown told me about the painted eggs. Rosemary Baker-Monaghan let me into the Liberty Theater in Astoria, and Renaissance man Michael Foster guided me around the place.

Very special thanks are due to Dan and Fran Makara and to the Grace Jones Richardson Trust for much-needed research funds. That vote of confidence gave this project liftoff. Huge gratitude is also due to Maggie and Frank Allen and the Institutes for Journalism and Natural Resources—they made this trip possible.

The public libraries in New York, Boston, and San Francisco also proved resourceful in helping me track down Knowles material, and Mark Neuzil of the University of St. Thomas (in St. Paul, Minnesota, not the Caribbean!) provided me with newspaper microfilm and a copy of his excellent paper on Knowles.

John Motavalli found me period works about Buffalo Bill and Charles Kellogg, the "Nature Singer." Katharine Lee and her daughter, Alice Lee, helped me interview Mary Jane "Fuzzy" Walker and research the Ilwaco Heritage Museum's voluminous files.

Oscar "Andy" Hammerstein III gave me the benefit of his considerable scholarship on his illustrious family. Terry Harbin, film historian, helped me understand Ithaca, New York's brief moment in the sun as a moviemaking capital, when Elaine Hammerstein and other stars strode its snowy streets. David Nasaw, professor at the City University of New York Graduate Center and author of *The Chief,* sent me some great clues to unlocking William Randolph Hearst's role in the making of the eugenics-promoting film *The Black Stork.* Also very helpful in that regard was Martin Pernick, professor of history at the University of Michigan and author of the book *The Black Stork.*

In Maine, the Wilton Farm and Home Museum's Pam Brown was helpful, and pointed me toward the Knowles collector Sean Minear, who serves as president of the Historical Society of Weld. Paul Taitt was kind enough to photograph three of the Wilton museum's paintings. I also enjoyed talking to two Knowles descendants, jazz bassist Donald Knowles (Joseph Knowles was his father's great-uncle) and wildlife artist Susan Knowles Jordan, Donald's daughter, who was inspired by the Nature Man's example.

Christopher Nyerges and Eustace Conway helped me understand the challenges of the modern-day nature man. This book would probably not exist had it not been for Roderick Nash's classic text *Wilderness and the American Mind,* which first put Joseph Knowles in context. Professor Nash also took my calls and e-mails and offered some considerable insights. The late Hans Koning was a crucially important mentor for me at several turning points in my writing career.

Other people who very kindly shared remembrances and opinions include: Prince Edward Island historian Boyde Beck, Marlene Burrell of the *Chinook Observer,* Allen Dickinson, Jay Franklin of J. Franklin Fine Art, Jack London biographer Alex Kershaw, Annabelle and Doreen Lovingfoss of the Monticello Hotel in Longview, author Ralph H. Lutts, Carolyn Maddux, genealogist Hazel Standeven (who describes Knowles as "a fabricator" and "a character"), Sandra Tellvik of the Ilwaco Heritage Museum, author Orin Starn of Duke University, Jim Tantillo of Cornell University, author Louis Warren of the University of California at Davis, and author Richard White of Stanford.

Keith Wallman at this book's first berth, Carroll & Graf, made me move the digressions into the footnotes and helped make the book fun to read: Thank him for all the illuminating illustrations. Fellow Da Capo author Alan Bisbort helped me find a home at his publishing house. Laura Stine at Da Capo moved the book briskly through the production stages. Finally, no book of mine is complete unless it thanks the stellar services of my agent, Sabine Hrechdakian, who not only helped organize my jumbled thoughts but guided my manuscript to a safe berth.

INDEX

⸻ ◆ ⸻